South

CLAS︱︱︱︱CTION

Southern Living

CLASSIC COLLECTION

PUBLISHED BY HANLEY WOOD
One Thomas Circle, NW, Suite 600
Washington, DC 20005

General Manager, Plans Services, David Rook
Associate Publisher, Development, Jennifer Pearce
Manager, Customer Service, Michael Morgan
Director, Marketing, Mark Wilkin
Editor, Simon Hyoun
Publications Manager, Brian Haefs
Production Manager, Theresa Emerson
Senior Plan Merchandiser, Nicole Phipps
Plan Merchandiser, Hillary Huff
Graphic Artist, Joong Min
Manager, Plans & Web Operations, Susan Jasmin
Director, Audience Development, Erik Schulze

HANLEY WOOD CORPORATE
Chief Executive Officer, Frank Anton
Chief Financial Officer, Matthew Flynn
Chief Administrative Officer, Frederick Moses
Chief Information Officer, Jeffrey Craig
Executive Vice President/Corporate Sales, Ken Beach
Vice President/Finance, Brad Lough
Vice President/Legal, Mike Bender
Interim Vice President/Human Resources, Bill McGrath

Most Hanley Wood titles are available at quantity discounts with
bulk purchases for educational, business, or sales promotional use. For information,
please contact Jennifer Pearce at jpearce@hanleywood.com.

VC GRAPHICS, INC.
Creative Director, Veronica Vannoy
Graphic Designer, Jennifer Gerstein
Graphic Designer, Denise Reiffenstein
Graphic Designer, Jeanne-Erin Worster

PHOTO CREDITS
Front Cover Images: Main, Design HPK3800248 (p. 272); Lower Left, Design HPK3800274 (p. 298).
Back Cover Images: Main and Lower Right, HPK3800248 (p. 272); Middle Right, Design HPK3800254 (p. 278).
Unless otherwise specified, all photography © Southern Living.

DESIGN
Cover Design, Deana Callison for Southern Living
Book Design, Denise Reiffenstein, VC Graphics, Inc.

DISTRIBUTION CENTER
PBD
Hanley Wood Consumer Group
3280 Summit Ridge Parkway
Duluth, Georgia 30096

10 9 8 7 6 5 4 3 2 1

Printed in the United States of America

Library of Congress Control Number: 2007930105

ISBN-10: 1-931131-77-5
ISBN-13: 978-1-931131-77-3

Southern Living®
CLASSIC COLLECTION

More Than 340 of Our Best House Plans

CLASSIC COLLECTION

See page 293 to view this plan.

Southern CLASSICS

See page 134 to view this plan.

See page 316 to view this plan.

SEE PAGE 134 TO VIEW THIS PLAN.

F or years, *Southern Living* magazine has celebrated the warmth and stately elegance of the American South, treating its devoted readers to a taste of what makes this region so timeless.

Throughout that time, *Southern Living* has been collecting exclusive home plans from the South's top architects and designers. From formal and elegant traditional homes, to casual and stylish cottages, the *Southern Living* plan collection has become an inspiration for admirers of southern architecture.

This volume represents the largest single collection of these winning house plans ever published—more than 340 designs selected by hand from the Southern Living house plan portfolio. Each home strikes the perfect balance between historical influences—Neoclassical, Colonial, European—and contemporary design trends.

Along with beautifully presented formal rooms, every plan recognizes the needs of today's homeowner. From mudrooms to offices, from pantries to flexible-use areas, these house plans were designed with everyday living firmly in mind.

Embodying "Southern hospitality" just as clearly, the homes also incorporate abundant entertaining space—covered porches, keeping rooms, formal and informal dining areas, and other seasonal spaces present easy opportunities for extended family gatherings and entertaining. On some plans, exclusive access to a porch creates a private retreat for homeowners.

The four sections of this book have been ordered by total square footage. The first section, "Cottage Homes" (page 10), presents lovely house plans under 2,205 square feet. The plans are designed to make the most of available space: open layouts heighten the sense of spaciousness, and stairways are tucked into corners to maximize living space. Ample windows and porches blur the line between indoor and outdoor living.

Section two, "Timeless Homes" (page 90), incorporates family starters from 2,206 to 2,800 square feet. These house plans bring a wealth of flexibility into their living spaces, making them equally appropriate as higher-end starter homes or for families. Large kitchens provide sufficient counter space for multiple cooks. Sunrooms, family rooms, third and fourth bedrooms all serve well as studies, home offices, libraries, or private retreats from the busier living areas.

SEE PAGE 316 TO VIEW THIS PLAN.

Section three, "Family Homes" (page 166), offers just that—house plans of 2,801 to 3,600 square feet that are ideal for families of any size. The designs vary widely: master suites are placed either conveniently near the other bedrooms, or at the opposite side of the floor plan for a more private retreat. Both casual and more formal dining areas abound. Master baths range from practical rooms with their own walk-in closets to more elegant spaces with twin vanities and large tubs.

SEE PAGE 134 TO VIEW THIS PLAN.

SEE PAGE 134 TO VIEW THIS PLAN.

The final section, "Luxury Homes" (page 268), showcases gorgeous estates over 3,600 square feet that offer the very height of Southern comfort. Stunning exteriors provide tremendous curb appeal. Large, inviting hearths warm central gathering spaces. Media rooms and gamerooms provide the perfect spots for entertaining guests. Owners of these homes will feel as if they live in a resort.

Take your time as you look through these pages. For within, you will find far more than a mere catalog of homes. From section to section, from plan to plan, you will find a wealth of grace, elegance, and what it means enjoy the best of Southern living.

SEE PAGE 134 TO VIEW THIS PLAN.

SEE PAGE 72 TO VIEW THIS PLAN.

Cottage
Homes

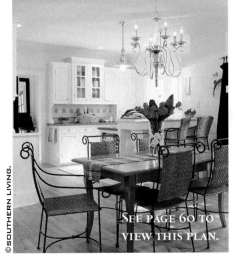

*Q*uaint cottages...rustic cabins...charming retreats... Within this section of homes under 2,205 square feet, you'll find house plan styles tailor-made for either first-time homebuyers or those looking for a vacation home. The variety of Southern Living homes offers welcoming front porches and comfortable floor plans.

Start with the Beachside Bungalow on page 13, where the name says it all. This house plan offers everything you need to relax at the beach—from well-defined bedroom, kitchen, and living areas, to a front porch perfect for enjoying the seaside view.

Starting small does not mean skimping on style, as the Couples Cottage on page 65 amply demonstrates. With multiple covered porches—including one off each upstairs bedroom—the outdoor living space is bound to be just as appreciated as the living space indoors.

Cozy and charming, yet incredibly chic, these house plans prove how much can be packed into a well-designed house plan, no matter how small.

SEE PAGE 60 TO VIEW THIS PLAN.

SEE PAGE 77 TO VIEW THIS PLAN.

412
square feet

Architectural Rendering: Roland Davis

DESIGNED BY WILLIAM H. PHILLIPS

Plan # **HPK3800001**

Square Footage: 412

Bedrooms: 1

Bathrooms: 1

Width: 23' - 0"

Depth: 36' - 0"

Foundation: Crawlspace

Price Code: A2

1-800-850-1491 • EPLANS.COM

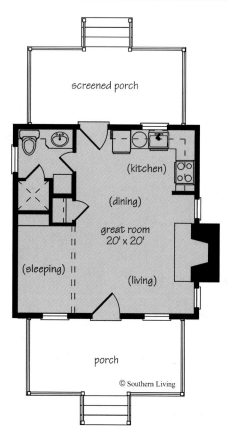

screened porch

(kitchen)

(dining)

great room
20' x 20'

(sleeping)

(living)

porch

© Southern Living

⋆ BEACHSIDE BUNGALOW ⋆

484 square feet

DESIGNED BY MOSER DESIGN GROUP FOR COASTAL LIVING MAGAZINE

Plan # **HPK3800002**

Square Footage: 484

Bedrooms: 1

Bathrooms: 1

Width: 23' - 0"

Depth: 22' - 0"

Foundation: Crawlspace

Price Code: A2

1-800-850-1491 • EPLANS.COM

Bedroom
11' x 11'

Kitchen 8' x 11'

Living Room
12' x 13'

Bath

Porch

© Southern Living

539 square feet

ARCHITECTURAL RENDERING: ROLAND DAVIS

DESIGNED BY WILLIAM H. PHILLIPS

Plan # HPK3800003

Square Footage: 539

Bedrooms: 1

Bathrooms: 1

Width: 29' - 0"

Depth: 31' - 0"

Foundation: Crawlspace

Price Code: A2

1-800-850-1491 • EPLANS.COM

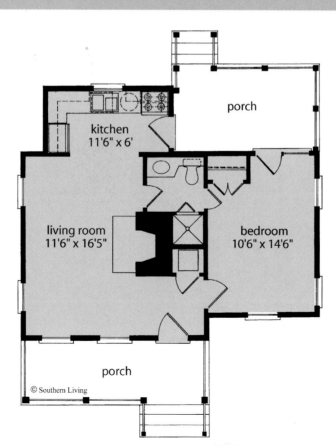

kitchen
11'6" x 6'

porch

living room
11'6" x 16'5"

bedroom
10'6" x 14'6"

porch

© Southern Living

CROOKED CREEK

631 square feet

DESIGNED BY WILLIAM H. PHILLIPS

Plan # HPK3800004

First Floor: 409 sq. ft.

Second Floor: 222 sq. ft.

Total: 631 sq. ft.

Bedrooms: 1

Bathrooms: 1 ½

Width: 25' - 0"

Depth: 26' - 0"

Foundation: Crawlspace

Price Code: A2

1-800-850-1491 • EPLANS.COM

kitchen

great room
15'6" x 16'

up

porch

© Southern Living

FIRST FLOOR

bedroom
11'10" x 12'8"

dn.

SECOND FLOOR

ᗌ Eagle's Nest ᗏ

634 square feet

ARCHITECTURAL RENDERING: ROLAND DAVIS

DESIGNED BY WILLIAM H. PHILLIPS

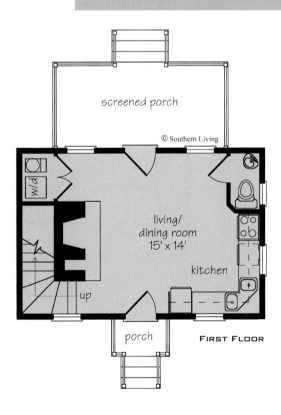

FIRST FLOOR

- screened porch
- © Southern Living
- living/dining room 15' x 14'
- kitchen
- w/d
- up
- porch

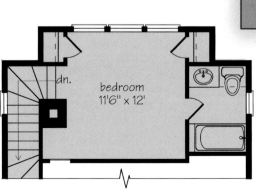

SECOND FLOOR

- dn.
- bedroom 11'6" x 12'

Plan# HPK3800005

First Floor: 384 sq. ft.

Second Floor: 250 sq. ft.

Total: 634 sq. ft.

Bedrooms: 1

Bathrooms: 1½

Width: 24' - 0"

Depth: 29' - 0"

Foundation: Crawlspace

Price Code: A3

1-800-850-1491 • EPLANS.COM

SMOKEY CREEK

640 square feet

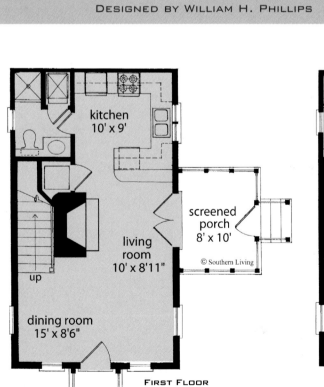

DESIGNED BY WILLIAM H. PHILLIPS

Plan # HPK3800006

First Floor: 448 sq. ft.

Second Floor: 192 sq. ft.

Total: 640 sq. ft.

Bedrooms: 1

Bathrooms: 2

Width: 24' - 0"

Depth: 28' - 0"

Foundation: Crawlspace

Price Code: A2

1-800-850-1491 • EPLANS.COM

kitchen
10' x 9'

screened porch
8' x 10'

living room
10' x 8'11"

© Southern Living

up

dining room
15' x 8'6"

FIRST FLOOR

bedroom loft
12' x 10'

dn.

open to below

SECOND FLOOR

LITTLE RED

800
square feet

DESIGNED BY WILLIAM H. PHILLIPS

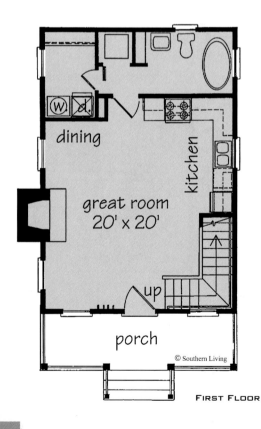

FIRST FLOOR

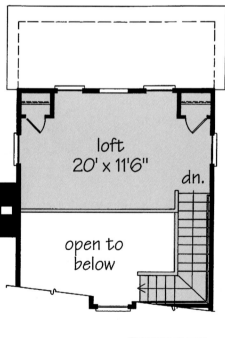

SECOND FLOOR

Plan# **HPK3800007**

First Floor: 562 sq. ft.

Second Floor: 238 sq. ft.

Total: 800 sq. ft.

Bedrooms: 1

Bathrooms: 1

Width: 23' - 0"

Depth: 33' - 0"

Foundation: Crawlspace

Price Code: A3

1-800-850-1491 • EPLANS.COM

808
square feet

ARCHITECTURAL RENDERING: KEN PIEPER

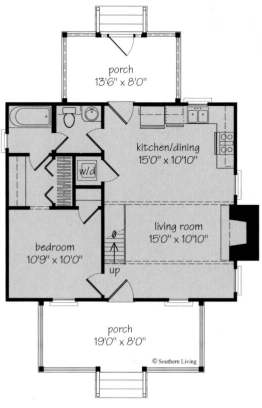

DESIGNED BY WILLIAM H. PHILLIPS

Plan # HPK3800008

First Floor: 603 sq. ft.

Second Floor: 205 sq. ft.

Total: 808 sq. ft.

Bedrooms: 1

Bathrooms: 1

Width: 27' - 0"

Depth: 39' - 0"

Foundation: Crawlspace

Price Code: A3

1-800-850-1491 • EPLANS.COM

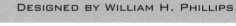

porch
13'6" x 8'0"

kitchen/dining
15'0" x 10'10"

w/d

living room
15'0" x 10'10"

bedroom
10'9" x 10'0"

up

porch
19'0" x 8'0"

© Southern Living

FIRST FLOOR

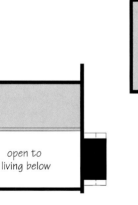

loft/ storage
10'9" x 11'9"

dn

open to
living below

SECOND FLOOR

❧ MILL SPRINGS ❧

967 square feet

ARCHITECTURAL RENDERING: KEN PIEPER

DESIGNED BY WILLIAM H. PHILLIPS

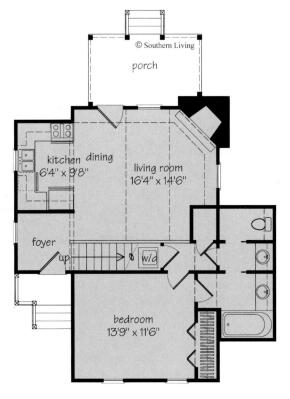

FIRST FLOOR

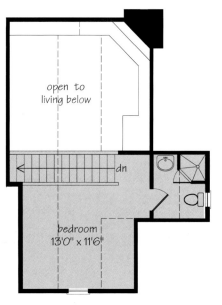

SECOND FLOOR

Plan# HPK3800009

First Floor: 716 sq. ft.

Second Floor: 251 sq. ft.

Total: 967 sq. ft.

Bedrooms: 2

Bathrooms: 2

Width: 30' - 0"

Depth: 39' - 0"

Foundation: Crawlspace

Price Code: A3

1-800-850-1491 • EPLANS.COM

❧ DEER RUN ❧

ARCHITECTURAL RENDERING: ROLAND DAVIS

DESIGNED BY WILLIAM H. PHILLIPS

Plan # HPK3800010

First Floor: 763 sq. ft.

Second Floor: 210 sq. ft.

Total: 973 sq. ft.

Bedrooms: 2

Bathrooms: 2

Width: 30' - 0"

Depth: 36' - 0"

Foundation: Crawlspace

Price Code: A2

1-800-850-1491 • EPLANS.COM

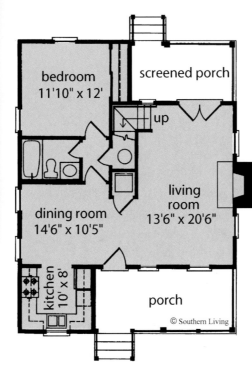

bedroom
11'10" x 12'

screened porch

up

dining room
14'6" x 10'5"

living room
13'6" x 20'6"

kitchen
10' x 8'

porch

© Southern Living

FIRST FLOOR

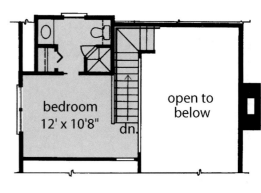

bedroom
12' x 10'8"

open to below

dn.

SECOND FLOOR

974 square feet

ARCHITECTURAL RENDERING: ROLAND DAVIS

DESIGNED BY WILLIAM H. PHILLIPS

Plan# HPK3800011

First Floor: 680 sq. ft.

Second Floor: 294 sq. ft.

Total: 974 sq. ft.

Bedrooms: 1

Bathrooms: 1 ½

Width: 35' - 0"

Depth: 28' - 0"

Foundation: Crawlspace

Price Code: A3

1-800-850-1491 • EPLANS.COM

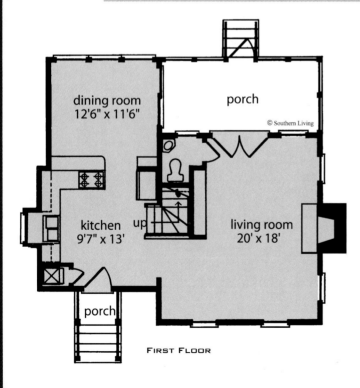

dining room
12'6" x 11'6"

porch

© Southern Living

kitchen
9'7" x 13'

up

living room
20' x 18'

porch

FIRST FLOOR

dn.

bedroom
11' x 16'2"

SECOND FLOOR

ARCHITECTURAL RENDERING: KEN PIEPER

1,086
square feet

DESIGNED BY WILLIAM H. PHILLIPS

Plan# HPK3800012

Square Footage: 1,086

Bedrooms: 2

Bathrooms: 2

Width: 34' - 0"

Depth: 52' - 0"

Foundation: Crawlspace

Price Code: C1

1-800-850-1491 • EPLANS.COM

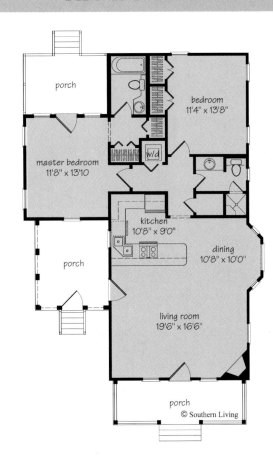

porch

bedroom
11'4" x 13'8"

master bedroom
11'8" x 13'10"

w/d

kitchen
10'8" x 9'0"

dining
10'8" x 10'0"

porch

living room
19'6" x 16'6"

porch

© Southern Living

~Foxglove Cottage~

1,087 square feet

ARCHITECTURAL RENDERING: LYNETTE GIROURARD

DESIGNED BY JOHN TEE, ARCHITECT

FIRST FLOOR

great room 19'7" x 13'4"

screen porch

dining 14'0" x 10'0"

kitchen 11'4" x 8'8"

up

dn

porch

© Southern Living

SECOND FLOOR

master bedroom 14'4" x 15'2"

dn

BASEMENT

bedroom 11'10" x 12'8"

bedroom 14'0" x 11'7"

up

w d

Plan# **HPK3800013**

First Floor: 631 sq. ft.

Second Floor: 456 sq. ft.

Total: 1,087 sq. ft.

Bedrooms: 1

Bathrooms: 1 ½

Width: 39' - 0"

Depth: 30' - 0"

Foundation: Unfinished Basement

Price Code: A3

1-800-850-1491 • EPLANS.COM

FOX RIVER

1,122 square feet

DESIGNED BY WILLIAM H. PHILLIPS

Plan# HPK3800014

First Floor: 870 sq. ft.

Second Floor: 252 sq. ft.

Total: 1,122 sq. ft.

Bedrooms: 2

Bathrooms: 2

Width: 34' - 0"

Depth: 34' - 0"

Foundation: Crawlspace

Price Code: C1

1-800-850-1491 • EPLANS.COM

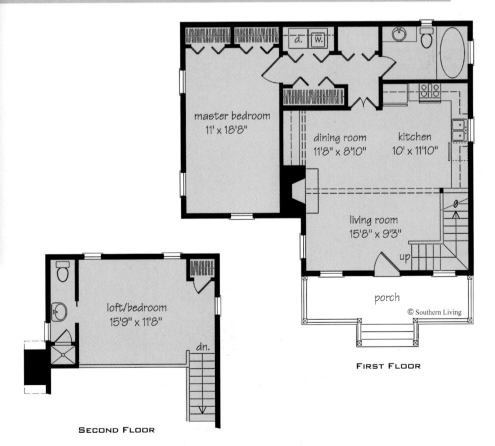

master bedroom
11' x 18'8"

dining room
11'8" x 8'10"

kitchen
10' x 11'10"

living room
15'8" x 9'3"

up

porch

© Southern Living

FIRST FLOOR

loft/bedroom
15'9" x 11'8"

dn.

SECOND FLOOR

❧ HUNTING CREEK ALTERNATE ❧

1,165 square feet

ARCHITECTURAL RENDERING: GREG HAVENS

DESIGNED BY WILLIAM H. PHILLIPS

Plan# HPK3800015

First Floor: 896 sq. ft.

Second Floor: 269 sq. ft.

Total: 1,165 sq. ft.

Bedrooms: 2

Bathrooms: 2

Width: 31' - 0"

Depth: 36' - 0"

Foundation: Crawlspace

Price Code: C1

1-800-850-1491 • EPLANS.COM

bedroom
14'6" x 11'6"

porch

up

w/d

living room
12'2" x 16'4"

dining room
17'10" x 10'0"

kitchen
12'3" x 7'8"

porch

© Southern Living

FIRST FLOOR

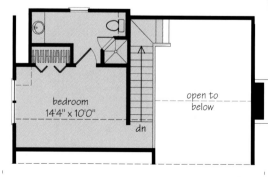

bedroom
14'4" x 10'0"

open to below

dn

SECOND FLOOR

ARCHITECTURAL RENDERING: LOIS WATSON

1,173 square feet

DESIGNED BY SULLIVAN DESIGN COMPANY

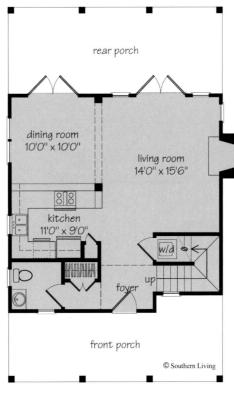
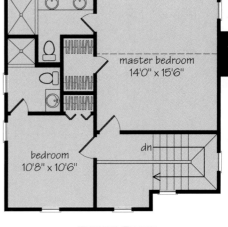

Plan# HPK3800016

First Floor: 630 sq. ft.

Second Floor: 543 sq. ft.

Total: 1,173 sq. ft.

Bedrooms: 2

Bathrooms: 2 ½

Width: 28' - 0"

Depth: 26' - 0"

Foundation: Crawlspace

Price Code: A3

1-800-850-1491 • EPLANS.COM

First Floor

rear porch

dining room
10'0" x 10'0"

living room
14'0" x 15'6"

kitchen
11'0" x 9'0"

w/d

up

foyer

front porch

© Southern Living

Second Floor

master bedroom
14'0" x 15'6"

bedroom
10'8" x 10'6"

dn

1,176 square feet

ARCHITECTURAL RENDERING: MUIR STEWART

DESIGNED BY GEORGE GRAVES, AIA FOR COASTAL LIVING MAGAZINE

FIRST FLOOR

Screened Porch
Covered Entry
Courtyard Deck
Deck
Bath
Foyer
Master Bedroom 11' x 17'
Up
Garage
Shower
Bench Seat
© Southern Living

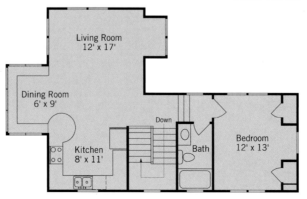

SECOND FLOOR

Living Room 12' x 17'
Dining Room 6' x 9'
Down
Bath
Bedroom 12' x 13'
Kitchen 8' x 11'

Plan# HPK3800350

First Floor: 405 sq. ft.

Second Floor: 771 sq. ft.

Total: 1,176 sq. ft.

Bedrooms: 2

Bathrooms: 2

Width: 26' - 0"

Depth: 43' - 0"

Foundation: Pier & Beam

Price Code: C3

1-800-850-1491 • EPLANS.COM

~ᴅDOGTROT᙮~

1,256
square feet

DESIGNED BY WILLIAM H. PHILLIPS

Plan# HPK3800017

Square Footage: 1,256

Bedrooms: 2

Bathrooms: 2

Width: 42' - 0"

Depth: 48' - 0"

Foundation: Crawlspace

Price Code: A3

1-800-850-1491 • EPLANS.COM

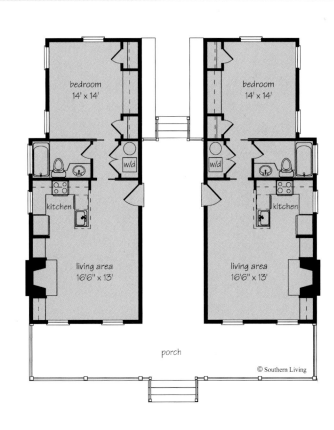

bedroom
14' x 14'

bedroom
14' x 14'

w/d

w/d

kitchen

kitchen

living area
16'6" x 13'

living area
16'6" x 13'

porch

© Southern Living

~SWEET WATER~

1,257
square feet

DESIGNED BY WILLIAM H. PHILLIPS

© Southern Living

FIRST FLOOR

porch

kitchen/dining
21' x 10'

living room
18'11" x 21'6"

up

porch

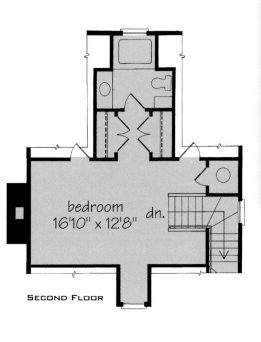

bedroom
16'10" x 12'8"   dn.

SECOND FLOOR

Plan# HPK3800018

First Floor: 787 sq. ft.

Second Floor: 470 sq. ft.

Total: 1,257 sq. ft.

Bedrooms: 1

Bathrooms: 2

Width: 29' - 0"

Depth: 32' - 0"

Foundation: Crawlspace

Price Code: A3

1-800-850-1491 • EPLANS.COM

1,286
square feet

DESIGNED BY MOSER DESIGN GROUP

Plan # HPK3800019

Square Footage: 1,286

Bedrooms: 2

Bathrooms: 2

Width: 41' - 0"

Depth: 58' - 0"

Foundation: Crawlspace

Price Code: C1

1-800-850-1491 • EPLANS.COM

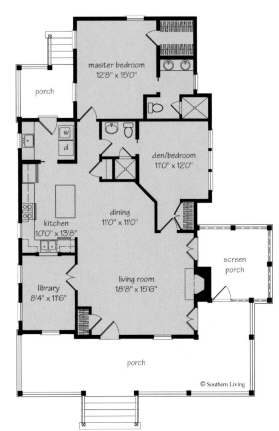

porch

master bedroom
12'8" x 15'0"

W
d

den/bedroom
11'0" x 12'0"

dining
11'0" x 11'0"

kitchen
10'0" x 13'8"

screen
porch

library
8'4" x 11'6"

living room
18'8" x 15'6"

porch

© Southern Living

~RUSTIC BEACH COTTAGE~

1,398
square feet

ARCHITECTURAL RENDERING: MIUR STEWART

MIUR STEWART

DESIGNED BY JOHN TEE, ARCHITECT, FOR COASTAL LIVING MAGAZINE

Plan # HPK3800020

First Floor: 1,030 sq. ft.

Second Floor: 368 sq. ft.

Total: 1,398 sq. ft.

Bedrooms: 2

Bathrooms: 2

Width: 46' - 0"

Depth: 40' - 0"

Foundation: Crawlspace

Price Code: C1

1-800-850-1491 • EPLANS.COM

FIRST FLOOR

deck

dining room
13' x 12'6"

up

family room
15'6" x 23'

screened porch

kitchen
11' x 9"

w.
d.

bedroom
12' x 15'4"

porch

© Southern Living

SECOND FLOOR

open
to below

master
bedroom
13'4" x 15'

dn.

CARIBBEAN GETAWAY

1,336 square feet

Plan# HPK3800021

First Floor: 693 sq. ft.

Second Floor: 643 sq. ft.

Total: 1,336 sq. ft.

Bedrooms: 2

Bathrooms: 2 ½

Width: 29' - 0"

Depth: 41' - 0"

Foundation: Slab

Price Code: A3

1-800-850-1491 • EPLANS.COM

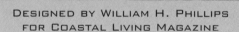

DESIGNED BY WILLIAM H. PHILLIPS
FOR COASTAL LIVING MAGAZINE

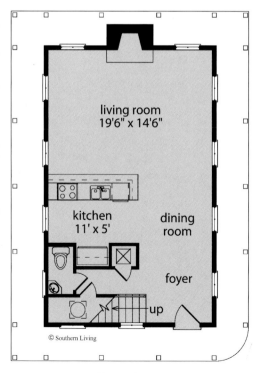

living room
19'6" x 14'6"

kitchen
11' x 5'

dining room

foyer

up

© Southern Living

FIRST FLOOR

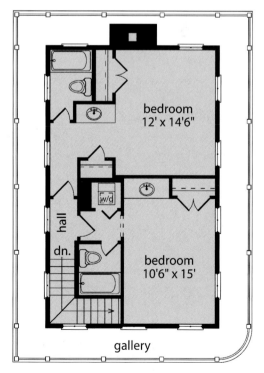

bedroom
12' x 14'6"

w/d

hall

dn.

bedroom
10'6" x 15'

gallery

SECOND FLOOR

❧ HEATHER PLACE ❧

1,486
square feet

DESIGNED BY JOHN TEE, ARCHITECT

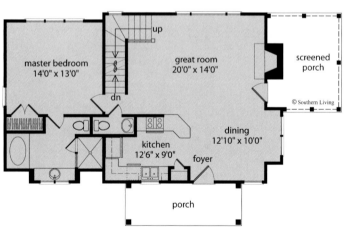

FIRST FLOOR

- master bedroom 14'0" x 13'0"
- great room 20'0" x 14'0"
- screened porch
- © Southern Living
- dining 12'10" x 10'0"
- kitchen 12'6" x 9'0"
- foyer
- porch
- up
- dn

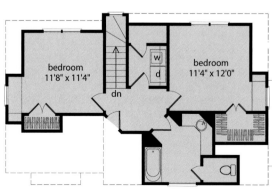

SECOND FLOOR

- bedroom 11'8" x 11'4"
- bedroom 11'4" x 12'0"
- w / d
- dn

Plan# HPK3800022

First Floor: 890 sq. ft.

Second Floor: 596 sq. ft.

Total: 1,486 sq. ft.

Bedrooms: 3

Bathrooms: 2 ½

Width: 50' - 0"

Depth: 31' - 0"

Foundation: Unfinished Basement

Price Code: A3

1-800-850-1491 • EPLANS.COM

RIVER BIRCH

1,500
square feet

ARCHITECTURAL RENDERING: KEN PIEPER

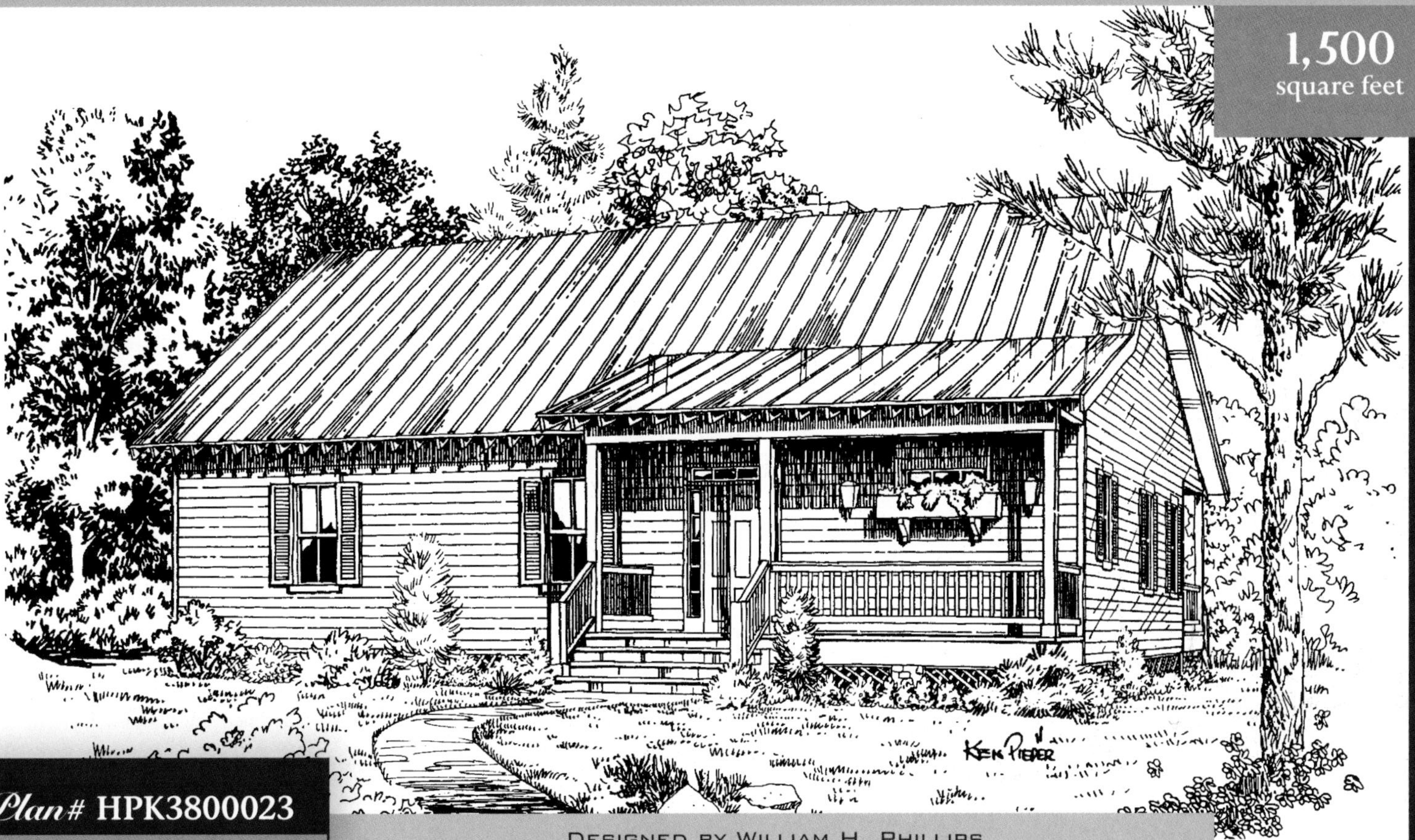
KEN PIEPER

Plan# HPK3800023

DESIGNED BY WILLIAM H. PHILLIPS

Square Footage: 1,500

Bedrooms: 3

Bathrooms: 2

Width: 50' - 0"

Depth: 46' - 0"

Foundation: Crawlspace

Price Code: C1

1-800-850-1491 • EPLANS.COM

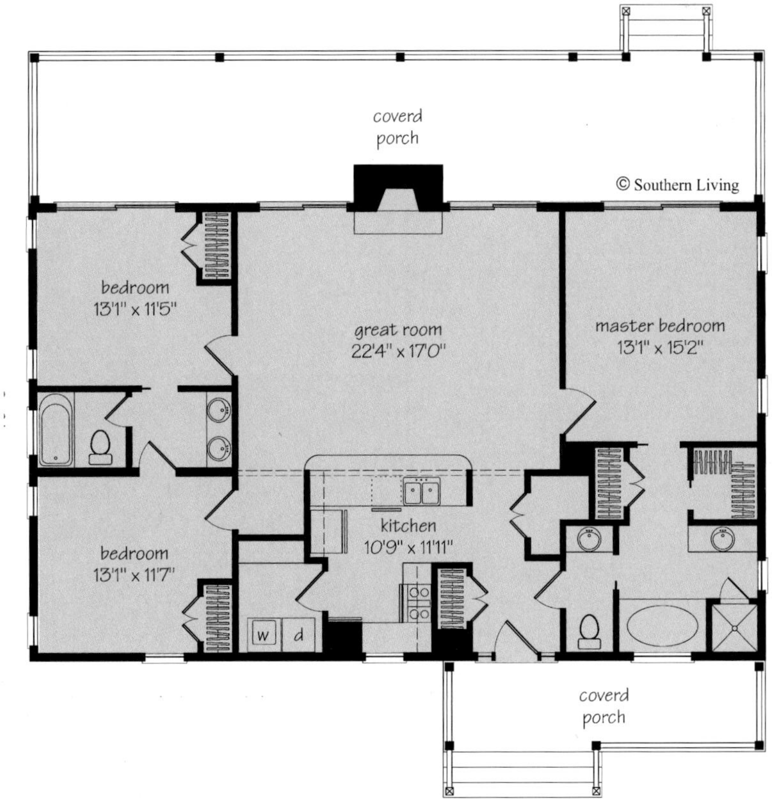
coverd
porch
© Southern Living
bedroom
13'1" x 11'5"
great room
22'4" x 17'0"
master bedroom
13'1" x 15'2"
kitchen
10'9" x 11'11"
bedroom
13'1" x 11'7"
w
d
coverd
porch

❦ FORSYTHIA ❦

1,521 square feet

ARCHITECTURAL RENDERING: ROLAND DAVIS

DESIGNED BY WILLIAM H. PHILLIPS

Plan# HPK3800024

First Floor: 1,016 sq. ft.

Second Floor: 505 sq. ft.

Total: 1,521 sq. ft.

Bedrooms: 3

Bathrooms: 2 ½

Width: 33' - 0"

Depth: 48' - 0"

Foundation: Crawlspace

Price Code: C1

1-800-850-1491 • EPLANS.COM

deck

living room
19' x 14'

master bedroom
12' x 14'

dining room
13' x 10'

d. w.

kitchen
10' x 8'

foyer

up

porch

© Southern Living

FIRST FLOOR

open to below

bedroom
10' x 12'

dn.

bedroom
12' x 15'6"

SECOND FLOOR

1,540 square feet

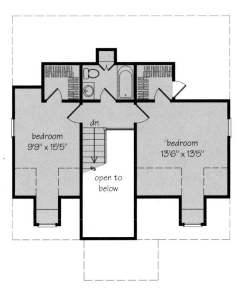

DESIGNED BY WILLIAM H. PHILLIPS

Plan# HPK3800025

First Floor: 1,024 sq. ft.

Second Floor: 516 sq. ft.

Total: 1,540 sq. ft.

Bedrooms: 3

Bathrooms: 2 ½

Width: 33' - 0"

Depth: 47' - 0"

Foundation: Crawlspace

Price Code: A3

1-800-850-1491 • EPLANS.COM

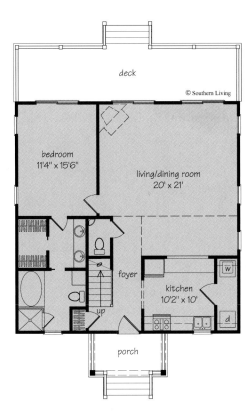

deck

© Southern Living

bedroom
11'4" x 15'6"

living/dining room
20' x 21'

foyer

kitchen
10'2" x 10'

w

d

up

porch

FIRST FLOOR

bedroom
9'9" x 15'5"

dn

open to
below

bedroom
13'6" x 13'5"

SECOND FLOOR

1,585
square feet

ARCHITECTURAL RENDERING: GREG HAVENS

DESIGNED BY WILLIAM H. PHILLIPS

Plan # HPK3800026

First Floor: 1,128 sq. ft.

Second Floor: 457 sq. ft.

Total: 1,585 sq. ft.

Bedrooms: 2

Bathrooms: 2 ½

Width: 39' - 0"

Depth: 45' - 0"

Foundation: Crawlspace

Price Code: C1

1-800-850-1491 • EPLANS.COM

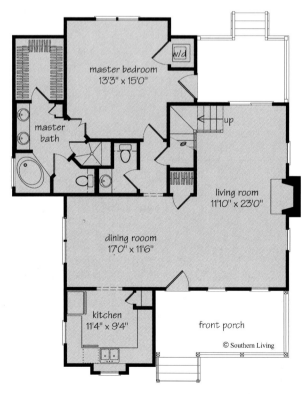

master bedroom
13'3" x 15'0"

w/d

master bath

living room
11'10" x 23'0"

dining rooom
17'0" x 11'6"

kitchen
11'4" x 9'4"

front porch

© Southern Living

up

FIRST FLOOR

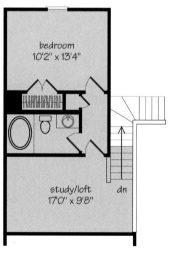

bedroom
10'2" x 13'4"

study/loft
17'0" x 9'8"

dn

SECOND FLOOR

~ ASHLEY RIVER COTTAGE ~

ARCHITECTURAL RENDERING: RICK HERR

1,605 square feet

Plan # HPK3800027

First Floor: 1,093 sq. ft.

Second Floor: 512 sq. ft.

Total: 1,605 sq. ft.

Bedrooms: 3

Bathrooms: 2 ½

Width: 33' - 0"

Depth: 51' - 0"

Foundation: Pier (same as Piling)

Price Code: C1

1-800-850-1491 • EPLANS.COM

DESIGNED BY ALLISON-RAMSEY ARCHITECTS, INC.

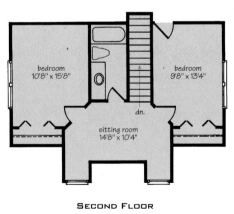

SECOND FLOOR

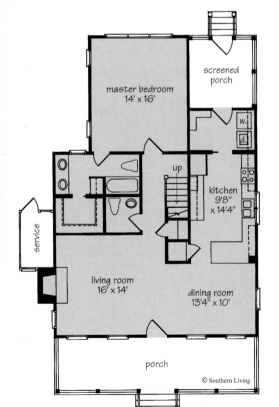

FIRST FLOOR

© Southern Living

·SUGARPLUM·

ARCHITECTURAL RENDERING: ROLAND DAVIS

DESIGNED BY William H. Phillips

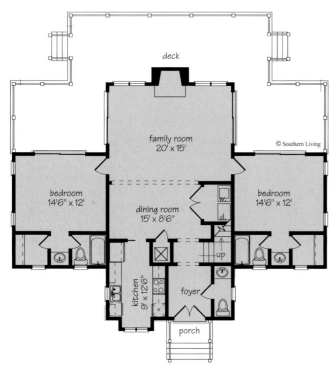

deck

family room
20' x 15'

© Southern Living

bedroom
14'6" x 12'

dining room
15' x 8'6"

bedroom
14'6" x 12'

kitchen
9' x 12'6"

up

foyer

porch

FIRST FLOOR

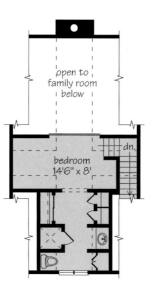

open to
family room
below

bedroom
14'6" x 8'

dn.

SECOND FLOOR

Plan# HPK3800028

First Floor: 1,281 sq. ft.

Second Floor: 364 sq. ft.

Total: 1,645 sq. ft.

Bedrooms: 3

Bathrooms: 3 ½

Width: 52' - 0"

Depth: 49' - 0"

Foundation: Crawlspace

Price Code : A3

1-800-850-1491 • EPLANS.COM

~ELLSWORTH COTTAGE~

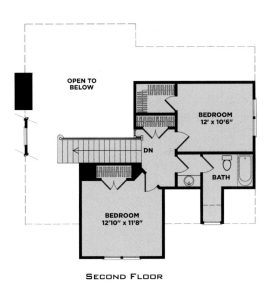

DESIGNED BY CALDWELL-CLINE ARCHITECTS AND DESIGNERS FOR COTTAGE LIVING MAGAZINE

Plan # HPK3800029

First Floor: 1,135 sq. ft.

Second Floor: 510 sq. ft.

Total: 1,645 sq. ft.

Bedrooms: 3

Bathrooms: 2 ½

Width: 38' - 0"

Depth: 50' - 0"

Foundation: Unfinished Basement

Price Code: C1

1-800-850-1491 • EPLANS.COM

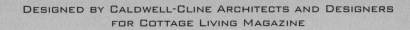

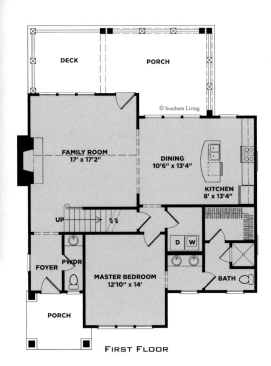

DECK

PORCH

© Southern Living

FAMILY ROOM
17' x 17'2"

DINING
10'6" x 13'4"

KITCHEN
8' x 13'4"

UP

D | W

FOYER

PWDR

MASTER BEDROOM
12'10" x 14'

BATH

PORCH

FIRST FLOOR

OPEN TO BELOW

BEDROOM
12' x 10'6"

DN

BATH

BEDROOM
12'10" x 11'8"

SECOND FLOOR

~ THE SAGE HOUSE ~

1,672 square feet

ARCHITECTURAL RENDERING: LYNETTE GIROUARD

DESIGNED BY JOHN TEE, ARCHITECT

Plan # HPK3800031

First Floor: 1,020 sq. ft.

Second Floor: 652 sq. ft.

Total: 1,672 sq. ft.

Bedrooms: 3

Bathrooms: 2 ½

Width: 36' - 0"

Depth: 34' - 0"

Foundation: Unfinished Basement

Price Code: C3

1-800-850-1491 • EPLANS.COM

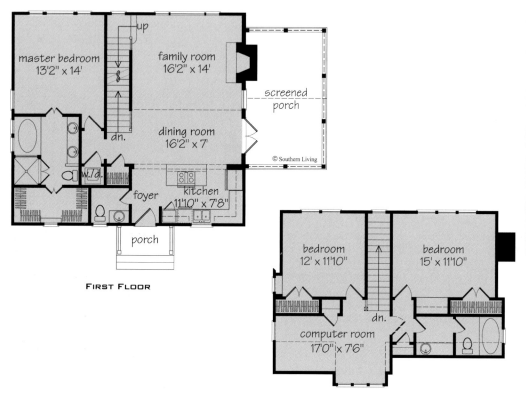

FIRST FLOOR

master bedroom 13'2" x 14'

family room 16'2" x 14'

screened porch

© Southern Living

dining room 16'2" x 7'

up

dn.

w./d.

foyer

kitchen 11'10" x 7'8"

porch

SECOND FLOOR

bedroom 12' x 11'10"

bedroom 15' x 11'10"

dn.

computer room 17'0" x 7'6"

1,686
square feet

DESIGNED BY WILLIAM H. PHILLIPS

Plan# **HPK3800032**

First Floor: 1,120 sq. ft.

Second Floor: 566 sq. ft.

Total: 1,686 sq. ft.

Bedrooms: 3

Bathrooms: 2 ½

Width: 40' - 0"

Depth: 39' - 0"

Foundation: Crawlspace

Price Code: A3

1-800-850-1491 • EPLANS.COM

deck

living room
17'6" x 12'6

up

master
bedroom
15' x 13'

dining
room
10' x 10'6"

kitchen
8 x 10'

foyer

d. w.

porch

© Southern Living

FIRST FLOOR

bedroom
12'6" x 13'

dn.

bedroom
11' x 12'

SECOND FLOOR

1,705 square feet

DESIGNED BY ALLISON-RAMSEY ARCHITECTS, INC.

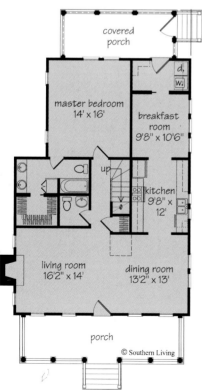

covered porch

master bedroom
14' x 16'

breakfast room
9'8" x 10'6"

d.
w.

up

kitchen
9'8" x 12'

living room
16'2" x 14'

dining room
13'2" x 13'

porch

© Southern Living

FIRST FLOOR

bonus room
11'4" x 21'10"

bedroom
10' x 13'

bedroom
9'8" x 13'4"

dn.

sitting room

SECOND FLOOR

Plan # HPK3800033

First Floor: 1,195 sq. ft.

Second Floor: 510 sq. ft.

Total: 1,705 sq. ft.

Bonus Space: 290 sq. ft.

Bedrooms: 3

Bathrooms: 2 ½

Width: 33' - 0"

Depth: 59' - 0"

Foundation: Crawlspace

Price Code: C3

1-800-850-1491 • EPLANS.COM

TIDEWATER RETREAT

1,710 square feet

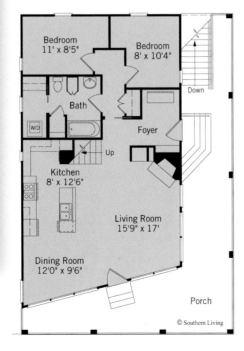

Plan# HPK3800034

First Floor: 975 sq. ft.

Second Floor: 643 sq. ft.

Third Floor: 92 sq. ft.

Total: 1,710 sq. ft.

Bedrooms: 3

Bathrooms: 2

Width: 33' - 0"

Depth: 50' - 0"

Foundation: Pier (same as Piling)

Price Code: C3

1-800-850-1491 • EPLANS.COM

DESIGNED BY LOONEY RICKS KISS ARCHITECTS, INC.
FOR COASTAL LIVING MAGAZINE

FIRST FLOOR

- Bedroom 11' x 8'5"
- Bedroom 8' x 10'4"
- Down
- Bath
- W/D
- Foyer
- Up
- Kitchen 8' x 12'6"
- Living Room 15'9" x 17'
- Dining Room 12'0" x 9'6"
- Porch

© Southern Living

SECOND FLOOR

- Bunk Room 15'8" x 6'3"
- Down
- Up
- Bath
- Master Bedroom 12' x 12'
- Storage

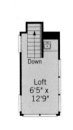

THIRD FLOOR

- Down
- Loft 6'5" x 12'9"

·ASHTON·

1,715
square feet

ARCHITECTURAL RENDERING: RICK HERR

DESIGNED BY CALDWELL-CLINE ARCHITECTS AND DESIGNERS

FIRST FLOOR

deck

covered porch

dining/breakfast
11'4" x 12'0"

master bedroom
13'4" x 14'0"

sleeping porch
10'0" x 14'0"

great room
19'4" x 18'0"

kitchen
11'4" x 10'6"

entry
up

dn

carriage house

covered porch

storage

© Southern Living

SECOND FLOOR

open to below

bedroom
12'0" x 12'0"

bedroom
11'8" x 12'6"

dn

Plan # HPK3800035

First Floor: 1,215 sq. ft.

Second Floor: 500 sq. ft.

Total: 1,715 sq. ft.

Bedrooms: 3

Bathrooms: 2 ½

Width: 65' - 0"

Depth: 46' - 0"

Foundation: Crawlspace, Slab, Unfinished Basement

Price Code: C1

1-800-850-1491 • EPLANS.COM

CEDARBROOK

1,715 square feet

DESIGNED BY CALDWELL-CLINE ARCHITECTS AND DESIGNERS

Plan# HPK3800036

First Floor: 1,215 sq. ft.

Second Floor: 500 sq. ft.

Total: 1,715 sq. ft.

Bedrooms: 3

Bathrooms: 2 ½

Width: 66' - 0"

Depth: 46' - 0"

Foundation: Crawlspace, Unfinished Basement

Price Code: C1

1-800-850-1491 • EPLANS.COM

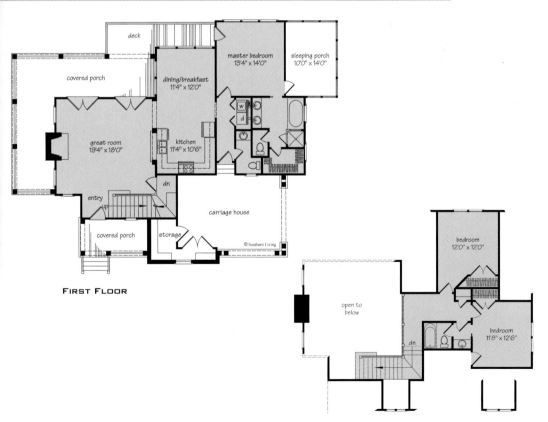

deck

covered porch

dining/breakfast
11'4" x 12'0"

master bedroom
13'4" x 14'0"

sleeping porch
10'0" x 14'0"

great room
19'4" x 18'0"

kitchen
11'4" x 10'6"

entry

dn

up

covered porch

storage

carriage house

© Southern Living

FIRST FLOOR

open to below

bedroom
12'0" x 12'0"

dn

bedroom
11'8" x 12'6"

SECOND FLOOR

BEAUFORT COTTAGE

1,720 square feet

Designed by Allison-Ramsey Architects, Inc. for Cottage Living Magazine

ARCHITECTURAL RENDERING: RICHARD CHENOWETH

Plan# **HPK3800037**

First Floor: 1,101 sq. ft.

Second Floor: 619 sq. ft.

Total: 1,720 sq. ft.

Bedrooms: 3

Bathrooms: 2 ½

Width: 28' - 0"

Depth: 61' - 0"

Foundation: Crawlspace

Price Code: C1

1-800-850-1491 • EPLANS.COM

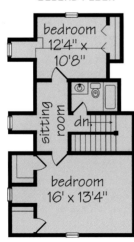

SECOND FLOOR

bedroom 12'4" x 10'8"

sitting room

dn

bedroom 16' x 13'4"

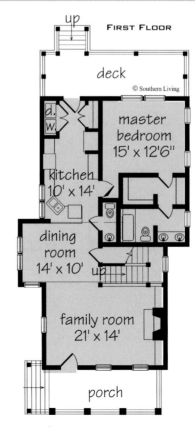

FIRST FLOOR

up

deck

© Southern Living

d. w.

master bedroom 15' x 12'6"

kitchen 10' x 14'

dining room 14' x 10'

up

family room 21' x 14'

porch

SAWGRASS COTTAGE

ARCHITECTURAL RENDERING: MUIR STEWART

DESIGNED BY GEORGE GRAVES, AIA FOR COASTAL LIVING MAGAZINE

Plan # HPK3800038

First Floor: 782 sq. ft.

Second Floor: 945 sq. ft.

Total: 1,727 sq. ft.

Bedrooms: 3

Bathrooms: 3

Width: 30' - 0"

Depth: 53' - 0"

Foundation: Crawlspace

Price Code: C3

1-800-850-1491 • EPLANS.COM

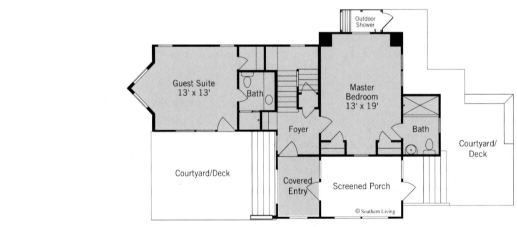

Outdoor Shower

Guest Suite
13' x 13'

Bath

Master Bedroom
13' x 19'

Foyer

Bath

Courtyard/Deck

Courtyard/Deck

Covered Entry

Screened Porch

© Southern Living

FIRST FLOOR

Bedroom
13' x 14'

Bath

Kitchen
10' x 13'

Dining Area
7' x 9'

Living Room
10' x 16'

SECOND FLOOR

~ROSEMARY COTTAGE~

1,754
square feet

DESIGNED BY SULLIVAN DESIGN COMPANY

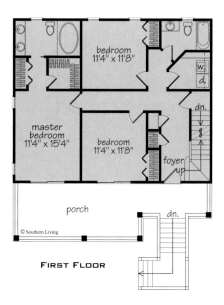

FIRST FLOOR

bedroom
11'4" x 11'8"

master bedroom
11'4" x 15'4"

bedroom
11'4" x 11'8"

foyer
up

porch

dn.

© Southern Living

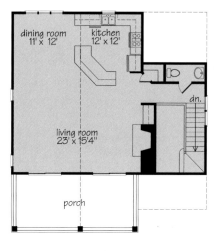

SECOND FLOOR

dining room
11' x 12'

kitchen
12' x 12'

living room
23' x 15'4"

dn.

porch

Plan# HPK3800039

First Floor: 980 sq. ft.

Second Floor: 774 sq. ft.

Total: 1,754 sq. ft.

Bedrooms: 3

Bathrooms: 2 ½

Width: 35' - 0"

Depth: 38' - 0"

Foundation: Pier
(same as Piling)

Price Code: C1

1-800-850-1491 • EPLANS.COM

SILVERHILL

ARCHITECTURAL RENDERING: LOIS WATSON

DESIGNED BY SULLIVAN DESIGN COMPANY

Plan # HPK3800040

First Floor: 1,154 sq. ft.

Second Floor: 621 sq. ft.

Total: 1,775 sq. ft.

Bedrooms: 3

Bathrooms: 2 ½

Width: 44' - 0"

Depth: 49' - 0"

Foundation: Crawlspace

Price Code: C3

1-800-850-1491 • EPLANS.COM

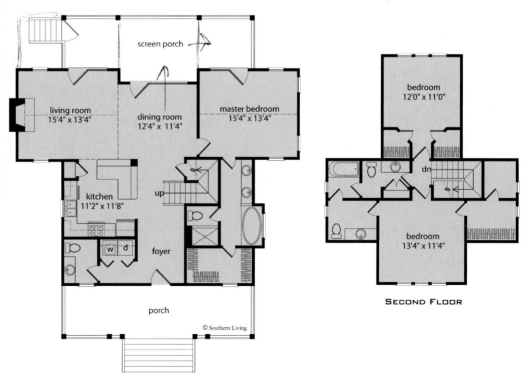

FIRST FLOOR

screen porch

living room
15'4" x 13'4"

dining room
12'4" x 11'4"

master bedroom
15'4" x 13'4"

kitchen
11'2" x 11'8"

up

foyer

porch

© Southern Living

SECOND FLOOR

bedroom
12'0" x 11'0"

dn

bedroom
13'4" x 11'4"

~Camellia Cottage~

1,792
square feet

Designed by William H. Phillips

Plan # HPK3800041

First Floor: 896 sq. ft.

Second Floor: 896 sq. ft.

Total: 1,792 sq. ft.

Bedrooms: 3

Bathrooms: 2 ½

Width: 34' - 0"

Depth: 43' - 0"

Foundation: Crawlspace

Price Code: A3

1-800-850-1491 • EPLANS.COM

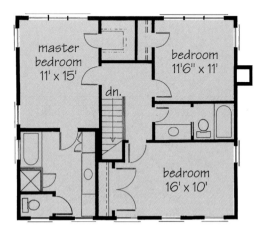

First Floor

deck

dining room
13'6" x 15'

living room
15'10" x 16'

kitchen
13' x 11'6"

foyer

up

w. d.

storage

porch

© Southern Living

Second Floor

master
bedroom
11' x 15'

bedroom
11'6" x 11'

dn.

bedroom
16' x 10'

❧ BUCKSPORT COTTAGE ❧

ARCHITECTURAL RENDERING: MILES MELTON

DESIGNED BY MOSER DESIGN GROUP

Plan# HPK3800042

First Floor: 1,066 sq. ft.

Second Floor: 728 sq. ft.

Total: 1,794 sq. ft.

Bedrooms: 3

Bathrooms: 2 ½

Width: 39' - 0"

Depth: 44' - 0"

Foundation: Crawlspace

Price Code: C1

1-800-850-1491 • EPLANS.COM

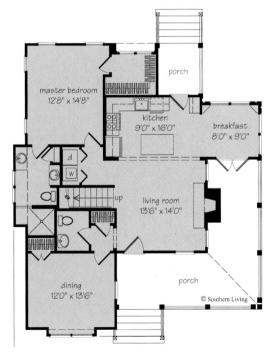

porch

master bedroom
12'8" x 14'8"

kitchen
9'0" x 16'0"

breakfast
8'0" x 9'0"

d

w

living room
13'6" x 14'0"

dining
12'0" x 13'6"

porch

© Southern Living

FIRST FLOOR

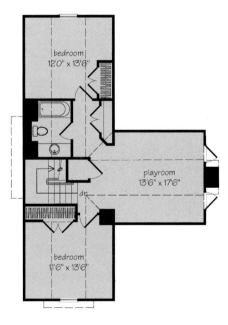

bedroom
12'0" x 13'6"

playroom
13'6" x 17'6"

dn

bedroom
11'6" x 13'6"

SECOND FLOOR

WISTERIA

1,802 square feet

ARCHITECTURAL RENDERING: LYNETTE GIROUARD

DESIGNED BY JOHN TEE, ARCHITECT

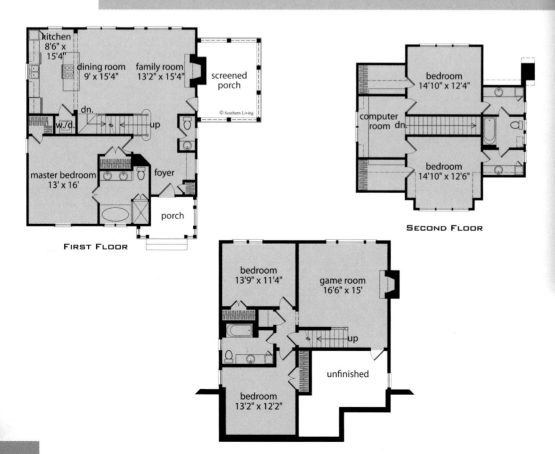

FIRST FLOOR

kitchen 8'6" x 15'4"

dining room 9' x 15'4"

family room 13'2" x 15'4"

screened porch

© Southern Living

dn.

w./d.

up

master bedroom 13' x 16'

foyer

porch

SECOND FLOOR

bedroom 14'10" x 12'4"

computer room   dn.

bedroom 14'10" x 12'6"

bedroom 13'9" x 11'4"

game room 16'6" x 15'

up

unfinished

bedroom 13'2" x 12'2"

Plan # HPK3800043

First Floor: 1,108 sq. ft.

Second Floor: 694 sq. ft.

Total: 1,802 sq. ft.

Bedrooms: 3

Bathrooms: 2 ½

Width: 44' - 0"

Depth: 39' - 0"

Foundation: Unfinished Basement

Price Code: C3

1-800-850-1491 • EPLANS.COM

CAPESIDE COTTAGE

1,825
square feet

Plan# **HPK3800044**

First Floor: 1,320 sq. ft.

Second Floor: 505 sq. ft.

Total: 1,825 sq. ft.

Optional Guest Cottage: 525 sq. ft.

Bedrooms: 3

Bathrooms: 3

Width: 58' - 0"

Depth: 73' - 0"

Foundation: Pier (same as Piling)

Price Code: A4

1-800-850-1491 • EPLANS.COM

DESIGNED BY SPITZMILLER AND NORRIS, INC.
FOR COASTAL LIVING MAGAZINE

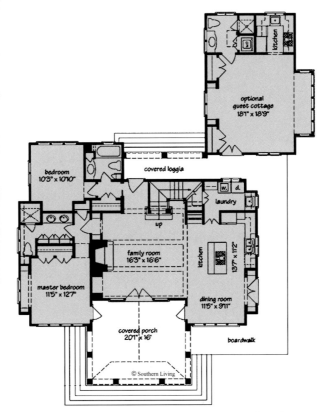

optional guest cottage
18'1" x 18'9"

covered loggia

w. d.

laundry

bedroom
10'3" x 10'10"

up

family room
16'3" x 16'6"

kitchen

master bedroom
11'5" x 12'7"

dining room
11'5" x 9'11"

covered porch
20'1" x 16'

boardwalk

© Southern Living

FIRST FLOOR

dn.

bedroom
11'3" x 13'10"

loft area

SECOND FLOOR

GRESHAM CREEK COTTAGE

1,831 square feet

DESIGNED BY MOSER DESIGN GROUP

FIRST FLOOR

- master bedroom 13'0" x 15'0"
- kitchen 11'0" x 15'0"
- den 11'0" x 14'0"
- dining 11'0" x 13'0"
- screen porch 9'0" x 10'0"
- living room 15'0" x 16'0"
- porch

© Southern Living

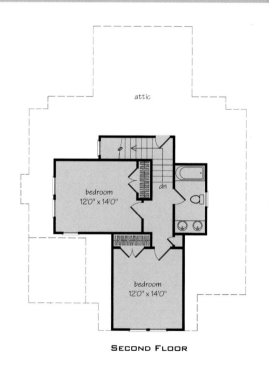

SECOND FLOOR

- attic
- bedroom 12'0" x 14'0"
- bedroom 12'0" x 14'0"

Plan# HPK3800045

First Floor: 1,350 sq. ft.

Second Floor: 481 sq. ft.

Total: 1,831 sq. ft.

Bedrooms: 3

Bathrooms: 2 ½

Width: 38' - 0"

Depth: 58' - 0"

Foundation: Crawlspace

Price Code: A3

1-800-850-1491 • EPLANS.COM

1,842 square feet

ARCHITECTURAL RENDERING: ROLAND DAVIS

DESIGNED BY WILLIAM H. PHILLIPS

Plan # HPK3800046

First Floor: 1,092 sq. ft.

Second Floor: 750 sq. ft.

Total: 1,842 sq. ft.

Bedrooms: 3

Bathrooms: 2 ½

Width: 44' - 0"

Depth: 41' - 0"

Foundation: Crawlspace

Price Code: C1

1-800-850-1491 • EPLANS.COM

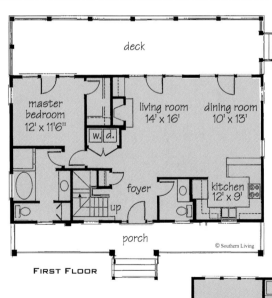

deck

master bedroom 12' x 11'6"

living room 14' x 16'

dining room 10' x 13'

w. d.

foyer

kitchen 12' x 9'

up

porch

© Southern Living

FIRST FLOOR

bedroom 12' x 15'

open to below

bedroom 12' x 16'

dn.

SECOND FLOOR

PIEDMONT COTTAGE

1,855 square feet

DESIGNED BY CALDWELL-CLINE ARCHITECTS AND DESIGNERS FOR COTTAGE LIVING MAGAZINE

Plan # HPK3800047

First Floor: 1,338 sq. ft.

Second Floor: 517 sq. ft.

Total: 1,855 sq. ft.

Bedrooms: 3

Bathrooms: 2 ½

Width: 59' - 0"

Depth: 45' - 0"

Foundation: Unfinished Basement

Price Code: C3

1-800-850-1491 • EPLANS.COM

First Floor

- PORCH 15'5" X 19'6"
- LIVING ROOM 18'2" X 17'6"
- MASTER BEDROOM 15'6" x 15'6"
- UP
- DN
- W D
- MASTER BATH
- DINING ROOM 12'10" X 11'4"
- FOYER
- KITCHEN 11'8" x 11'0"
- PWDR
- PORCH 19'2" X 11'5"

© Southern Living

Second Floor

- OPEN TO BELOW
- BEDROOM 13'2" X 11'7"
- DN
- PWDR
- BEDROOM 12'0" X 11'4"

TURTLE LAKE COTTAGE

ARCHITECTURAL RENDERING: MILES MELTON

1,871 square feet

DESIGNED BY MOSER DESIGN GROUP

Plan # HPK3800048

First Floor: 1,308 sq. ft.

Second Floor: 563 sq. ft.

Total: 1,871 sq. ft.

Bedrooms: 3

Bathrooms: 2 ½

Width: 43' - 0"

Depth: 64' - 0"

Foundation: Crawlspace

Price Code: C1

1-800-850-1491 • EPLANS.COM

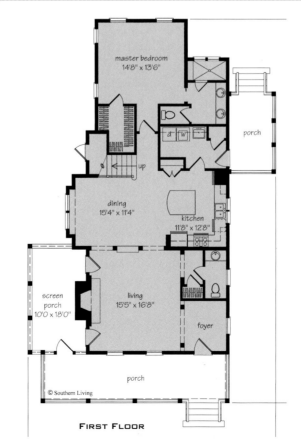

master bedroom
14'8" x 13'6"

porch

dining
15'4" x 11'4"

kitchen
11'8" x 12'8"

up

screen porch
10'0 x 18'0"

living
15'5" x 16'8"

foyer

© Southern Living

porch

FIRST FLOOR

dn

bedroom
14'0" x 11'6"

bedroom
15'6" x 11'4"

SECOND FLOOR

1,872
square feet

DESIGNED BY CIRCA STUDIOS

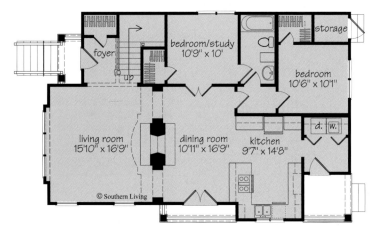

FIRST FLOOR

foyer

up

bedroom/study
10'9" x 10'

storage

bedroom
10'6" x 10'1"

living room
15'10" x 16'9"

dining room
10'11" x 16'9"

kitchen
9'7" x 14'8"

d. w.

© Southern Living

SECOND FLOOR

dn.

open to
below

loft

master bedroom
15'8" x 19'1"

storage

THE WINONNA PARK offers all

the amenities characteristic of larger homes, but in a manageable footprint. A wall of front-facing windows in the living room ensures plenty of natural light. Tucked under the eaves upstairs, the master suite features a double-door entry, a vaulted ceiling, and a private bath with luxurious oval tub.

Plan # HPK3800049

First Floor: 1,174 sq. ft.

Second Floor: 698 sq. ft.

Total: 1,872 sq. ft.

Bedrooms: 3

Bathrooms: 2

Width: 30' - 0"

Depth: 46' - 0"

Foundation: Crawlspace

Price Code: A2

1-800-850-1491 • EPLANS.COM

⚜ RIVER CLIFF COTTAGE ⚜

1,910
square feet

ARCHITECTURAL RENDERING: MILES MELTON

DESIGNED BY MOUZON DESIGN FOR BILTMORE ESTATE

Plan# HPK3800050

First Floor: 1,288 sq. ft.

Second Floor: 622 sq. ft.

Total: 1,910 sq. ft.

Bedrooms: 3

Bathrooms: 3 ½

Width: 41' - 0"

Depth: 74' - 0"

Foundation: Crawlspace

Price Code: L4

1-800-850-1491 • EPLANS.COM

BILTMORE™
For Your Home

WINDSONG COTTAGE

1,927
square feet

Plan# HPK3800051

First Floor: 1,016 sq. ft.

Second Floor: 911 sq. ft.

Total: 1,927 sq. ft.

Bedrooms: 4

Bathrooms: 3

Width: 40' - 0"

Depth: 51' - 0"

Foundation: Crawlspace

Price Code: A3

1-800-850-1491 • EPLANS.COM

DESIGNED BY SULLIVAN DESIGN COMPANY
FOR COASTAL LIVING MAGAZINE

FIRST FLOOR

SECOND FLOOR

© Southern Living

·ELIZABETH'S PLACE·

1,938
square feet

ARCHITECTURAL RENDERING: MILES MELTON

DESIGNED BY MITCHELL GINN

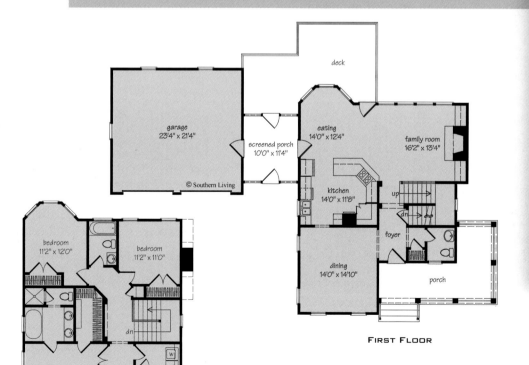

deck

garage
23'4" x 21'4"

screened porch
10'0" x 11'4"

eating
14'0" x 12'4"

family room
16'2" x 13'4"

© Southern Living

kitchen
14'0" x 11'8"

up

dn

foyer

dining
14'0" x 14'10"

porch

FIRST FLOOR

bedroom
11'2" x 12'0"

bedroom
11'2" x 11'0"

dn

w

d

master bedroom
14'0" x 14'10"

SECOND FLOOR

Plan # HPK3800052

First Floor: 983 sq. ft.

Second Floor: 955 sq. ft.

Total: 1,938 sq. ft.

Bedrooms: 3

Bathrooms: 2 ½

Width: 70' - 0"

Depth: 51' - 0"

Foundation: Unfinished Basement

Price Code: C1

1-800-850-1491 • EPLANS.COM

~COUPLES COTTAGE~

2,090
square feet

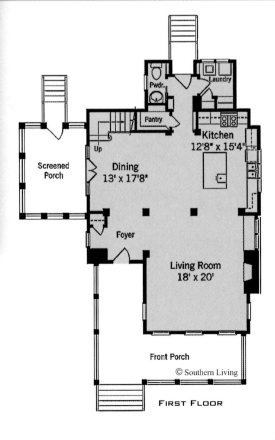

DESIGNED BY MOSER DESIGN GROUP
FOR COASTAL LIVING MAGAZINE

Plan# HPK3800053

First Floor: 1,162 sq. ft.

Second Floor: 928 sq. ft.

Total: 2,090 sq. ft.

Bedrooms: 2

Bathrooms: 2 ½

Width: 43' - 0"

Depth: 56' - 0"

Foundation: Crawlspace

Price Code: C3

1-800-850-1491 • EPLANS.COM

Screened Porch

Up

Pantry

Pwdr.

Laundry

Kitchen
12'8" x 15'4"

Dining
13' x 17'8"

Foyer

Living Room
18' x 20'

Front Porch

© Southern Living

FIRST FLOOR

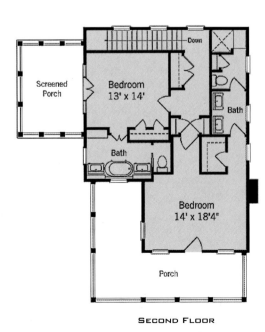

Screened Porch

Down

Bedroom
13' x 14'

Bath

Bath

Bedroom
14' x 18'4"

Porch

SECOND FLOOR

BERMUDA BLUFF COTTAGE

1,998 square feet

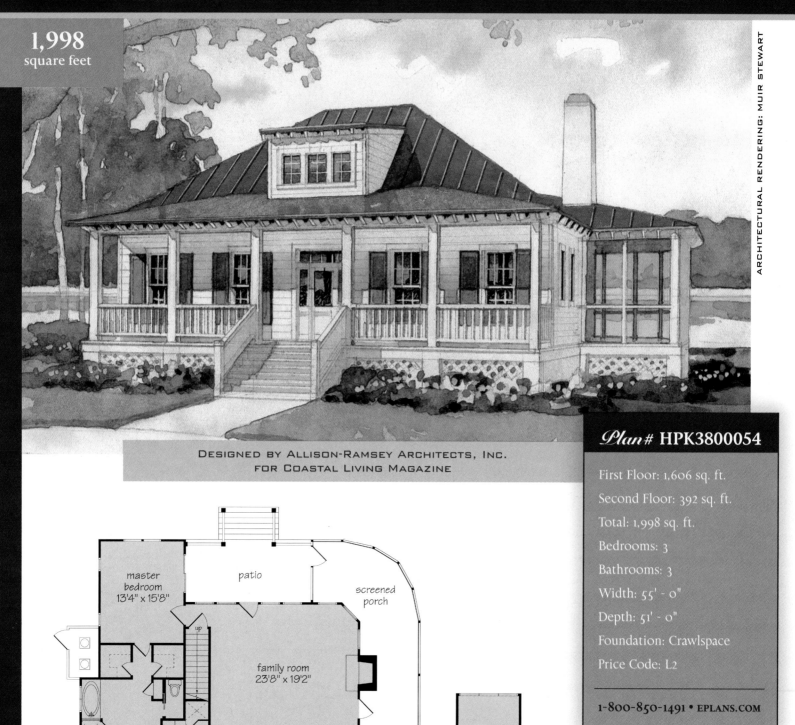

DESIGNED BY ALLISON-RAMSEY ARCHITECTS, INC.
FOR COASTAL LIVING MAGAZINE

Plan # HPK3800054

First Floor: 1,606 sq. ft.

Second Floor: 392 sq. ft.

Total: 1,998 sq. ft.

Bedrooms: 3

Bathrooms: 3

Width: 55' - 0"

Depth: 51' - 0"

Foundation: Crawlspace

Price Code: L2

1-800-850-1491 • EPLANS.COM

First Floor

- master bedroom 13'4" x 15'8"
- patio
- screened porch
- up
- family room 23'8" x 19'2"
- office/bedroom 17'4" x 11'
- foyer
- kitchen 14'4" x 14'4"
- W. d.
- porch

© Southern Living

FIRST FLOOR

Second Floor

- bedroom 12' x 15'9"
- dn.

SECOND FLOOR

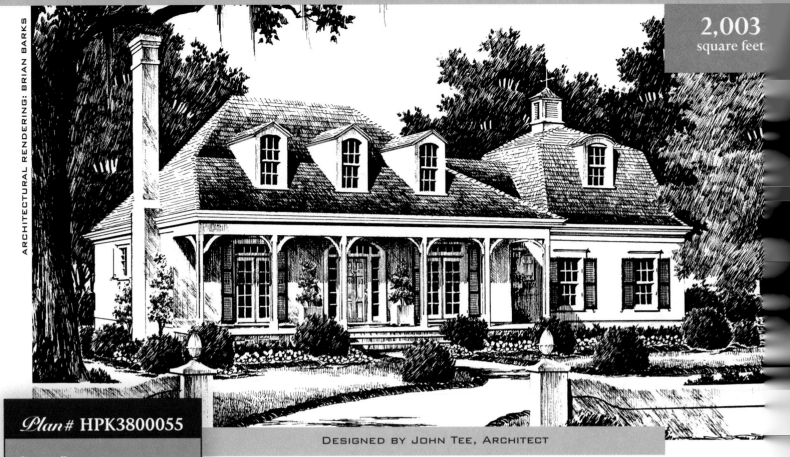

ARCHITECTURAL RENDERING: BRIAN BARKS

2,003
square feet

DESIGNED BY JOHN TEE, ARCHITECT

Plan # HPK3800055

Square Footage: 2,003

Bedrooms: 2

Bathrooms: 2 ½

Width: 66' - 0"

Depth: 50' - 0"

Foundation: Crawlspace

Price Code: A4

1-800-850-1491 • EPLANS.COM

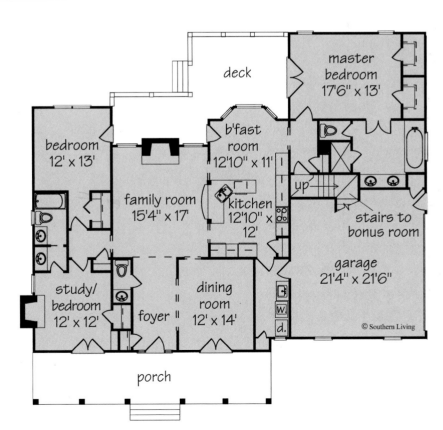

deck

master bedroom
17'6" x 13'

bedroom
12' x 13'

b'fast room
12'10" x 11'

family room
15'4" x 17'

kitchen
12'10" x 12'

up

stairs to bonus room

study/bedroom
12' x 12'

foyer

dining room
12' x 14'

garage
21'4" x 21'6"

© Southern Living

porch

2,010
square feet

ARCHITECTURAL RENDERING: LOIS WATSON

DESIGNED BY SULLIVAN DESIGN COMPANY

Plan # **HPK3800056**

Square Footage: 2,010

Bonus Space: 277 sq. ft.

Bedrooms: 3

Bathrooms: 3

Width: 60' - 0"

Depth: 75' - 0"

Foundation: Crawlspace

Price Code: C3

1-800-850-1491 • EPLANS.COM

porch

deck

master bedroom
13'4" x 16'4"

sunroom
13'4" x 10'8"

family room
17'4" x 19'11"

breakfast
room
7' x 10'8"

kitchen
13'3" x
12'8"

foyer

bedroom
11' x 12'8"

dining room
10'3" x 12'3"

bedroom
11'4" x 12'

dn.

bonus room
13'8" x 20'4"

up

d. w.

porch

garage
20'4" x 20'4"

© Southern Living

ARCHITECTURAL RENDERING: MUIR STEWART

2,032 square feet

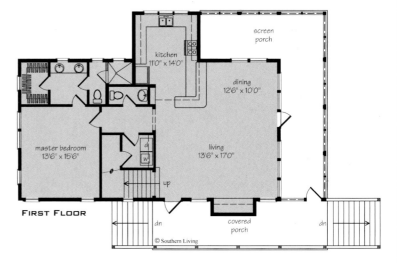

Plan# HPK3800057

First Floor: 1,222 sq. ft.

Second Floor: 810 sq. ft.

Total: 2,032 sq. ft.

Bedrooms: 3

Bathrooms: 2 ½

Width: 40' - 0"

Depth: 54' - 0"

Foundation: Pier (same as Piling)

Price Code: C3

1-800-850-1491 • EPLANS.COM

DESIGNED BY GEORGE GRAVES, AIA
FOR COASTAL LIVING MAGAZINE

FIRST FLOOR

screen porch

kitchen 11'0" x 14'0"

dining 12'6" x 10'0"

master bedroom 13'6" x 15'6"

living 13'6" x 17'0"

up

dn

covered porch

dn

© Southern Living

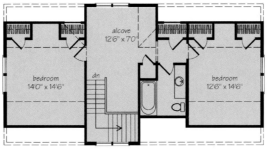

SECOND FLOOR

alcove 12'6" x 7'0"

bedroom 14'0" x 14'6"

dn

bedroom 12'6" x 14'6"

❦ AZALEA ❧

2,014
square feet

ARCHITECTURAL RENDERING: ROLAND DAVIS

DESIGNED BY WILLIAM H. PHILLIPS

Plan # HPK3800058

First Floor: 1,225 sq. ft.

Second Floor: 789 sq. ft.

Total: 2,014 sq. ft.

Bonus Space: 168 sq. ft.

Bedrooms: 3

Bathrooms: 2 ½

Width: 35' - 0"

Depth: 50' - 0"

Foundation: Crawlspace

Price Code: C1

1-800-850-1491 • EPLANS.COM

porch

© Southern Living

master
bedroom
12' x 17'

living room
19'6" x 13'

dining room
11' x 9'

d.
w.

kitchen
11' x 12'

foyer   up

porch

FIRST FLOOR

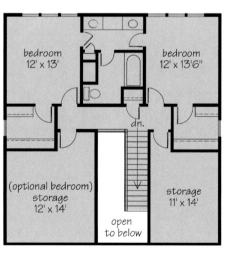

bedroom
12' x 13'

bedroom
12' x 13'6"

dn.

(optional bedroom)
storage
12' x 14'

storage
11' x 14'

open
to below

SECOND FLOOR

WALTERBORO RIDGE

2,051 square feet

DESIGNED BY MOSER DESIGN GROUP

Plan # HPK3800059

First Floor: 1,441 sq. ft.

Second Floor: 610 sq. ft.

Total: 2,051 sq. ft.

Bedrooms: 3

Bathrooms: 2 ½

Width: 35' - 0"

Depth: 56' - 0"

Foundation: Crawlspace

Price Code: C1

1-800-850-1491 • EPLANS.COM

master bedroom
16'0" x 12'8"

sun room
12'0" x 10'8"

kitchen
13'0" x 14'0"

up

dining
11'0" x 14'0"

den/bedroom
12'0" x 14'0"

living
16'4" x 18'0"

porch

© Southern Living

FIRST FLOOR

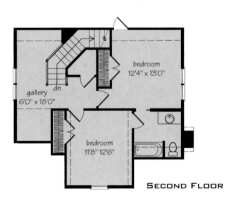

bedroom
12'4" x 13'0"

gallery
6'0" x 18'0"

dn

bedroom
11'8" 12'6"

SECOND FLOOR

⊰ WEST BAY LANDING ⊱

2,051
square feet

ARCHITECTURAL RENDERING: MILES MELTON

DESIGNED BY LAKE FLATO ARCHITECTS, INC.
FOR ST. JOE LAND COMPANY

Plan# HPK3800060

First Floor: 1,197 sq. ft.

Second Floor: 854 sq. ft.

Total: 2,051 sq. ft.

Bedrooms: 3

Bathrooms: 3 ½

Width: 32' - 0"

Depth: 99' - 0"

Foundation: Pier
(same as Piling)

Price Code: L4

1-800-850-1491 • EPLANS.COM

office
7'11" x
5'2"

family room
16' x 12'9"

dining room
12'10" x
15'10"

kitchen
12'7" x 12'2"

master bedroom
12'9" x
15'11"

up

screened porch

mudroom
9'10" x
10'2"

dn.

dn.

© Southern Living

FIRST FLOOR

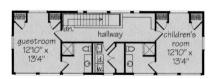

dn.

guestroom
12'10" x
13'4"

hallway

children's room
12'10" x
13'4"

SECOND FLOOR

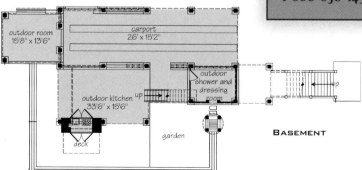

outdoor room
15'8" x 13'6"

carport
26' x 15'2"

outdoor shower and dressing room

up

outdoor kitchen
33'6" x 15'6"

up

deck

garden

BASEMENT

BARRIER ISLAND ESCAPE

2,060
square feet

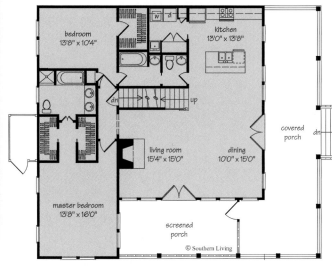

DESIGNED BY ALLISON-RAMSEY ARCHITECTS, INC.
FOR COASTAL LIVING MAGAZINE

Plan# HPK3800061

First Floor: 1,463 sq. ft.

Second Floor: 597 sq. ft.

Total: 2,060 sq. ft.

Bedrooms: 2

Bathrooms: 2

Width: 50' - 0"

Depth: 43' - 0"

Foundation: Pier
(same as Piling)

Price Code: C3

1-800-850-1491 • EPLANS.COM

bedroom
13'8" x 10'4"

kitchen
13'0" x 13'8"

w   d

dn   up

living room
15'4" x 15'0"

dining
10'0" x 15'0"

covered
porch

dn

master bedroom
13'8" x 16'0"

screened
porch

© Southern Living

FIRST FLOOR

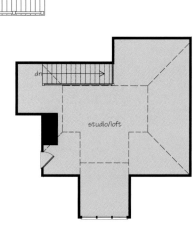

dn

studio/loft

SECOND FLOOR

2,066 square feet

ARCHITECTURAL RENDERING: MILES MELTON

DESIGNED BY MOSER DESIGN GROUP

Plan # HPK3800062

First Floor: 1,667 sq. ft.

Second Floor: 399 sq. ft.

Total: 2,066 sq. ft.

Bedrooms: 4

Bathrooms: 3

Width: 43' - 0"

Depth: 63' - 0"

Foundation: Crawlspace

Price Code: C1

1-800-850-1491 • EPLANS.COM

First Floor

porch 9'8" x 12'4"

master bedroom 13'8" x 15'0"

w d

kitchen 14'8" x 16'8"

bedroom 12'0" x 12'4"

up

dining 10'0" x 13'4"

living 20'4" x 20'4"

bedroom 12'0" x 13'6"

porch

© Southern Living

Second Floor

bedroom 12'8" x 13'8"

dn

gallery 7'4" x 10'8"

⚜ GLENCOE SPRINGS ⚜

2,066 square feet

ARCHITECTURAL RENDERING: LOIS WATSON

DESIGNED BY SULLIVAN DESIGN COMPANY

Plan# HPK3800063

First Floor: 1,581 sq. ft.

Second Floor: 485 sq. ft.

Total: 2,066 sq. ft.

Bedrooms: 3

Bathrooms: 3

Width: 39' - 0"

Depth: 60' - 0"

Foundation: Pier (same as Piling)

Price Code: C1

1-800-850-1491 • EPLANS.COM

master bedroom
15'0" x 13'8"

screen porch

great room
18'0" x 14'8"

up

kitchen
15'2" x 11'8"

bedroom
11'4" x 12'8"

foyer

dining room
11'0" x 10'4"

dn

d
w

porch

© Southern Living

FIRST FLOOR

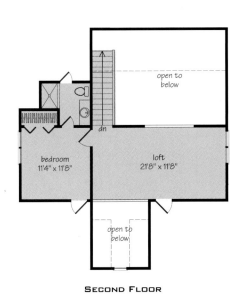

open to below

bedroom
11'4" x 11'8"

loft
21'8" x 11'8"

dn

open to below

SECOND FLOOR

RED BAY COTTAGE

2,074
square feet

DESIGNED BY SULLIVAN DESIGN COMPANY

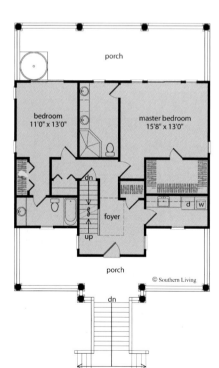

Plan# HPK3800064

First Floor: 956 sq. ft.

Second Floor: 896 sq. ft.

Third Floor: 222 sq. ft.

Total: 2,074 sq. ft.

Bedrooms: 3

Bathrooms: 3

Width: 35' - 0"

Depth: 49' - 0"

Foundation: Pier
(same as Piling)

Price Code: C1

1-800-850-1491 • EPLANS.COM

porch

bedroom
11'0" x 13'0"

master bedroom
15'8" x 13'0"

dn

foyer

up

porch

© Southern Living

dn

FIRST FLOOR

porch

bedroom
11'0" x 12'10"

living room
14'0" x 22'10"

dn

kitchen
11'0" x 11'0"

balcony

SECOND FLOOR

balcony

cupola
11'8" x 19'7"

THIRD FLOOR

COTTON HILL COTTAGE

2,083
square feet

DESIGNED BY BRYAN & CONTRERAS, LLC

Plan# HPK3800065

First Floor: 1,161 sq. ft.

Second Floor: 922 sq. ft.

Total: 2,083 sq. ft.

Bedrooms: 3

Bathrooms: 3

Width: 36' - 4"

Depth: 46' - 6"

Foundation: Crawlspace

Price Code: C1

1-800-850-1491 • EPLANS.COM

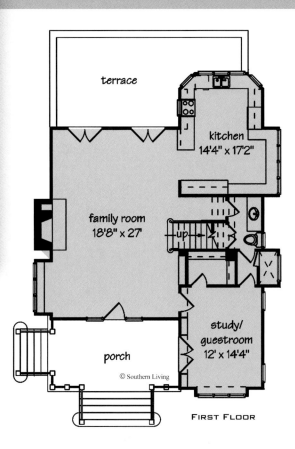

terrace

kitchen
14'4" x 17'2"

family room
18'8" x 27

up

study/
guestroom
12' x 14'4"

porch

© Southern Living

FIRST FLOOR

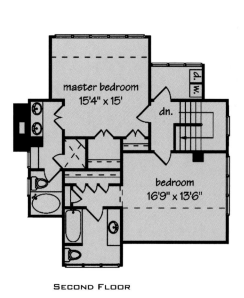

master bedroom
15'4" x 15'

dn.

bedroom
16'9" x 13'6"

SECOND FLOOR

MISS MAGGIE'S HOUSE

2,089
square feet

DESIGNED BY MITCHELL GINN

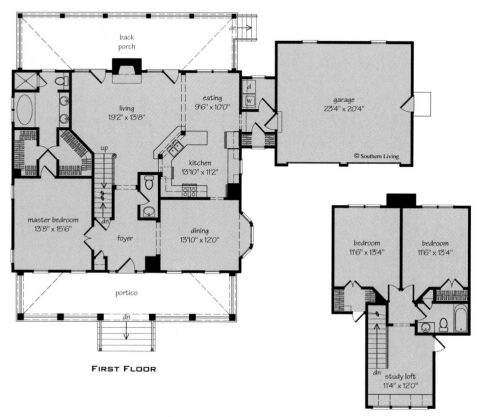

FIRST FLOOR

- back porch
- living 19'2" x 13'8"
- eating 9'6" x 10'0"
- garage 23'4" x 20'4"
- © Southern Living
- kitchen 13'10" x 11'2"
- up
- master bedroom 13'8" x 15'6"
- foyer
- dining 13'10" x 12'0"
- dn
- portico
- dn

SECOND FLOOR

- bedroom 11'6" x 13'4"
- bedroom 11'6" x 13'4"
- dn
- study loft 11'4" x 12'0"

Plan # HPK3800066

First Floor: 1,444 sq. ft.

Second Floor: 645 sq. ft.

Total: 2,089 sq. ft.

Bedrooms: 3

Bathrooms: 2 ½

Width: 70' - 0"

Depth: 52' - 0"

Foundation: Unfinished Basement

Price Code: C1

1-800-850-1491 • EPLANS.COM

~·CHINABERRY·~

ARCHITECTURAL RENDERING: ROLAD DAVIS

2,099 square feet

DESIGNED BY WILLIAM H. PHILLIPS

Plan# HPK3800067

First Floor: 1,191 sq. ft.

Second Floor: 908 sq. ft.

Total: 2,099 sq. ft.

Bedrooms: 3

Bathrooms: 2 ½

Width: 35' - 0"

Depth: 56' - 0"

Foundation: Crawlspace

Price Code: C1

1-800-850-1491 • EPLANS.COM

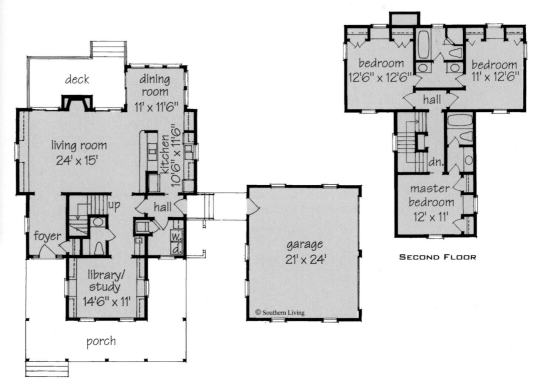

deck

dining room
11' x 11'6"

living room
24' x 15'

kitchen
10'6" x 11'6"

up

hall

foyer

W.d.

library/
study
14'6" x 11'

porch

garage
21' x 24'

© Southern Living

FIRST FLOOR

bedroom
12'6" x 12'6"

bedroom
11' x 12'6"

hall

dn.

master
bedroom
12' x 11'

SECOND FLOOR

❦ CHESTNUT HILL ALTERNATE ❦

2,105 square feet

ARCHITECTURAL RENDERING: BRIAN BARKS

DESIGNED BY JOHN TEE, ARCHITECT

Plan # **HPK3800351**

First Floor: 1,365 sq. ft.

Second Floor: 740 sq. ft.

Total: 2,105 sq. ft.

Bonus Space: 338 sq. ft.

Bedrooms: 3

Bathrooms: 2 ½

Width: 62' - 0"

Depth: 64' - 0"

Foundation: Unfinished Basement

Price Code: L4

1-800-850-1491 • EPLANS.COM

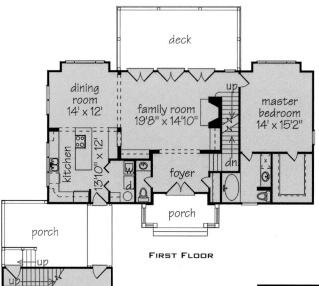

deck

dining room 14' x 12'

family room 19'8" x 14'10"

master bedroom 14' x 15'2"

kitchen 13'10" x 12'

up

dn

foyer

porch

FIRST FLOOR

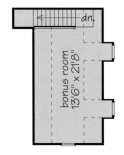

bonus room 13'6" x 21'8"

dn.

porch

up

up

garage 22' x 26'

© Southern Living

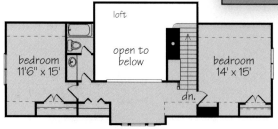

loft

bedroom 11'6" x 15'

open to below

bedroom 14' x 15'

dn.

SECOND FLOOR

⇌ BAYSIDE COTTAGE ⇌

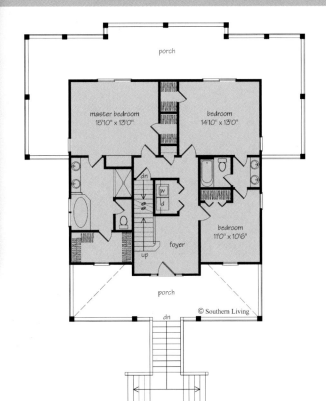

2,105 square feet

Plan# HPK3800068

First Floor: 1,173 sq. ft.

Second Floor: 932 sq. ft.

Total: 2,105 sq. ft.

Bedrooms: 4

Bathrooms: 3

Width: 51' - 0"

Depth: 53' - 0"

Foundation: Pier (same as Piling)

Price Code: C1

1-800-850-1491 • EPLANS.COM

DESIGNED BY SULLIVAN DESIGN COMPANY
FOR COASTAL LIVING MAGAZINE

porch

master bedroom
15'10" x 13'0"

bedroom
14'10" x 13'0"

dn

w
d

up

foyer

bedroom
11'0" x 10'6"

porch

dn

© Southern Living

FIRST FLOOR

balcony

dining
7'2" x 10'0"

living room
21'8" x 16'4"

kitchen
10'10" x 14'2"

dn

bedroom
10'8" x 13'6"

open to below

SECOND FLOOR

❧ WILLIAMS BLUFF ❧

2,144 square feet

ARCHITECTURAL RENDERING: MILES MELTON

MILES MELTON

DESIGNED BY MOSER DESIGN GROUP

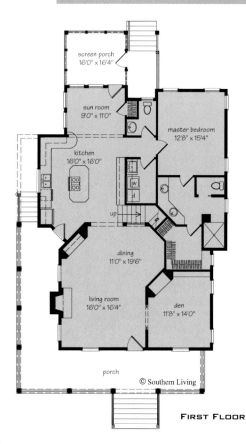

screen porch
16'0" x 16'4"

sun room
9'0" x 11'0"

kitchen
16'0" x 16'0"

master bedroom
12'8" x 15'4"

up

dining
11'0" x 19'6"

living room
16'0" x 16'4"

den
11'8" x 14'0"

porch

© Southern Living

FIRST FLOOR

attic

bedroom
12'0" x 13'4"

gallery

dn

bedroom
11'4" x 12'4"

SECOND FLOOR

Plan# HPK3800069

First Floor: 1,534 sq. ft.

Second Floor: 610 sq. ft.

Total: 2,144 sq. ft.

Bedrooms: 3

Bathrooms: 2 ½

Width: 40' - 0"

Depth: 67' - 0"

Foundation: Crawlspace

Price Code: C1

1-800-850-1491 • EPLANS.COM

LOWCOUNTRY COTTAGE

2,148
square feet

DESIGNED BY MOSER DESIGN GROUP FOR COTTAGE LIVING MAGAZINE

Plan# HPK3800070

First Floor: 1,631 sq. ft.

Second Floor: 517 sq. ft.

Total: 2,148 sq. ft.

Bedrooms: 2

Bathrooms: 2 ½

Width: 45' - 0"

Depth: 73' - 0"

Foundation: Crawlspace

Price Code: C1

1-800-850-1491 • EPLANS.COM

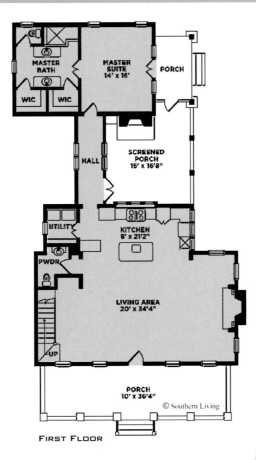

FIRST FLOOR

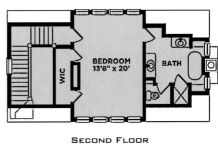

SECOND FLOOR

OAKLEAF

2,165 square feet

ARCHITECTURAL RENDERING: ROLAND DAVIS

DESIGNED BY WILLIAM H. PHILLIPS

deck

dining room 13' x 17'

family room 19'6" x 18'6"

master bedroom 12'6" x 19'

b'fast 9'6" x 10'6"

kitchen 11' x 14'6"

foyer

w d

porch

bedroom 11' x 15'6"

bedroom 11' x 12'6"

garage 21' x 25'

© Southern Living

Plan# **HPK3800071**

Square Footage: 2,165

Bedrooms: 3

Bathrooms: 2 ½

Width: 67' - 0"

Depth: 79' - 0"

Foundation: Crawlspace

Price Code: C1

1-800-850-1491 • EPLANS.COM

Maple Hill

ARCHITECTURAL RENDERING: LOIS WATSON

2,169 square feet

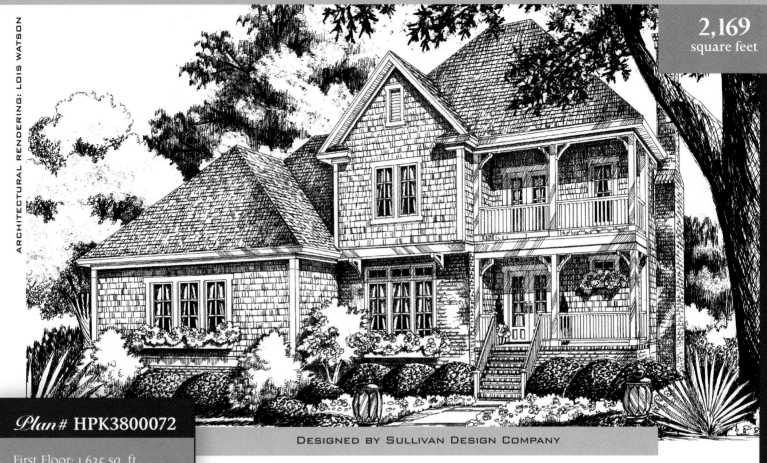

DESIGNED BY SULLIVAN DESIGN COMPANY

Plan # HPK3800072

First Floor: 1,635 sq. ft.

Second Floor: 534 sq. ft.

Total: 2,169 sq. ft.

Bonus Space: 241 sq. ft.

Bedrooms: 3

Bathrooms: 2 ½

Width: 57' - 0"

Depth: 63' - 0"

Foundation: Crawlspace

Price Code: C1

1-800-850-1491 • EPLANS.COM

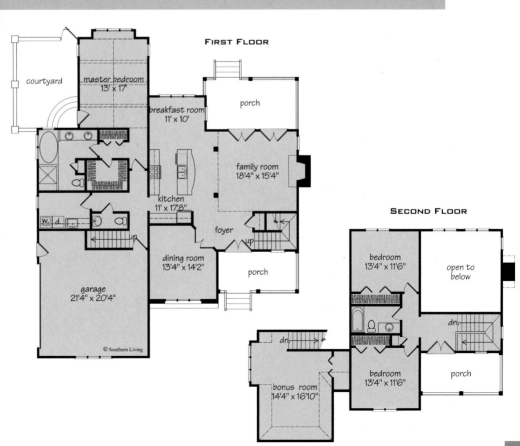

FIRST FLOOR

courtyard

master bedroom
13' x 17'

breakfast room
11' x 10'

porch

kitchen
11' x 17'8"

family room
18'4" x 15'4"

foyer

up

up

w.d.

dining room
13'4" x 14'2"

porch

garage
21'4" x 20'4"

© Southern Living

SECOND FLOOR

bedroom
13'4" x 11'6"

open to below

dn.

dn.

bonus room
14'4" x 16'10"

bedroom
13'4" x 11'6"

porch

2,188
square feet

ARCHITECTURAL RENDERING: MUIR STEWART

DESIGNED BY ALLISON-RAMSEY ARCHITECTS, INC.
FOR COASTAL LIVING MAGAZINE

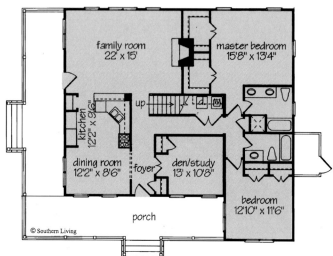

© Southern Living

FIRST FLOOR

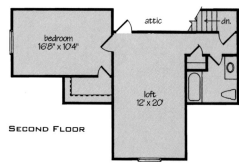

SECOND FLOOR

Plan # HPK3800073

First Floor: 1,604 sq. ft.

Second Floor: 584 sq. ft.

Total: 2,188 sq. ft.

Bedrooms: 3

Bathrooms: 3

Width: 52' - 0"

Depth: 42' - 0"

Foundation: Crawlspace

Price Code: C3

1-800-850-1491 • EPLANS.COM

⚘ CARLISLE HOUSE ⚘

2,196 square feet

ARCHITECTURAL RENDERING: MILES MELTON

DESIGNED BY MOSER DESIGN GROUP

Plan# HPK3800074

First Floor: 1,658 sq. ft.

Second Floor: 538 sq. ft.

Total: 2,196 sq. ft.

Bonus Space: 178 sq. ft.

Bedrooms: 3

Bathrooms: 2 ½

Width: 44' - 0"

Depth: 62' - 0"

Foundation: Crawlspace

Price Code: C1

1-800-850-1491 • EPLANS.COM

porch

master bedroom
13'0" x 16'0"

w d

kitchen
11'6" x 12'0"

breakfast
6'0" x 10'0"

family room
20'6" x 16'4"

up

living
17'0" x 12'4"

dining
12'0" x 12'8"

porch

© Southern Living

FIRST FLOOR

open to below

bonus room
17'0" x 10'6"

dn

bedroom
11'4" x 13'2"

bedroom
12'2" x 12'8"

SECOND FLOOR

⋅Summer Cottage⋅

2,195 square feet

MUIR STEWART

Designed by George Graves, AIA
for Coastal Living Magazine

Plan# HPK3800075

First Floor: 1,226 sq. ft.

Second Floor: 969 sq. ft.

Total: 2,195 sq. ft.

Bedrooms: 3

Bathrooms: 3

Width: 32' - 0"

Depth: 59' - 0"

Foundation: Crawlspace

Price Code: C1

1-800-850-1491 • EPLANS.COM

Screened Porch

© Southern Living

Living Room
16' x 17'

Dining Room
15'6" x 10'

Kitchen
11' x 12'

Foyer

Up

Bath

Entry
Porch

Bedroom
12' x 17'

FIRST FLOOR

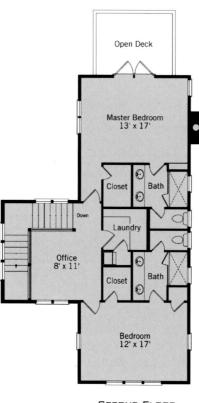

Open Deck

Master Bedroom
13' x 17'

Closet

Bath

Down

Laundry

Office
8' x 11'

Closet

Bath

Bedroom
12' x 17'

SECOND FLOOR

·AIKEN RIDGE·

2,202
square feet

DESIGNED BY MOSER DESIGN GROUP

Plan# HPK3800076

First Floor: 1,580 sq. ft.

Second Floor: 622 sq. ft.

Total: 2,202 sq. ft.

Bedrooms: 3

Bathrooms: 3 ½

Width: 40' - 0"

Depth: 60' - 0"

Foundation: Crawlspace

Price Code: C3

1-800-850-1491 • EPLANS.COM

FIRST FLOOR

SECOND FLOOR

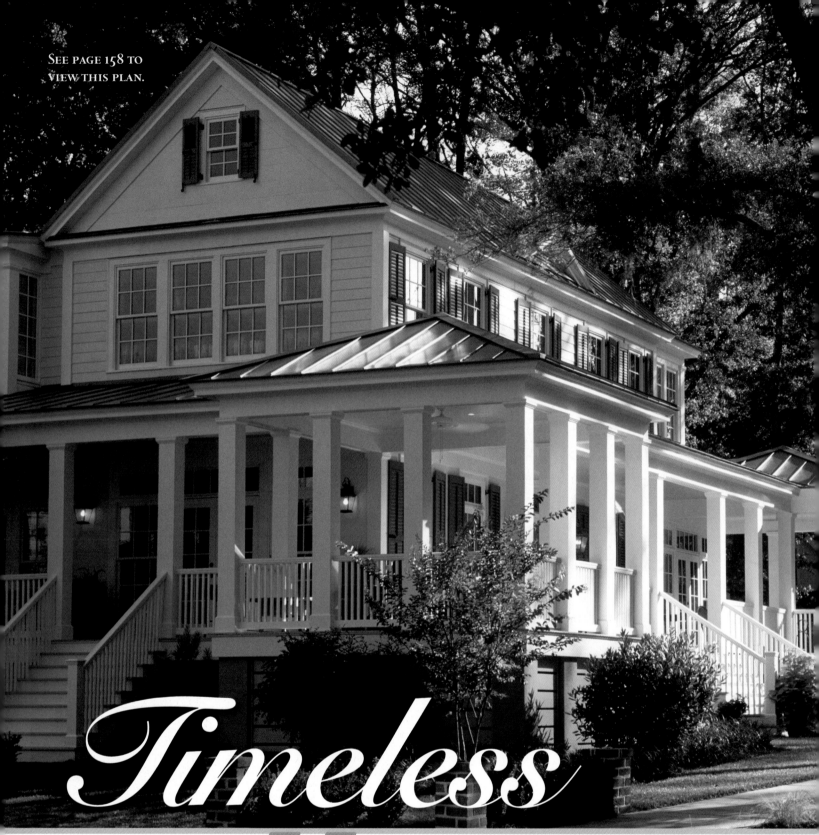

SEE PAGE 158 TO VIEW THIS PLAN.

Timeless
Homes

SEE PAGE 134 TO VIEW THIS PLAN.

© SOUTHERN LIVING

Whether you're ready to graduate from your first home or you wish to start with something truly special, Timeless Homes (from 2,206 to 2,800 square feet) offer spacious bedrooms, elegant, open kitchens, and more.

Consider the Richmond, on page 101. With covered porches in front and back, a large sunroom, and generous counterspace in the kitchen, the plan is ideal for entertaining. Three bedrooms and a garage make it an excellent family home, as well.

Timeless Homes are all about flexibility, and the house plans in this section adapt well to any lifestyle.

© SOUTHERN LIVING

SEE PAGE 134 TO VIEW THIS PLAN.

© COASTAL LIVING

SEE PAGE 158 TO VIEW THIS PLAN.

2,208
square feet

ARCHITECTURAL RENDERING: MILES MELTON

DESIGNED BY JOHN TEE, ARCHITECT

Plan # **HPK3800077**

Square Footage: 2,208

Bedrooms: 3

Bathrooms: 2 ½

Width: 80' - 0"

Depth: 48' - 0"

Foundation: Crawlspace

Price Code: C3

1-800-850-1491 • EPLANS.COM

covered porch

breakfast
13'8" x 10'6"

optional up

kitchen
13'8" x 11'0"

family room
18'0" x 18'0"

master bedroom
14'4" x 18'0"

garage
21'4" x 22'0"

© Southern Living

dining
13'8" x 13'0"

foyer
7'4" x 12'6"

bedroom/study
12'0" x 13'0"

bedroom
13'0" x 15'4"

front porch

ARCHITECTURAL RENDERING: MILES MELTON

2,218
square feet

DESIGNED BY MOSER DESIGN GROUP

Plan # HPK3800078

First Floor: 1,412 sq. ft.

Second Floor: 806 sq. ft.

Total: 2,218 sq. ft.

Bedrooms: 3

Bathrooms: 3 ½

Width: 44' - 0"

Depth: 51' - 0"

Foundation: Crawlspace

Price Code: C3

1-800-850-1491 • EPLANS.COM

master bedroom
13'0" x 16'4"

porch

up

kitchen
14'0" x 15'0"

screened
porch
11'0" x 17'6"

living
16'10" x 19'0"

entry
porch

dining
12'0" x 12'4"

© Southern Living

FIRST FLOOR

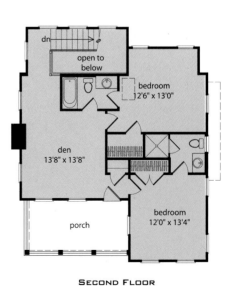

dn

open to
below

bedroom
12'6" x 13'0"

den
13'8" x 13'8"

porch

bedroom
12'0" x 13'4"

SECOND FLOOR

2,460
square feet

ARCHITECTURAL RENDERING: RICK HERR

Designed by Allison-Ramsey Architects, Inc.

Plan # **HPK3800236**

First Floor: 1,747 sq. ft.

Second Floor: 713 sq. ft.

Total: 2,460 sq. ft.

Bedrooms: 4

Bathrooms: 3

Width: 46' - 0"

Depth: 60' - 0"

Foundation: Pier (same as Piling)

Price Code: C3

1-800-850-1491 • EPLANS.COM

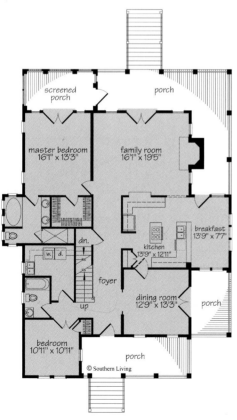

screened porch

porch

master bedroom
16'1" x 13'3"

family room
16'1" x 19'5"

breakfast
13'9" x 7'7"

kitchen
13'9" x 12'11"

dn.

w. d.

foyer

up

dining room
12'9" x 13'3"

porch

bedroom
10'11" x 10'11"

porch

© Southern Living

First Floor

bedroom
13'5" x 17'1"

dn.

bedroom
13'2" x 14'6"

Second Floor

SHILOH CREEK

2,236
square feet

Plan# HPK3800080

First Floor: 1,732 sq. ft.

Second Floor: 504 sq. ft.

Total: 2,236 sq. ft.

Bedrooms: 3

Bathrooms: 2 ½

Width: 48' - 0"

Depth: 72' - 0"

Foundation: Unfinished Basement

Price Code: C1

1-800-850-1491 • EPLANS.COM

DESIGNED BY STEPHEN FULLER, INC.

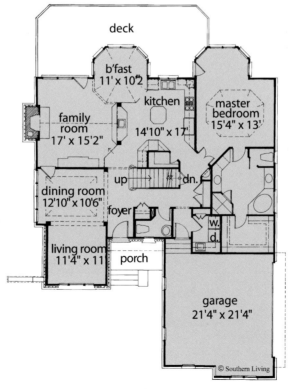

deck

b'fast
11' x 10'2"

kitchen
14'10" x 17'

master bedroom
15'4" x 13'

family room
17' x 15'2"

up / dn.

dining room
12'10" x 10'6"

foyer

w. d.

living room
11'4" x 11'

porch

garage
21'4" x 21'4"

© Southern Living

FIRST FLOOR

bedroom
11'2" x 1'2"

dn.

open to below

bedroom
10'8" x 12'

SECOND FLOOR

NEW ROUND HILL

2,242 square feet

ARCHITECTURAL RENDERING: MILES MELTON

DESIGNED BY JOHN TEE, ARCHITECT

Plan# HPK3800081

Square Footage: 2,242

Bonus Space: 295 sq. ft.

Bedrooms: 3

Bathrooms: 2 full + 2 half

Width: 76' - 0"

Depth: 78' - 0"

Foundation: Crawlspace

Price Code: C3

1-800-850-1491 • EPLANS.COM

garage
22'8" x 23'0"

© Southern Living

covered porch

breakfast
12'0" x 11'0"

mudroom

optional up

kitchen
12'0" x 13'0"

family room
16'0" x 20'0"

master bedroom
14'0" x 18'0"

dining
15'0" x 14'0"

foyer
7'0" x 13'6"

bedroom/study
12'0" x 14'0"

bedroom
12'0" x 14'8"

porch

optional guest apartment
295 s.f.

dn

ARCHITECTURAL RENDERING: LOIS WATSON

2,289
square feet

DESIGNED BY SULLIVAN DESIGN COMPANY

Plan# HPK3800082

First Floor: 1,953 sq. ft.

Second Floor: 336 sq. ft.

Total: 2,289 sq. ft.

Bedrooms: 3

Bathrooms: 2

Width: 61' - 0"

Depth: 55' - 0"

Foundation: Crawlspace

Price Code: C1

1-800-850-1491 • EPLANS.COM

© Southern Living

FIRST FLOOR

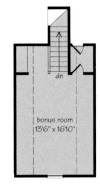

SECOND FLOOR

ANGEL OAK POINT

2,299
square feet

ARCHITECTURAL RENDERING: MILES MELTON

DESIGNED BY MOSER DESIGN GROUP

First Floor: 1,462 sq. ft.

Second Floor: 837 sq. ft.

Total: 2,299 sq. ft.

Bedrooms: 3

Bathrooms: 3 ½

Width: 33' - 0"

Depth: 71' - 0"

Foundation: Crawlspace

Price Code: C1

1-800-850-1491 • EPLANS.COM

FIRST FLOOR

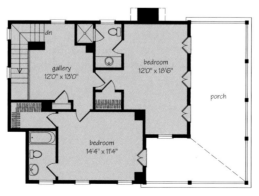

SECOND FLOOR

98   SOUTHERN LIVING *Classic Collection of House Plans*

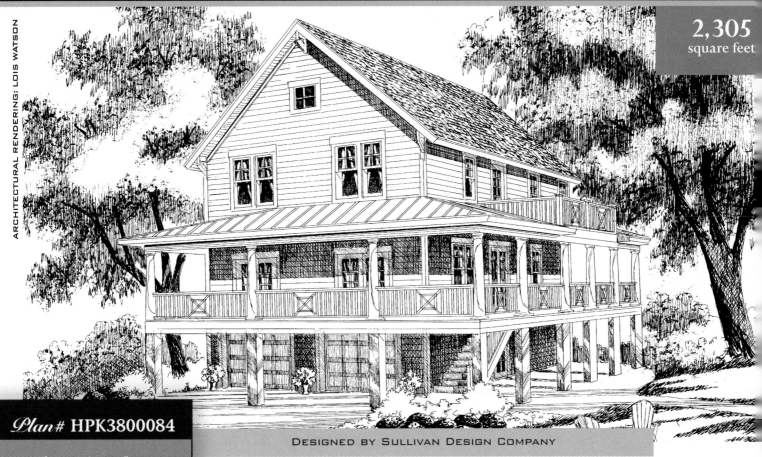

2,305 square feet

ARCHITECTURAL RENDERING: LOIS WATSON

DESIGNED BY SULLIVAN DESIGN COMPANY

Plan# HPK3800084

First Floor: 1,185 sq. ft.

Second Floor: 1,120 sq. ft.

Total: 2,305 sq. ft.

Bedrooms: 3

Bathrooms: 2 ½

Width: 34' - 0"

Depth: 57' - 0"

Foundation: Pier (same as Piling)

Price Code: C1

1-800-850-1491 • EPLANS.COM

future rec. room

mechanical

up

garage
24'4" x 22'0"

up

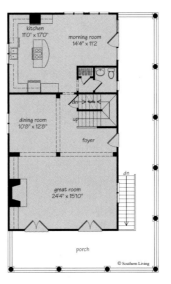

kitchen
11'0" x 17'0"

morning room
14'4" x 11'2

dining room
10'8" x 12'8"

dn
up

foyer

great room
24'4" x 15'10"

dn

porch

© Southern Living

FIRST FLOOR

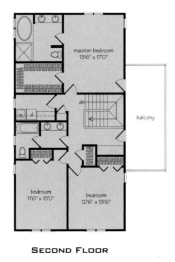

master bedroom
13'6" x 17'0"

dn

w d

balcony

bedroom
11'6" x 15'0"

bedroom
12'6" x 13'6"

SECOND FLOOR

2,315
square feet

DESIGNED BY LOONEY RICKS KISS ARCHITECTS, INC.

ARCHITECTURAL RENDERING: MILES MELTON

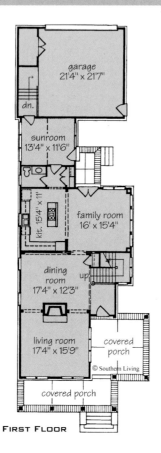

FIRST FLOOR

garage
21'4" x 21'7"

dn.

sunroom
13'4" x 11'6"

kit. 15'4" x 11'

family room
16' x 15'4"

dining room
17'4" x 12'3"

up

living room
17'4" x 15'9"

covered porch

covered porch

© Southern Living

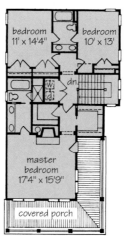

SECOND FLOOR

bedroom
11' x 14'4"

bedroom
10' x 13'

dn.

W/D

master bedroom
17'4" x 15'9"

covered porch

Plan# HPK3800085

First Floor: 1,234 sq. ft.

Second Floor: 1,081 sq. ft.

Total: 2,315 sq. ft.

Bedrooms: 3

Bathrooms: 2 ½

Width: 34' - 0"

Depth: 95' - 0"

Foundation: Crawlspace

Price Code: C3

1-800-850-1491 • EPLANS.COM

RICHMOND

ARCHITECTURAL RENDERING: ROD DENT

2,325 square feet

DESIGNED BY STEPHEN FULLER, INC.

Plan # HPK3800086

Square Footage: 2,325

Bedrooms: 3

Bathrooms: 2 ½

Width: 68' - 0"

Depth: 75' - 0"

Foundation: Unfinished Basement

Price Code: L1

1-800-850-1491 • EPLANS.COM

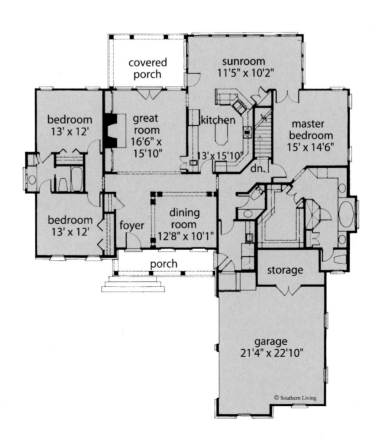

·WILDMERE COTTAGE·

2,345 square feet

DESIGNED BY MOSER DESIGN GROUP FOR COTTAGE LIVING MAGAZINE

Plan# **HPK3800087**

First Floor: 1,435 sq. ft.

Second Floor: 910 sq. ft.

Total: 2,345 sq. ft.

Bedrooms: 3

Bathrooms: 3 ½

Width: 44' - 0"

Depth: 68' - 0"

Foundation: Crawlspace

Price Code: C3

1-800-850-1491 • EPLANS.COM

SCREENED PORCH
13' x 12'6"

MUDROOM
9'2" x 8'4"

KITCHEN
11'0" x 11'7"

MASTER BATH

DN

UP

DINING
11' x 10'1"

D **W**

MASTER BEDROOM
14'4" x 16'5"

ENTRY

PWDR

LIVING
11' x 17'1"

PORCH
24'10"x 9'2"

© Southern Living

FIRST FLOOR

BEDROOM
17' x 12'6"

STORAGE

BATH

DN

PLAYROOM
11'0" X 11'10"

BATH

BEDROOM
17' x 13'10"

SECOND FLOOR

⌐ FRANKLIN HOUSE ⌐

2,352 square feet

DESIGNED BY MOUZON DESIGN

Plan # **HPK3800088**

First Floor: 1,704 sq. ft.

Second Floor: 648 sq. ft.

Total: 2,352 sq. ft.

Bedrooms: 3

Bathrooms: 3 ½

Width: 45' - 0"

Depth: 91' - 0"

Foundation: Crawlspace

Price Code: L4

1-800-850-1491 • EPLANS.COM

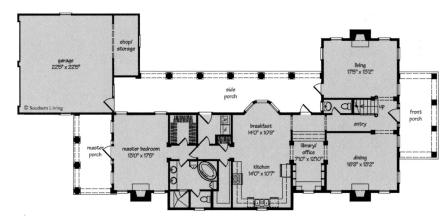

FIRST FLOOR

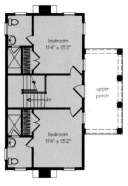

SECOND FLOOR

~ WINNSBORO HEIGHTS ~

2,355
square feet

ARCHITECTURAL RENDERING: MILES MELTON

DESIGNED BY MOSER DESIGN GROUP

FIRST FLOOR

SECOND FLOOR

Plan# **HPK3800089**

First Floor: 1,462 sq. ft.

Second Floor: 893 sq. ft.

Total: 2,355 sq. ft.

Bedrooms: 4

Bathrooms: 2 ½

Width: 42' - 0"

Depth: 60' - 0"

Foundation: Crawlspace

Price Code: C1

1-800-850-1491 • EPLANS.COM

⸙ VALENSOLE ⸙

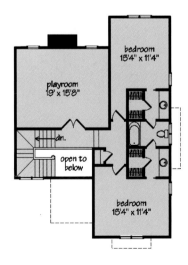

2,360
square feet

DESIGNED BY SULLIVAN DESIGN COMPANY

Plan # HPK3800090

First Floor: 1,391 sq. ft.

Second Floor: 969 sq. ft.

Total: 2,360 sq. ft.

Bedrooms: 3

Bathrooms: 2 ½

Width: 56' - 0"

Depth: 68' - 0"

Foundation: Crawlspace

Price Code: C3

1-800-850-1491 • EPLANS.COM

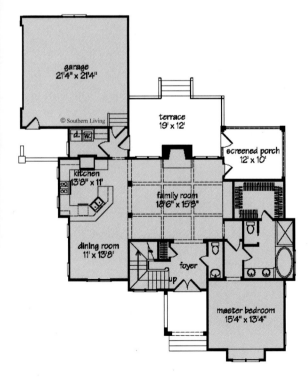

garage
21'4" x 21'4"

© Southern Living

terrace
19' x 12'

screened porch
12' x 10'

kitchen
13'8" x 11'

family room
18'6" x 15'8"

dining room
11' x 13'8"

foyer

up

master bedroom
15'4" x 13'4"

FIRST FLOOR

bedroom
15'4" x 11'4"

playroom
19' x 15'8"

dn.

open to below

bedroom
15'4" x 11'4"

SECOND FLOOR

⟨ TABOR LANE ⟩

2,360 square feet

ARCHITECTURAL RENDERING: MILES MELTON

MILES MELTON

DESIGNED BY MOSER DESIGN GROUP

Plan # HPK3800091

First Floor: 1,421 sq. ft.

Second Floor: 939 sq. ft.

Total: 2,360 sq. ft.

Bedrooms: 3

Bathrooms: 3 ½

Width: 42' - 0"

Depth: 60' - 0"

Foundation: Crawlspace

Price Code: A4

1-800-850-1491 • EPLANS.COM

---

master bedroom
15'6" x 14'0"

porch

screened porch
12'0" x 13'0"

kitchen
17'0" x 11'0"

d

w

up

living room
22'0" x 19'0"

dining
17'0" x 10'0"

porch

© Southern Living

FIRST FLOOR

dn

gallery

bedroom
14'2" x 13'5"

study
10'0" x 9'4"

bedroom
14'2" x 13'5"

porch

SECOND FLOOR

RAMBERT PLACE

2,364
square feet

DESIGNED BY MOSER DESIGN GROUP

Plan # HPK3800092

First Floor: 1,565 sq. ft.

Second Floor: 799 sq. ft.

Total: 2,364 sq. ft.

Bedrooms: 4

Bathrooms: 3 ½

Width: 36' - 0"

Depth: 60' - 0"

Foundation: Crawlspace

Price Code: C1

1-800-850-1491 • EPLANS.COM

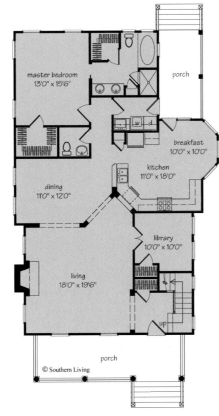

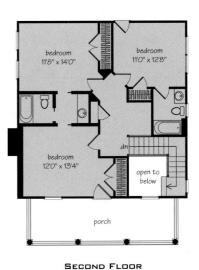

FIRST FLOOR

SECOND FLOOR

MABRY COTTAGE

2,372
square feet

DESIGNED BY LOONEY RICKS KISS ARCHITECTS, INC.
FOR COTTAGE LIVING MAGAZINE

Plan# HPK3800093

First Floor: 1,774 sq. ft.

Second Floor: 598 sq. ft.

Total: 2,372 sq. ft.

Bedrooms: 3

Bathrooms: 2 ½

Width: 38' - 0"

Depth: 73' - 0"

Foundation: Slab

Price Code: C3

1-800-850-1491 • EPLANS.COM

FIRST FLOOR

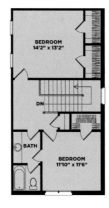

SECOND FLOOR

2,390 square feet

ARCHITECTURAL RENDERING: DON RANKIN

DESIGNED BY JOHN TEE, ARCHITECT

Plan# HPK3800094

Square Footage: 2,390

Bedrooms: 3

Bathrooms: 2 ½

Width: 80' - 0"

Depth: 56' - 0"

Foundation: Crawlspace, Unfinished Basement

Price Code: C3

1-800-850-1491 • EPLANS.COM

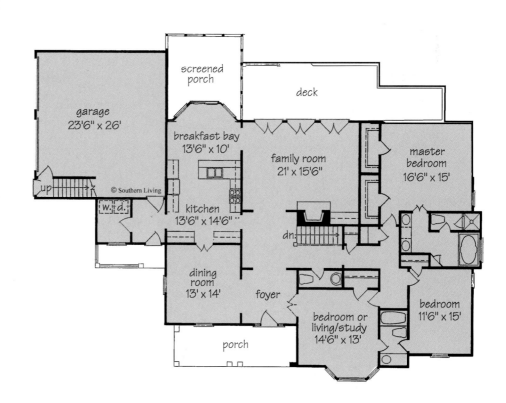

LAKESIDE COTTAGE

2,400 square feet

DESIGNED BY WILLIAM H. PHILLIPS

Plan# HPK3800095

Square Footage: 2,400

Bonus Space: 192 sq. ft.

Bedrooms: 3

Bathrooms: 2 ½

Width: 76' - 3"

Depth: 75' - 9"

Foundation: Crawlspace

Price Code: A4

1-800-850-1491 • EPLANS.COM

foyer

deck

skylit porch
21' x 10'

b'fast
10' x 10'

master
bedroom
14' x 17'

bedroom
12' x 13'

living room
24' x 17'

kitchen
12' x 20'

bedroom
12' x 13'

foyer

dining
room
13' x 16'

W.d.

porch

© Southern Living

up

garage
21' x 30'

12' x 16'

ARCHITECTURAL RENDERING: MILES MELTON

2,401 square feet

DESIGNED BY MOSER DESIGN GROUP

Plan# HPK3800096

First Floor: 1,764 sq. ft.

Second Floor: 637 sq. ft.

Total: 2,401 sq. ft.

Bedrooms: 3

Bathrooms: 2 ½

Width: 49' - 0"

Depth: 80' - 0"

Foundation: Crawlspace

Price Code: C3

1-800-850-1491 • EPLANS.COM

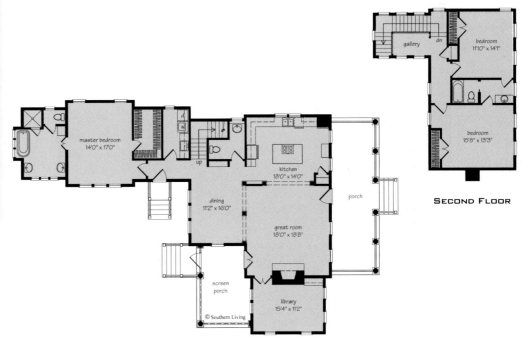

SECOND FLOOR

gallery · dn
bedroom 11'10" x 14'1"
bedroom 15'8" x 13'3"

FIRST FLOOR

master bedroom 14'0" x 17'0"
up
kitchen 18'0" x 14'0"
porch
dining 11'2" x 16'0"
great room 18'0" x 18'8"
© Southern Living
screen porch
library 15'4" x 11'2"

❖NEW OXFORD❖

2,404 square feet

DESIGNED BY JOHN TEE, ARCHITECT

porch

bedroom
13'0" x 12'0"

family room
21'4" x 17'4"

breakfast
11'8" x 11'0"

master bedroom
14'4" x 18'0"

kitchen
13'8" x 12'8"

bedroom
13'0" x 15'8"

foyer
6'8" x 16'0"

dining
12'0" x 15'4"

up

porch

up

garage
21'4" x 24'0"

© Southern Living

Plan# HPK3800097

Square Footage: 2,404

Bedrooms: 3

Bathrooms: 2 ½

Width: 70' - 0"

Depth: 63' - 0"

Foundation: Unfinished Basement

Price Code: L1

1-800-850-1491 • EPLANS.COM

MONTEREAU

ARCHITECTURAL RENDERING: MILES MELTON

DESIGNED BY JOHN TEE, ARCHITECT

Plan# HPK3800098

Square Footage: 2,404

Bedrooms: 3

Bathrooms: 2 ½

Width: 70' - 0"

Depth: 63' - 0"

Foundation: Unfinished Basement

Price Code: L1

1-800-850-1491 • EPLANS.COM

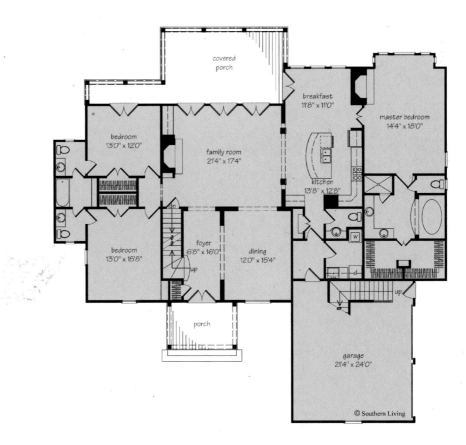

GLEN VIEW COTTAGE

2,414 square feet

DESIGNED BY MOSER DESIGN GROUP FOR Cottage Living MAGAZINE

Plan # HPK3800099

First Floor: 1,712 sq. ft.

Second Floor: 702 sq. ft.

Total: 2,414 sq. ft.

Bedrooms: 3

Bathrooms: 2 ½

Width: 45' - 0"

Depth: 67' - 0"

Foundation: Crawlspace

Price Code: C1

1-800-850-1491 • EPLANS.COM

FIRST FLOOR

- SCREENED PORCH 11'4"x13'8"
- UTILITY
- PANTRY
- PWDR
- UP
- DINING ROOM 11'8"x14'
- MASTER BATH
- WIC
- WIC
- MASTER BEDROOM 14'x17'
- LIVING ROOM 17'6"x18'
- KITCHEN 14'x15'
- DEN 12'x13'8"
- PORCH 9'6" DEEP

SECOND FLOOR

- OPEN TO BELOW
- BATH
- DN
- LANDING 11'x16'
- BEDROOM #2 13'6"x14'8"
- STORAGE
- BEDROOM #3 11'8"x13'8"

2,420 square feet

ARCHITECTURAL RENDERING: BRIAN BARKS

DESIGNED BY GARY/RAGSDALE, INC.

Plan# HPK3800100

Square Footage: 2,420

Bedrooms: 4

Bathrooms: 2 ½

Width: 60' - 0"

Depth: 63' - 0"

Foundation: Crawlspace

Price Code: C3

1-800-850-1491 • EPLANS.COM

master bedroom
18' x 14'4"

family room
16' x 19'

covered porch

breakfast room
10'6" x 11'4"

opt. sunroom/office
11' x 20'

bedroom
11' x 12'

kitchen
13'8" x 17

up

bedroom
11' x 12'

entry

w d

garage
19'8" x 22'6"

study/bedroom
11' x 14'4"

dining room
11' x 13'4"

© Southern Living

porch

covered porch

sunroom
11' x 20'

OPTIONAL LAYOUT

FOREST RIDGE

2,593 square feet

ARCHITECTURAL RENDERING: LOIS WATSON

DESIGNED BY SULLIVAN DESIGN COMPANY

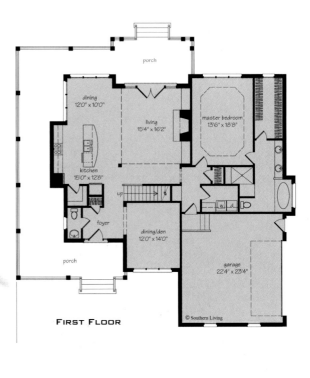

FIRST FLOOR

SECOND FLOOR

Plan# HPK3800175

First Floor: 1,679 sq. ft.

Second Floor: 914 sq. ft.

Total: 2,593 sq. ft.

Bonus Space: 357 s q. ft.

Bedrooms: 4

Bathrooms: 3 ½

Width: 60' - 0"

Depth: 62' - 0"

Foundation: Crawlspace

Price Code: C1

1-800-850-1491 • EPLANS.COM

2,421
square feet

ARCHITECTURAL RENDERING: GREG HAVENS

Plan # HPK3800102

First Floor: 1,814 sq. ft.

Second Floor: 607 sq. ft.

Total: 2,421 sq. ft.

Bedrooms: 3

Bathrooms: 2 ½

Width: 62' - 0"

Depth: 54' - 0"

Foundation: Unfinished Basement

Price Code: C3

1-800-850-1491 • EPLANS.COM

DESIGNED BY BRYAN & CONTRERAS, LLC

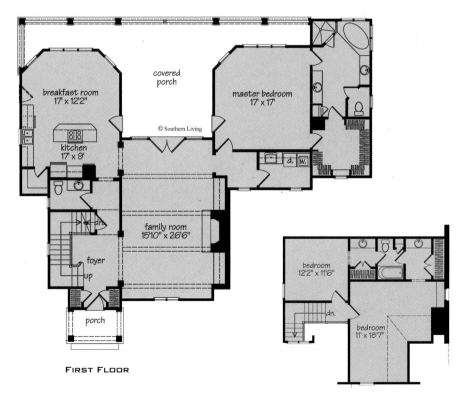

breakfast room
17' x 12'2"

covered porch

master bedroom
17' x 17'

kitchen
17' x 9'

© Southern Living

family room
15'10" x 26'6"

foyer
up

porch

d. w.

FIRST FLOOR

bedroom
12'2" x 11'6"

dn.

bedroom
11' x 18'7"

SECOND FLOOR

2,430
square feet

ARCHITECTURAL RENDERING: RICK HERR

DESIGNED BY BRYAN & CONTRERAS, LLC

Plan# HPK3800103

First Floor: 1,835 sq. ft.

Second Floor: 595 sq. ft.

Total: 2,430 sq. ft.

Bonus/Future Space: 725 sq. ft.

Bedrooms: 3

Bathrooms: 2 ½

Width: 67' - 0"

Depth: 68' - 0"

Foundation: Unfinished Basement

Price Code: C3

1-800-850-1491 • EPLANS.COM

FIRST FLOOR

SECOND FLOOR

LAUREL WOODS

2,430
square feet

DESIGNED BY BRYAN & CONTRERAS, LLC

Plan # HPK3800104

First Floor: 1,835 sq. ft.

Second Floor: 595 sq. ft.

Total: 2,430 sq. ft.

Bonus/Future Space:
690 sq. ft.

Bedrooms: 3

Bathrooms: 2 ½

Width: 60' - 0"

Depth: 68' - 0"

Foundation: Unfinished
Basement

Price Code: C3

1-800-850-1491 • EPLANS.COM

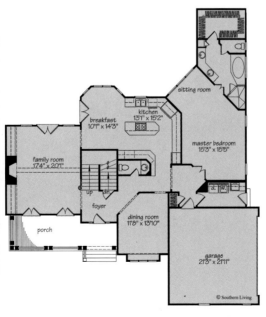

FIRST FLOOR

SECOND FLOOR

WOODRIDGE

2,440 square feet

DESIGNED BY CALDWELL-CLINE ARCHITECTS AND DESIGNERS

Plan# HPK3800105

Square Footage: 2,440

Bedrooms: 3

Bathrooms: 3

Width: 77' - 0"

Depth: 74' - 0"

Foundation: Unfinished Basement

Price Code: A4

1-800-850-1491 • EPLANS.COM

bedroom 11'4" x 12'

breakfast 11'2" x 10'

deck

master bedroom 15'4" x 14'

family room 15' x 19'

study 13' x 12'8"

foyer

bedroom 11'4" x 12'

kitchen 13'6" x 11'

dining room 12' x 14'6"

porch

w. d.

garage 21'4" x 22'4"

© Southern Living

❧ STAFFORD PLACE ❧

2,451
square feet

DESIGNED BY CALDWELL-CLINE ARCHITECTS AND DESIGNERS

Plan # HPK3800106

First Floor: 1,871 sq. ft.

Second Floor: 580 sq. ft.

Total: 2,451 sq. ft.

Bonus Space: 193 sq. ft.

Bedrooms: 3

Bathrooms: 2 ½

Width: 64' - 0"

Depth: 63' - 0"

Foundation: Unfinished Basement

Price Code: A4

1-800-850-1491 • EPLANS.COM

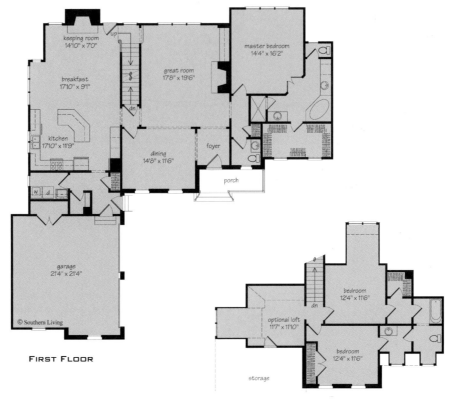

FIRST FLOOR

SECOND FLOOR

WESTBURY PARK

2,457 square feet

ARCHITECTURAL RENDERING: MILES MELTON

DESIGNED BY MOSER DESIGN GROUP

First Floor

- porch
- sunroom 16'0" x 10'8"
- master bedroom 14'8" x 16'10"
- kitchen 13'0" x 15'0"
- living 20'0" x 18'0"
- dining 14'0" x 11'4"
- covered porch

© Southern Living

Second Floor

- bedroom 12'4" x 13'0"
- attic space
- bedroom 11'6" x 14'0"

Plan # HPK3800107

First Floor: 1,905 sq. ft.

Second Floor: 552 sq. ft.

Total: 2,457 sq. ft.

Bedrooms: 3

Bathrooms: 2 ½

Width: 66' - 2"

Depth: 52' - 3"

Foundation: Crawlspace

Price Code: C3

1-800-850-1491 • EPLANS.COM

2,465
square feet

DESIGNED BY STEPHEN FULLER, INC.

Plan# HPK3800108

Square Footage: 2,465

Bonus Space: 374 sq. ft.

Bedrooms: 3

Bathrooms: 2 ½

Width: 69' - 0"

Depth: 61' - 0"

Foundation: Crawlspace, Slab, Unfinished Basement

Price Code: L2

1-800-850-1491 • EPLANS.COM

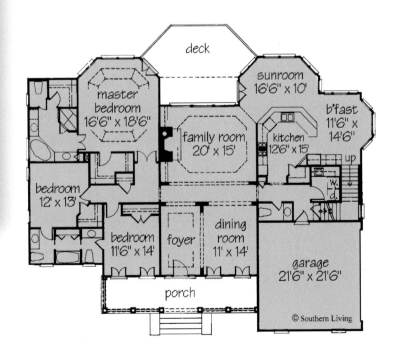

deck

master bedroom
16'6" x 18'6"

sunroom
16'6" x 10'

family room
20' x 15'

kitchen
12'6" x 15

b'fast
11'6" x 14'6"

up

bedroom
12' x 13'

w. d.

bedroom
11'6" x 14'

foyer

dining room
11' x 14'

garage
21'6" x 21'6"

porch

© Southern Living

bedroom
16' x 12'6"

dn.

2,474
square feet

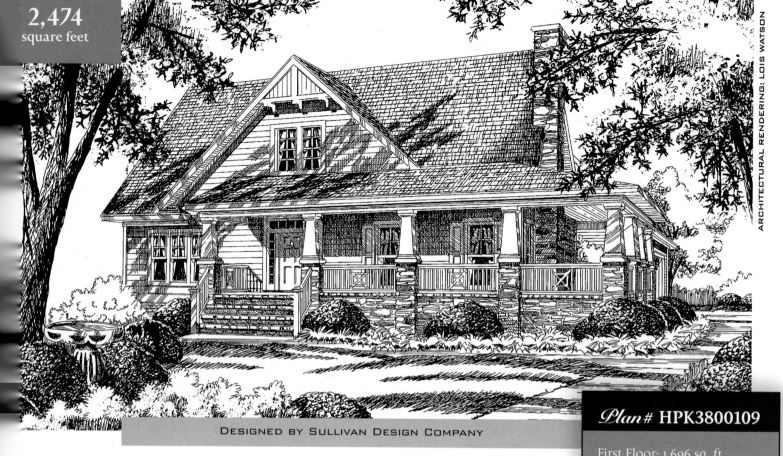

ARCHITECTURAL RENDERING: LOIS WATSON

DESIGNED BY SULLIVAN DESIGN COMPANY

garage
23' x 23'

© Southern Living

deck

up

d. w.

dining room
15'8" x 13'8"

kitchen
13'8" x 14'

master
bedroom
13'4" x 17

foyer

living room
18'10" x 18'4"

up

porch

FIRST FLOOR

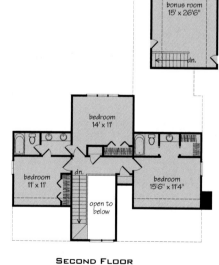

bonus room
15' x 26'6"

dn.

bedroom
14' x 11'

bedroom
11' x 11'

dn.

bedroom
15'6" x 11'4"

open to
below

SECOND FLOOR

Plan# HPK3800109

First Floor: 1,696 sq. ft.

Second Floor: 778 sq. ft.

Total: 2,474 sq. ft.

Bonus Space: 397 sq. ft.

Bedrooms: 4

Bathrooms: 3 ½

Width: 63' - 0"

Depth: 77' - 0"

Foundation: Crawlspace

Price Code: C3

1-800-850-1491 • EPLANS.COM

·OUR GULF COAST COTTAGE·

2,496
square feet

DESIGNED BY WILLIAM H. PHILLIPS

Plan # **HPK3800110**

Square Footage: 2,496

Bedrooms: 3

Bathrooms: 2 ½

Width: 50' - 0"

Depth: 74' - 0"

Foundation: Crawlspace

Price Code: C3

1-800-850-1491 • EPLANS.COM

© Southern Living

master bedroom
26'5" x 15'

courtyard

garden
pool

bedroom
14' x 13'

family room
28'5" x 13'

bedroom
13' x 14'

living
room
13' x 14'

foyer

dining
room
13' x 14'

~Camden Cottage~

2,530 square feet

DESIGNED BY MOUZON DESIGN FOR COTTAGE LIVING MAGAZINE

Plan# HPK3800111

First Floor: 1,508 sq. ft.

Second Floor: 1,022 sq. ft.

Total: 2,530 sq. ft.

Bedrooms: 4

Bathrooms: 3 ½

Width: 37' - 0"

Depth: 91' - 0"

Foundation: Crawlspace, Slab

Price Code: L4

1-800-850-1491 • EPLANS.COM

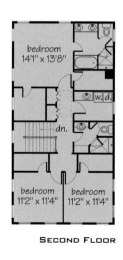

First Floor

garage
21'9" x 21'9"

© Southern Living

porch

master
bedroom
12'9" x 13'4"

breakfast
room
9'6" x
8'2"

keeping
room
14'6" x
14'2"

11'6"
x
8'2"
kitchen

office
7'10" x
9'6"

family room/dining room
15'4" x 23'

porch

Second Floor

bedroom
14'1" x 13'8"

w. d.

dn.

bedroom
11'2" x 11'4"

bedroom
11'2" x 11'4"

❧ ASBURY ❧

2,536
square feet

Plan # HPK3800112

First Floor: 1,466 sq. ft.

Second Floor: 1,070 sq. ft.

Total: 2,536 sq. ft.

Bonus Space: 306 sq. ft.

Bedrooms: 3

Bathrooms: 2 ½

Width: 63' - 0"

Depth: 58' - 0"

Foundation: Unfinished Basement

Price Code: C3

1-800-850-1491 • EPLANS.COM

DESIGNED BY SPITZMILLER AND NORRIS, INC.

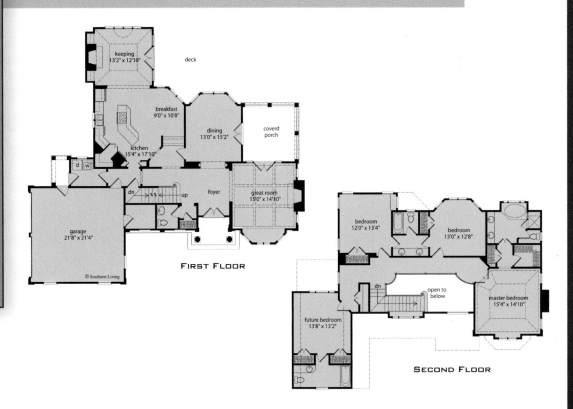

FIRST FLOOR

keeping 13'2" x 12'10"

deck

breakfast 9'0" x 10'8"

dining 13'0" x 15'2"

coverd porch

kitchen 15'4" x 17'10"

dn / up

foyer

great room 15'0" x 14'10"

garage 21'8" x 21'4"

© Southern Living

SECOND FLOOR

bedroom 12'0" x 13'4"

bedroom 13'0" x 12'8"

dn

open to below

master bedroom 15'4" x 14'10"

future bedroom 13'8" x 13'2"

MOORE'S CREEK

2,540 square feet

DESIGNED BY JOHN TEE, ARCHITECT

Plan# HPK3800113

Square Footage: 2,540

Bedrooms: 3

Bathrooms: 2 full + 2 half

Width: 84' - 0"

Depth: 53' - 0"

Foundation: Unfinished Basement

Price Code: C3

1-800-850-1491 • EPLANS.COM

HONEYSUCKLE HILL

ARCHITECTURAL RENDERING: ROD DENT

2,552 square feet

DESIGNED BY STEPHEN FULLER, INC.

Plan# HPK3800114

First Floor: 1,179 sq. ft.

Second Floor: 1,373 sq. ft.

Total: 2,552 sq. ft.

Bedrooms: 4

Bathrooms: 3 ½

Width: 61' - 0"

Depth: 46' - 0"

Foundation: Unfinished Basement

Price Code: C3

1-800-850-1491 • EPLANS.COM

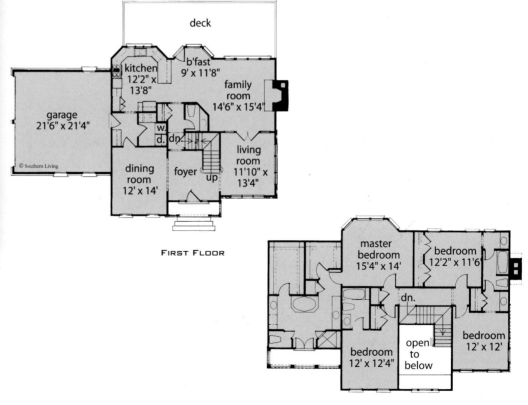

FIRST FLOOR

SECOND FLOOR

❧BELHAVEN PLACE❧

2,576 square feet

DESIGNED BY LOONEY RICKS KISS ARCHITECTS, INC.

FIRST FLOOR

- screened porch
- master bedroom 13' x 19'1"
- dining room 11'3" x 13'3"
- family room 17'2" x 21'6"
- kitchen 14'10" x 10'5"
- up
- foyer
- study/sitting room 14'7" x 12'11"
- porch
- d. w
- garage 22'6" x 21'8"
- storage

© Southern Living

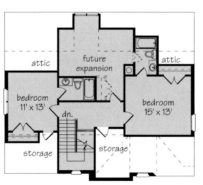

SECOND FLOOR

- attic
- future expansion
- attic
- bedroom 11' x 13'
- dn.
- bedroom 15' x 13'
- storage
- storage

Plan# HPK3800115

First Floor: 1,959 sq. ft.

Second Floor: 617 sq. ft.

Total: 2,576 sq. ft.

Bedrooms: 3

Bathrooms: 3 ½

Width: 63' - 0"

Depth: 83' - 0"

Foundation: Slab

Price Code: C3

1-800-850-1491 • EPLANS.COM

~STONE HARBOR~

2,587 square feet

ARCHITECTURAL RENDERING: MILES MELTON

DESIGNED BY SPITZMILLER AND NORRIS, INC.

Plan# HPK3800116

First Floor: 1,387 sq. ft.

Second Floor: 1,200 sq. ft.

Total: 2,587 sq. ft.

Bonus Space: 270 sq. ft.

Bedrooms: 3

Bathrooms: 2 ½

Width: 58' - 0"

Depth: 66' - 0"

Foundation: Unfinished Basement

Price Code: C3

1-800-850-1491 • EPLANS.COM

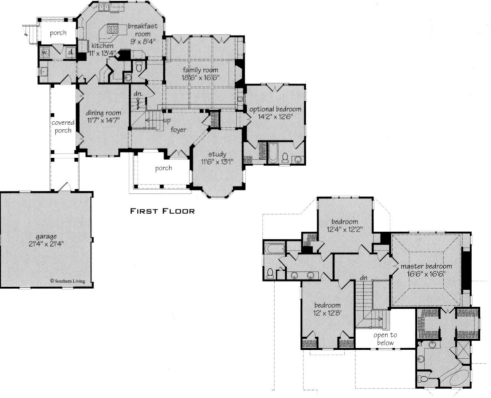

FIRST FLOOR

SECOND FLOOR

❧ Pine Hill Cottage ❧

2,589
square feet

ARCHITECTURAL RENDERING: LOIS WATSON

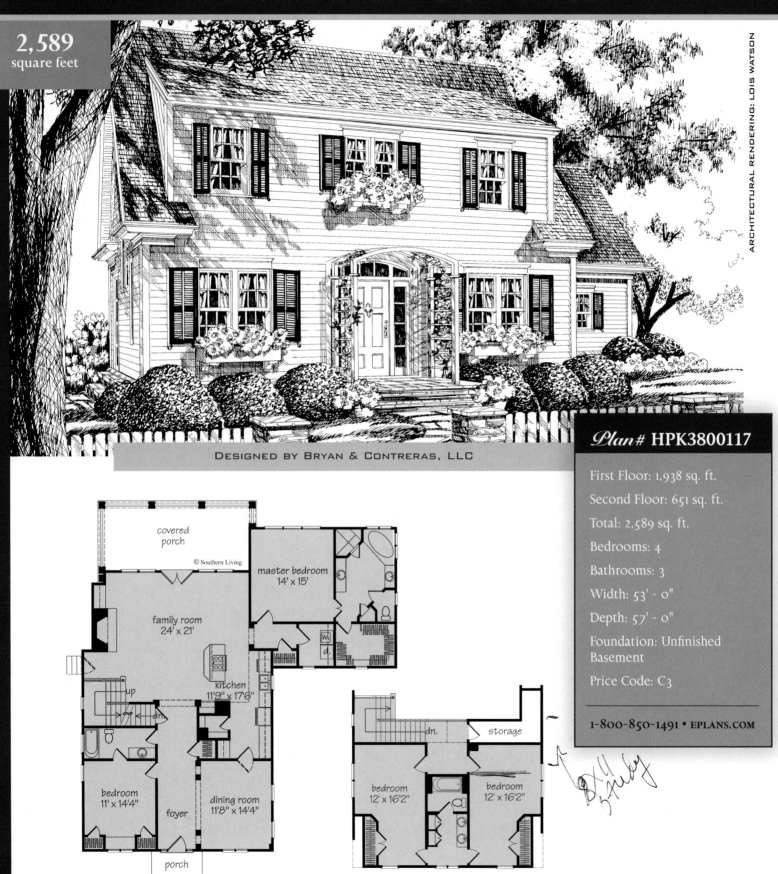

DESIGNED BY BRYAN & CONTRERAS, LLC

© Southern Living

covered porch

family room
24' x 21'

master bedroom
14' x 15'

up

dn.

kitchen
11'9" x 17'6"

W.
d.

bedroom
11' x 14'4"

foyer

dining room
11'8" x 14'4"

porch

FIRST FLOOR

dn.

storage

bedroom
12' x 16'2"

bedroom
12' x 16'2"

SECOND FLOOR

Plan# HPK3800117

First Floor: 1,938 sq. ft.

Second Floor: 651 sq. ft.

Total: 2,589 sq. ft.

Bedrooms: 4

Bathrooms: 3

Width: 53' - 0"

Depth: 57' - 0"

Foundation: Unfinished Basement

Price Code: C3

1-800-850-1491 • EPLANS.COM

~FAIRMONT HEIGHTS~

2,600
square feet

DESIGNED BY STEPHEN FULLER, INC.

Plan # HPK3800119

First Floor: 1,164 sq. ft.

Second Floor: 1,436 sq. ft.

Total: 2,600 sq. ft.

Bedrooms: 4

Bathrooms: 2 ½

Width: 52' - 0"

Depth: 40' - 0"

Foundation: Unfinished Basement

Price Code: L1

1-800-850-1491 • EPLANS.COM

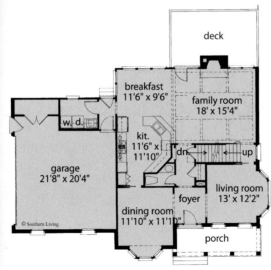

deck

breakfast
11'6" x 9'6"

family room
18' x 15'4"

w. d.

kit.
11'6" x 11'10"

dn.   up

garage
21'8" x 20'4"

living room
13' x 12'2"

foyer

dining room
11'10" x 11'10"

porch

© Southern Living

FIRST FLOOR

master bedroom
17'2" x 13'10"

bedroom
16'4" x 13'10"

dn.

bedroom
12'4" x 12'4"

bedroom
11'10" x 13'

SECOND FLOOR

2,592
square feet

DESIGNED BY JOHN TEE, ARCHITECT FOR THE PROGRESSIVE FARMER

SIMPLICITY AND SOPHISTICATION

combine in Sand Mountain, a sprawling one-story plan with many charms. This plan honors the richness of traditional design elements with its covered, columned porches, multiple fireplaces, and distinctive exterior, while show-casing contemporary design features such as an opulent master suite and spacious home office.

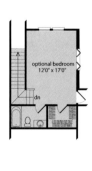

© THE PROGRESSIVE FARMER. THIS HOME, AS SHOWN IN THE PHOTOGRAPHY, MAY DIFFER FROM THE ACTUAL BLUEPRINTS. FOR MORE DETAILED INFORMATION, PLEASE CHECK THE FLOOR PLANS CAREFULLY.

Plan# HPK3800118

Square Footage: 2,592

Bonus Space: 295 sq. ft.

Bedrooms: 3

Bathrooms: 2 full + 2 half

Width: 80' - 0"

Depth: 78' - 0"

Foundation: Crawlspace

Price Code: L4

1-800-850-1491 • EPLANS.COM

©THE PROGRESSIVE FARMER

SOUTHERN LIVING *Classic Collection of House Plans*   135

2,602 square feet

ARCHITECTURAL RENDERING: MILES MELTON

DESIGNED BY BRYAN & CONTRERAS, LLC

Plan # HPK3800120

First Floor: 1,389 sq. ft.

Second Floor: 1,213 sq. ft.

Total: 2,602 sq. ft.

Bedrooms: 3

Bathrooms: 4

Width: 48' - 0"

Depth: 46' - 0"

Foundation: Crawlspace

Price Code: C1

1-800-850-1491 • EPLANS.COM

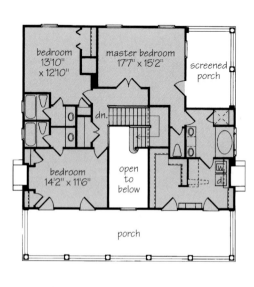

FIRST FLOOR

- patio
- dining room 10' x 15'2"
- family room 15'4" x 15'2"
- porch
- kitchen 17' x 9'1"
- up
- keeping room 17' x 10'
- foyer
- living room/library 17' x 14'
- porch
- © Southern Living

SECOND FLOOR

- bedroom 13'10" x 12'10"
- master bedroom 17'7" x 15'2"
- screened porch
- dn.
- bedroom 14'2" x 11'6"
- open to below
- w. d
- porch

2,622 square feet

ARCHITECTURAL RENDERING: MUIR STEWART

Plan # HPK3800354

First Floor: 870 sq. ft.

Second Floor: 1,170 sq. ft.

Third Floor: 582 sq. ft.

Total: 2,622 sq. ft.

Bedrooms: 3

Bathrooms: 2 full + 2 half

Width: 30' - 0"

Depth: 55' - 0"

Foundation: Pier (same as Piling)

Price Tier: A4

1-800-521-6797 • EPLANS.COM

DESIGNED BY MEL SNYDER, DOMAIN DESIGN
FOR COASTAL LIVING MAGAZINE

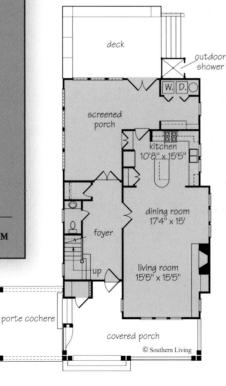

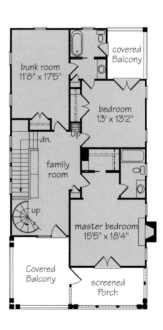

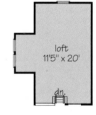

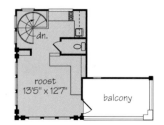

FIRST FLOOR

SECOND FLOOR

THIRD FLOOR

2,612
square feet

DESIGNED BY MOSER DESIGN GROUP FOR COASTAL LIVING MAGAZINE

Plan# **HPK3800122**

First Floor: 2,028 sq. ft.

Second Floor: 584 sq. ft.

Total: 2,612 sq. ft.

Bedrooms: 4

Bathrooms: 3 ½

Width: 65' - 0"

Depth: 77' - 0"

Foundation: Pier
(same as Piling)

Price Code: L4

1-800-850-1491 • EPLANS.COM

FIRST FLOOR

porch

guest
cottage
10' x 12'14"

up

screened
porch
17'4" x 15'6"

kitchen
21'2" x 9'2"

w.
d.

family room
22'2" x 22'

dining
room
11'6" x 22'

vestibule
4' x 8'9"

master
bedroom
15' x 13'10"

porch

up

porch

© Southern Living

open to
below

guest
cottage
loft

dn.

SECOND FLOOR

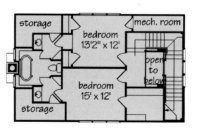

storage

bedroom
13'2" x 12'

mech. room

storage

bedroom
15' x 12'

open
to
below

ARCHITECTURAL RENDERING: MILES MELTON

2,614 square feet

DESIGNED BY GARY/RAGSDALE, INC.

Plan# HPK3800123

Square Footage: 2,614

Bedrooms: 4

Bathrooms: 3 ½

Width: 65' - 0"

Depth: 65' - 0"

Foundation: Crawlspace

Price Code: C3

1-800-850-1491 • EPLANS.COM

master bedroom
14'0" x 18'6"

covered porch

breakfast
9'10" x 11'4"

bedroom
13'0" x 11'0"

family room
15'8" x 20'0"

up

kitchen
11'0" x 13'4"

W
D

garage
20'0" x 29'0"

dining
11'0" x 13'0"

entry

bedroom
11'0" x 13'0"

bedroom
14'0" x 11'6"

© Southern Living

covered porch

·NEW LYNWOOD·

2,620 square feet

ARCHITECTURAL RENDERING: MILES MELTON

DESIGNED BY JOHN TEE, ARCHITECT

Plan # **HPK3800124**

Square Footage: 2,620

Bedrooms: 3

Bathrooms: 2 full + 2 half

Width: 72' - 0"

Depth: 70' - 0"

Foundation: Unfinished Basement

Price Code: C3

1-800-850-1491 • EPLANS.COM

·CLOVERDALE·

ARCHITECTURAL RENDERING: RICK HERR

2,620 square feet

Plan # HPK3800125

First Floor: 1,755 sq. ft.

Second Floor: 865 sq. ft.

Total: 2,620 sq. ft.

Bedrooms: 3

Bathrooms: 2 ½

Width: 68' - 0"

Depth: 53' - 0"

Foundation: Crawlspace

Price Code: C1

1-800-850-1491 • EPLANS.COM

DESIGNED BY CALDWELL-CLINE ARCHITECTS AND DESIGNERS

FIRST FLOOR

SECOND FLOOR

2,628
square feet

ARCHITECTURAL RENDERING: LOIS WATSON

DESIGNED BY BRYAN & CONTRERAS, LLC

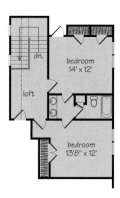

Plan# HPK3800126

First Floor: 2,026 sq. ft.

Second Floor: 602 sq. ft.

Total: 2,628 sq. ft.

Bedrooms: 3

Bathrooms: 2 ½

Width: 46' - 0"

Depth: 82' - 0"

Foundation: Unfinished Basement

Price Code: C3

1-800-850-1491 • EPLANS.COM

FIRST FLOOR

- covered porch
- master bedroom 15'10" x 16'2"
- covered porch
- breakfast room 13' x 11'11"
- © Southern Living
- up
- dn.
- w. d.
- family room 18'6" x 15'10"
- kitchen 16'10" x 16'10"
- covered porch
- foyer
- dining room 16' x 13'2"

SECOND FLOOR

- dn.
- loft
- bedroom 14' x 12'
- bedroom 13'8" x 12'

❦ NEW MEADOWLARK ❦

2,628
square feet

Plan# HPK3800127

Square Footage: 2,628

Bonus Space: 356 sq. ft.

Bedrooms: 3

Bathrooms: 2 ½

Width: 71' - 0"

Depth: 60' - 0"

Foundation: Crawlspace

Price Code: C3

1-800-850-1491 • EPLANS.COM

DESIGNED BY JOHN TEE, ARCHITECT

© Southern Living

NEW WYNTUCK

2,638
square feet

DESIGNED BY JOHN TEE, ARCHITECT

Plan # HPK3800128

Square Footage: 2,638

Bedrooms: 3

Bathrooms: 2 full + 2 half

Width: 78' - 0"

Depth: 53' - 0"

Foundation: Crawlspace

Price Code: C1

1-800-850-1491 • EPLANS.COM

MANDEVILLE PLACE

2,638 square feet

DESIGNED BY JOHN TEE, ARCHITECT

Plan # HPK3800129

Square Footage: 2,638

Bedrooms: 3

Bathrooms: 2 full + 2 half

Width: 78' - 0"

Depth: 51' - 0"

Foundation: Crawlspace

Price Code: C3

1-800-850-1491 • EPLANS.COM

SPRING LAKE COTTAGE

2,639 square feet

DESIGNED BY MOUZON DESIGN

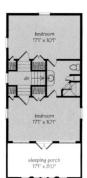

sleeping loft 11'4" x 6'4"
sleeping loft 11'4" x 6'4"

SECOND FLOOR

bedroom 17'1" x 10'1"
bedroom 17'1" x 10'1"
sleeping porch 17'1" x 8'0"

front porch
library 11'4" x 6'4"
entry hall
great room 29'1" x 17'4"
kitchen/breakfast 22'0" x 16'7"
master bath 17'1" x 13'7"
main screened porch 30'0" x 8'0"
gallery
dining 17'1" x 12'7"
terrace
master bedroom 17'1" x 12'7"
dining porch 18'0" x 8'0"
master porch 18'0" x 8'0"

© Southern Living

FIRST FLOOR

Plan# HPK3800130

First Floor: 1,978 sq. ft.

Second Floor: 661 sq. ft.

Total: 2,639 sq. ft.

Bedrooms: 3

Bathrooms: 2 ½

Width: 82' - 0"

Depth: 64' - 0"

Foundation: Unfinished Basement

Price Code: L4

1-800-850-1491 • EPLANS.COM

~ALTA VISTA~

ARCHITECTURAL RENDERING: MILES MELTON

DESIGNED BY MOUZON DESIGN FOR BILTMORE ESTATE

Plan # **HPK3800131**

First Floor: 1,823 sq. ft.

Second Floor: 822 sq. ft.

Total: 2,645 sq. ft.

Bedrooms: 3

Bathrooms: 2 ½

Width: 71' - 0"

Depth: 75' - 0"

Foundation: Crawlspace

Price Code: L4

1-800-850-1491 • EPLANS.COM

BILTMORE™
For Your Home

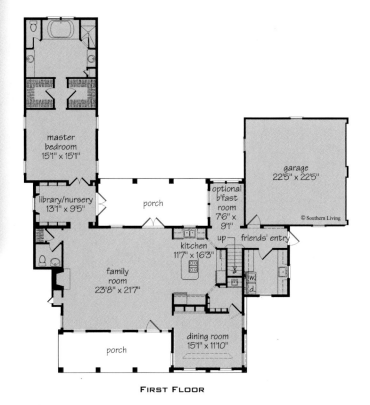

FIRST FLOOR

SECOND FLOOR

OVERTON PLACE

2,652 square feet

DESIGNED BY SULLIVAN DESIGN COMPANY

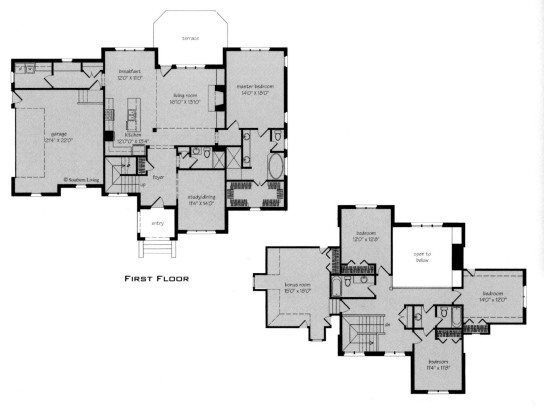

FIRST FLOOR

SECOND FLOOR

Plan # HPK3800132

First Floor: 1,733 sq. ft.

Second Floor: 919 sq. ft.

Total: 2,652 sq. ft.

Bonus Space: 335 sq. ft.

Bedrooms: 4

Bathrooms: 4

Width: 66' - 0"

Depth: 54' - 0"

Foundation: Crawlspace

Price Code: C3

1-800-850-1491 • EPLANS.COM

TURNBALL PARK

ARCHITECTURAL RENDERING: MILES MELTON

DESIGNED BY MOSER DESIGN GROUP

Plan# HPK3800133

First Floor: 1,537 sq. ft.

Second Floor: 1,123 sq. ft.

Total: 2,660 sq. ft.

Bedrooms: 3

Bathrooms: 2 ½

Width: 40' - 0"

Depth: 70' - 0"

Foundation: Crawlspace

Price Code: C3

1-800-850-1491 • EPLANS.COM

FIRST FLOOR

SECOND FLOOR

~ELDERBERRY PLACE~

2,673 square feet

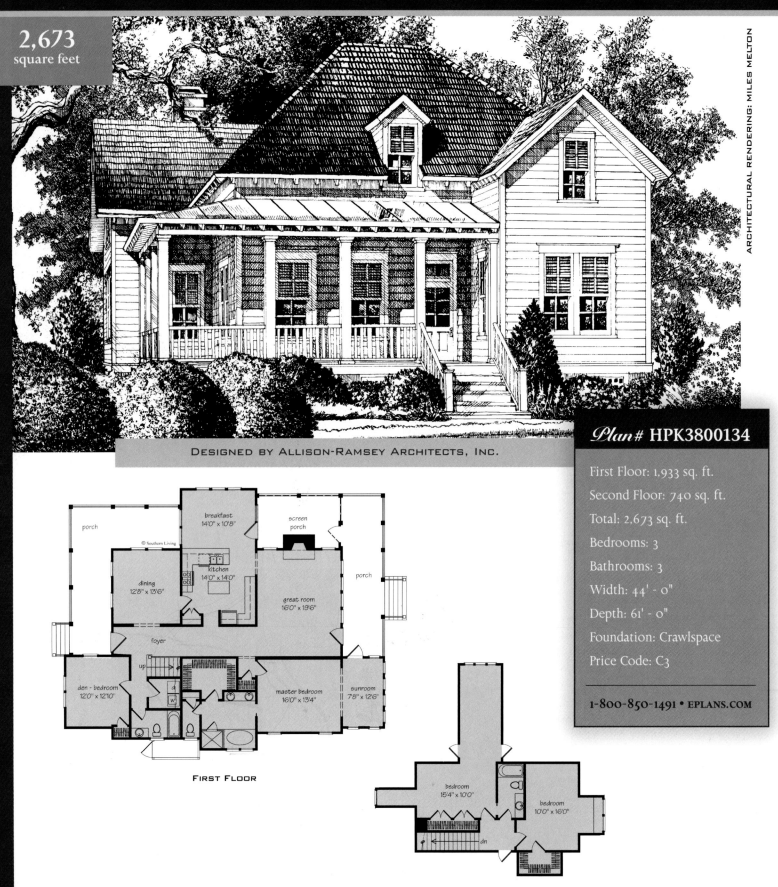

DESIGNED BY ALLISON-RAMSEY ARCHITECTS, INC.

Plan# HPK3800134

First Floor: 1,933 sq. ft.

Second Floor: 740 sq. ft.

Total: 2,673 sq. ft.

Bedrooms: 3

Bathrooms: 3

Width: 44' - 0"

Depth: 61' - 0"

Foundation: Crawlspace

Price Code: C3

1-800-850-1491 • EPLANS.COM

FIRST FLOOR

SECOND FLOOR

❧ ARBORVIEW ❧

2,675 square feet

DESIGNED BY GARY/RAGSDALE, INC.

Plan # HPK3800135

First Floor: 2,155 sq. ft.

Second Floor: 520 sq. ft.

Total: 2,675 sq. ft.

Bonus Space: 288 sq. ft.

Bedrooms: 3

Bathrooms: 2 ½

Width: 51' - 0"

Depth: 89' - 0"

Foundation: Crawlspace

Price Code: C3

1-800-850-1491 • EPLANS.COM

FIRST FLOOR

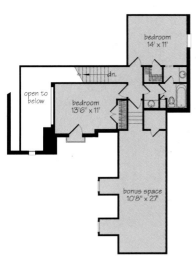

SECOND FLOOR

2,677 square feet

ARCHITECTURAL RENDERING: MILES MELTON

DESIGNED BY MOSER DESIGN GROUP

Plan # HPK3800136

First Floor: 1,554 sq. ft.

Second Floor: 1,123 sq. ft.

Total: 2,677 sq. ft.

Bedrooms: 4

Bathrooms: 3 ½

Width: 40' - 0"

Depth: 67' - 0"

Foundation: Crawlspace

Price Code: C1

1-800-850-1491 • EPLANS.COM

porch

master bedroom
12'10" x 15'10"

porch

breakfast
7'6" x 8'0"

kitchen
13'0" x 13'8"

dining
17'0" x 11'2"

living
16'2" x 18'0"

up

foyer

© Southern Living

porch

FIRST FLOOR

bedroom
13'8" x 25'0"

gallery
10'0" x 8'8"

bedroom
12'0" x 12'2"

dn

open to below

bedroom
14'0" x 11'10"

porch

SECOND FLOOR

~SADDLEBROOK HOUSE~

ARCHITECTURAL RENDERING: ROD DENT

2,679 square feet

DESIGNED BY STEPHEN FULLER, INC.

Plan# HPK3800137

First Floor: 1,434 sq. ft.

Second Floor: 1,245 sq. ft.

Total: 2,679 sq. ft.

Bonus Space: 210 sq. ft.

Bedrooms: 4

Bathrooms: 3

Width: 72' - 0"

Depth: 41' - 0"

Foundation: Unfinished Basement

Price Code: C3

1-800-850-1491 • EPLANS.COM

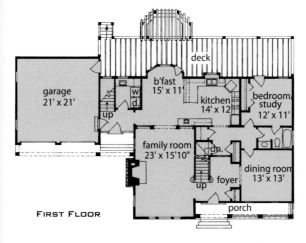

garage 21' x 21'

w. d.

up

deck

b'fast 15' x 11'

kitchen 14' x 12'

bedroom, study 12' x 11'

family room 23' x 15'10"

dn.

foyer

up

dining room 13' x 13'

porch

FIRST FLOOR

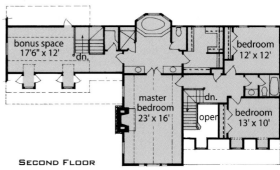

bonus space 17'6" x 12'

dn.

bedroom 12' x 12'

master bedroom 23' x 16'

dn.

open

bedroom 13' x 10'

SECOND FLOOR

2,696 square feet

ARCHITECTURAL RENDERING: ROLAND DAVIS

DESIGNED BY STEPHEN FULLER, INC.

deck

family room
18'6" x 18'9"

kitchen
10' x 16'

b'fast
9'9" x 11'6"

dn.

study
13'6" x 12'9"

dining room
13'6" x 14'9"

up

porch

© Southern Living

FIRST FLOOR

bedroom
12'6 x 12'6"

bedroom
13'6 x 12'9"

dn.

bedroom
11'6 x 13'9"

master bedroom
13'6 x 18'4"

SECOND FLOOR

Plan# HPK3800138

First Floor: 1,348 sq. ft.

Second Floor: 1,348 sq. ft.

Total: 2,696 sq. ft.

Bedrooms: 4

Bathrooms: 2 ½

Width: 43' - 0"

Depth: 37' - 0"

Foundation: Unfinished Basement

Price Code: C3

1-800-850-1491 • EPLANS.COM

2,700 square feet

ARCHITECTURAL RENDERING: DON RANKIN

DESIGNED BY JOHN TEE, ARCHITECT

Plan# HPK3800139

First Floor: 1,740 sq. ft.

Second Floor: 960 sq. ft.

Total: 2,700 sq. ft.

Bonus Space: 286 sq. ft.

Bedrooms: 4

Bathrooms: 3 ½

Width: 77' - 0"

Depth: 50' - 0"

Foundation: Crawlspace

Price Code: A4

1-800-850-1491 • EPLANS.COM

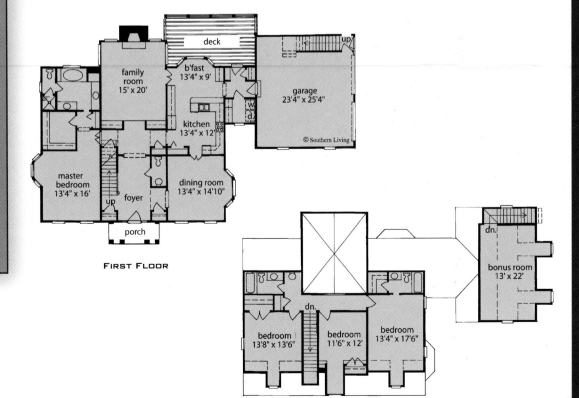

First Floor

deck

family room 15' x 20'

b'fast 13'4" x 9'

garage 23'4" x 25'4"

kitchen 13'4" x 12'

master bedroom 13'4" x 16'

foyer

dining room 13'4" x 14'10"

porch

© Southern Living

Second Floor

bonus room 13' x 22'

bedroom 13'8" x 13'6"

bedroom 11'6" x 12'

bedroom 13'4" x 17'6"

⤠ Bluff Towne Cottage ⤟

2,508
square feet

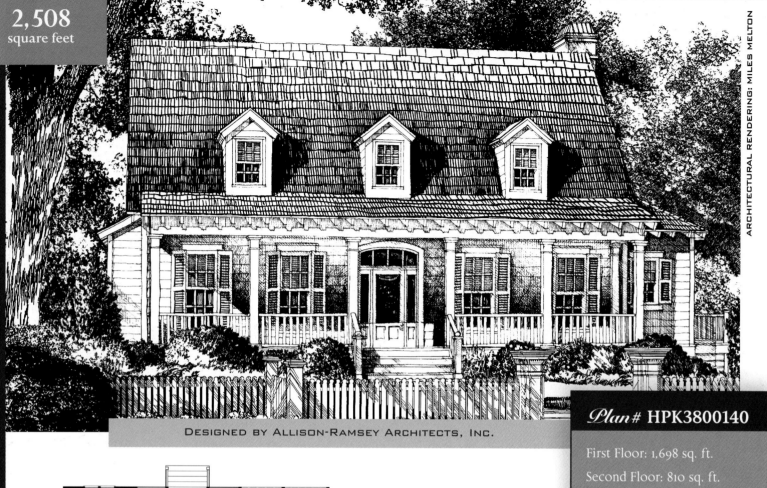

ARCHITECTURAL RENDERING: MILES MELTON

Designed by Allison-Ramsey Architects, Inc.

Plan# HPK3800140

First Floor: 1,698 sq. ft.

Second Floor: 810 sq. ft.

Total: 2,508 sq. ft.

Bedrooms: 3

Bathrooms: 3 ½

Width: 60' - 0"

Depth: 52' - 0"

Foundation: Crawlspace

Price Code: C3

1-800-850-1491 • EPLANS.COM

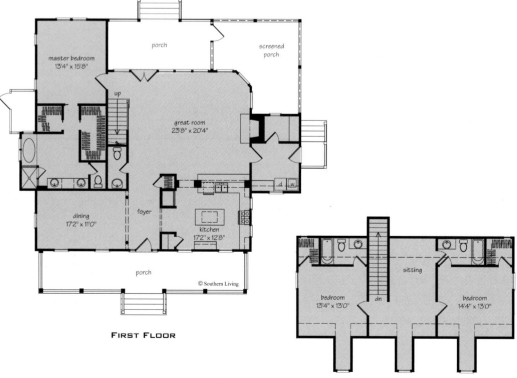

FIRST FLOOR

SECOND FLOOR

~ BIENVILLE ~

ARCHITECTURAL RENDERING: ROD DENT

2,729
square feet

Plan# HPK3800141

First Floor: 1,542 sq. ft.

Second Floor: 1,187 sq. ft.

Total: 2,729 sq. ft.

Bonus Space: 141 sq. ft.

Bedrooms: 3

Bathrooms: 3 ½

Width: 56' - 0"

Depth: 60' - 0"

Foundation: Unfinished Basement

Price Code: L1

1-800-850-1491 • EPLANS.COM

DESIGNED BY STEPHEN FULLER, INC.

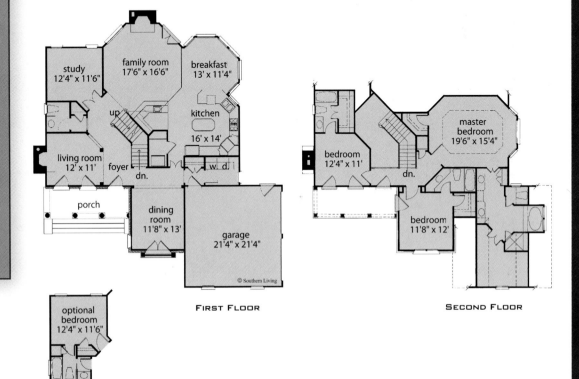

study 12'4" x 11'6"

family room 17'6" x 16'6"

breakfast 13' x 11'4"

kitchen 16' x 14'

up

living room 12' x 11'

foyer

dn.

w. d.

living room 12' x 11'

porch

dining room 11'8" x 13'

garage 21'4" x 21'4"

© Southern Living

master bedroom 19'6" x 15'4"

bedroom 12'4" x 11'

dn.

bedroom 11'8" x 12'

FIRST FLOOR

SECOND FLOOR

optional bedroom 12'4" x 11'6"

OPTIONAL LAYOUT

SEA ISLAND HOUSE

2,738 square feet

DESIGNED BY HISTORICAL CONCEPTS, LLC FOR COASTAL LIVING MAGAZINE

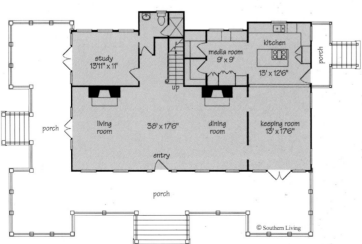

study
13'11" x 11'

media room
9' x 9'

kitchen
13' x 12'6"

porch

living room

38' x 17'6"

dining room

keeping room
13' x 17'6"

up

porch

entry

porch

© Southern Living

FIRST FLOOR

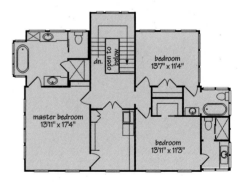

open to below

dn.

bedroom
13'7" x 11'4"

master bedroom
13'11" x 17'4"

bedroom
13'11" x 11'3"

SECOND FLOOR

FROM THE VERY FIRST GLANCE, this home captures the picture of low-country living in the South. Classic white siding sets off the column-lined wraparound porch. A second-floor pediment centers the focus on the front entry. Window shutters and a paneled front door further add to the perfectly charming facade.

The elegance continues inside, with a vast entry that opens into hearth-warmed living and dining rooms.

Plan # HPK3800142

First Floor: 1,584 sq. ft.

Second Floor: 1,154 sq. ft.

Total: 2,738 sq. ft.

Bedrooms: 3

Bathrooms: 4

Width: 69' - 0"

Depth: 45' - 0"

Foundation: Crawlspace

Price Code: SQ5

1-800-850-1491 • EPLANS.COM

The first-floor living room, keeping room, and study all open to the wraparound porch, maximizing gathering spaces indoors and out. An additional porch can be accessed from the kitchen in back.

The first-floor's layout offers smooth transitions between formal and informal spaces, from the open living room and dining room to the media room off the island kitchen, complete with two walk-in closets and two wall closets.

A stairway beyond the foyer leads to more private retreats upstairs, where a central laundry room is convenient to all. All three bedrooms on this level offer full baths. The master bath is particularly luxurious, including twin vanities, a shower stall, and separate tub.

HARBORSIDE COTTAGE

2,689 square feet

DESIGNED BY CALDWELL-CLINE ARCHITECTS AND DESIGNERS FOR COTTAGE LIVING MAGAZINE

Plan # HPK3800143

First Floor: 1,600 sq. ft.

Second Floor: 1,089 sq. ft.

Total: 2,689 sq. ft.

Bedrooms: 4

Bathrooms: 4

Width: 48' - 0"

Depth: 55' - 0"

Foundation: Crawlspace

Price Code: C1

1-800-850-1491 • EPLANS.COM

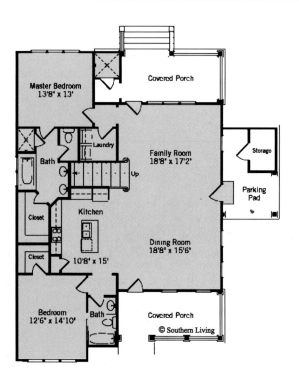

FIRST FLOOR

Master Bedroom 13'8" x 13'

Covered Porch

Laundry

Bath

Family Room 18'8" x 17'2"

Up

Storage

Parking Pad

Closet

Kitchen 10'8" x 15'

Closet

Dining Room 18'8" x 15'6"

Bedroom 12'6" x 14'10"

Bath

Covered Porch

© Southern Living

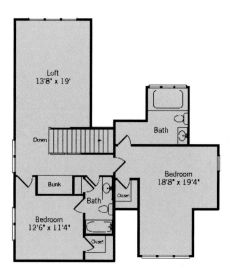

SECOND FLOOR

Loft 13'8" x 19'

Down

Bath

Bunk

Bath

Closet

Bedroom 18'8" x 19'4"

Bedroom 12'6" x 11'4"

Closet

~McKenzie Cottage~

MILES MELTON

2,750
square feet

Plan # HPK3800144

First Floor: 1,930 sq. ft.

Second Floor: 820 sq. ft.

Total: 2,750 sq. ft.

Bedrooms: 3

Bathrooms: 4

Width: 60' - 0"

Depth: 46' - 0"

Foundation: Crawlspace

Price Code: C1

1-800-850-1491 • EPLANS.COM

DESIGNED BY BRYAN & CONTRERAS, LLC

terrace

master bedroom
15'8" x 17'0"

dining
17'0" x 11'8"

kitchen
12'0" x 15'6"

breakfast
7'6" x 9'8"

master bath
15'6" x 13'2"

living
18'4" x 19'4"

w d

MAIN LEVEL (1,930 sq. ft.)

covered porch

© Southern Living

study/bedroom
12'0" x 14'0"

FIRST FLOOR

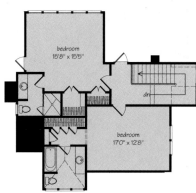

bedroom
15'8" x 15'5"

dn

bedroom
17'0" x 12'8"

SECOND FLOOR

WOODMERE CREEK

2,762 square feet

ARCHITECTURAL RENDERING: RICK HERR

DESIGNED BY BRYAN & CONTRERAS, LLC

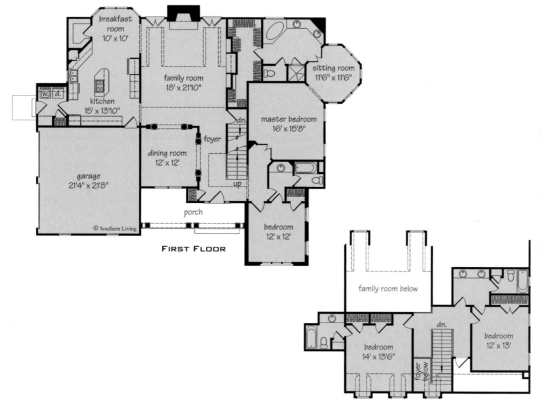

FIRST FLOOR

- breakfast room 10' x 10'
- family room 18' x 21'10"
- sitting room 11'6" x 11'6"
- kitchen 15' x 13'10"
- master bedroom 16' x 15'8"
- garage 21'4" x 21'8"
- dining room 12' x 12'
- foyer
- up
- dn.
- w. d.
- porch
- bedroom 12' x 12'
- © Southern Living

SECOND FLOOR

- family room below
- bedroom 14' x 13'6"
- bedroom 12' x 13'
- foyer below
- dn.

Plan # HPK3800145

First Floor: 2,110 sq. ft.

Second Floor: 652 sq. ft.

Total: 2,762 sq. ft.

Bedrooms: 4

Bathrooms: 4

Width: 69' - 0"

Depth: 53' - 0"

Foundation: Unfinished Basement

Price Code: C3

1-800-850-1491 • EPLANS.COM

SILVER SPRINGS

2,780 square feet

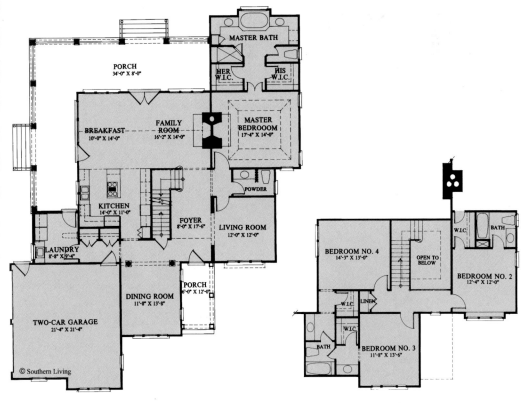

DESIGNED BY STEPHEN FULLER, INC.

Plan# HPK3800146

First Floor: 1,870 sq. ft.

Second Floor: 910 sq. ft.

Total: 2,780 sq. ft.

Bedrooms: 4

Bathrooms: 3 ½

Width: 58' - 0"

Depth: 71' - 0"

Foundation: Unfinished Basement

Price Code: C3

1-800-850-1491 • EPLANS.COM

FIRST FLOOR

SECOND FLOOR

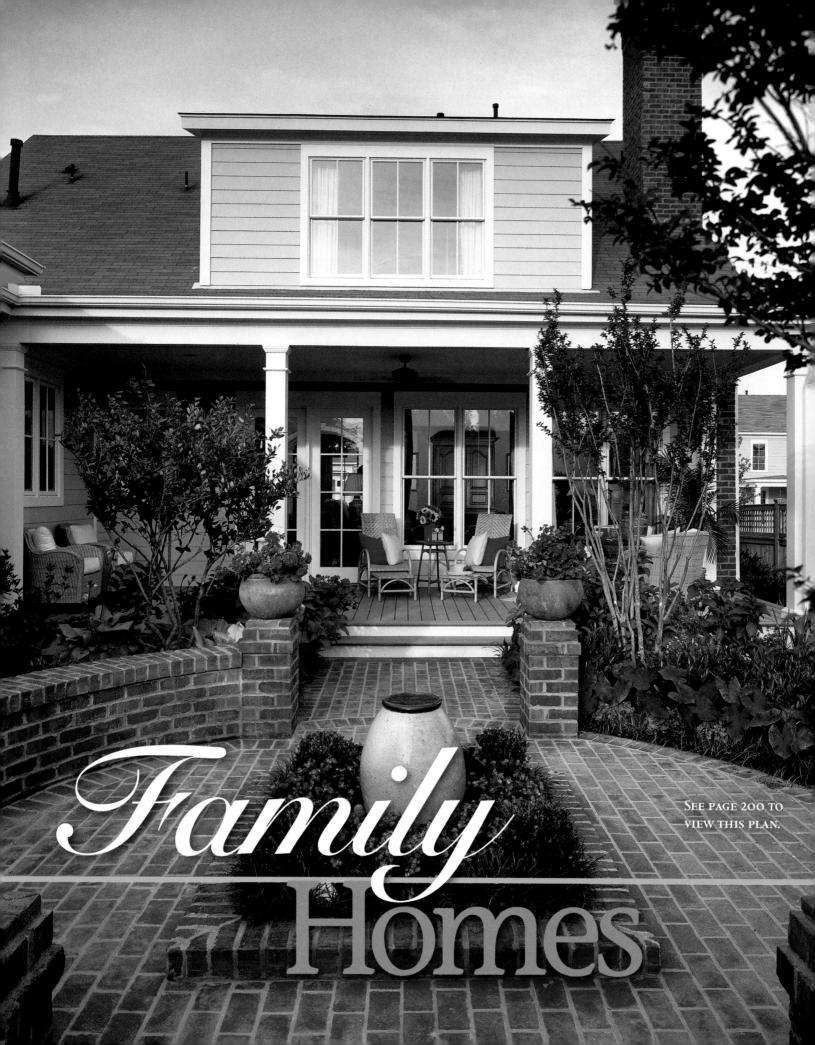

Family
Homes

SEE PAGE 200 TO
VIEW THIS PLAN.

This selection of homes ranges from 2,801 to 3,600 square feet and fits the needs of any size family.

The Covington Cove on page 179 features plenty of family-friendly amenities. From the three bedrooms conveniently clustered around the second-floor master suite, to the inclusion of formal and informal dining areas, this home adapts well to the needs of both family and guests.

Poppy Point, on page 204, reveals the lavish kind of comfort that can be attained at under 3,000 square feet.

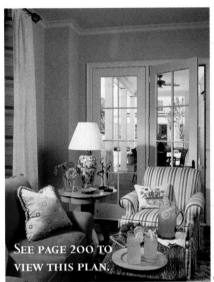

SEE PAGE 200 TO VIEW THIS PLAN.

© SOUTHERN LIVING

SEE PAGE 200 TO VIEW THIS PLAN.

© SOUTHERN LIVING

2,809
square feet

ARCHITECTURAL RENDERING: MILES MELTON

DESIGNED BY GARY/RAGSDALE, INC.

FIRST FLOOR

master bedroom
18' x 15'

master bath

garage
26' x 20'4"

© Southern Living

sun room
12' x 16'

family room
18'4" x 18'

dining room
11' x 16'

kitchen
13'10" x 17'4"

up

entry

porch

breakfast
12'2" x 9'2"

study
11'4" x 11'

SECOND FLOOR

bedroom
11' x 14'6"

unfinished room
26' x 10'8"

up

dn

bedroom
11' x 13'6"

open to
below

Plan # HPK3800147

First Floor: 2,299 sq. ft.

Second Floor: 510 sq. ft.

Total: 2,809 sq. ft.

Bonus Space: 277 sq. ft.

Bedrooms: 3

Bathrooms: 2 ½

Width: 50' - 6"

Depth: 88' - 6"

Foundation: Crawlspace

Price Code: C3

1-800-850-1491 • EPLANS.COM

ADDISON PLACE

2,819
square feet

DESIGNED BY LOONEY RICKS KISS ARCHITECTS, INC.

Plan# HPK3800148

First Floor: 2,117 sq. ft.

Second Floor: 702 sq. ft.

Total: 2,819 sq. ft.

Bedrooms: 3

Bathrooms: 3

Width: 65' - 0"

Depth: 51' - 0"

Foundation: Crawlspace

Price Code: C3

1-800-850-1491 • EPLANS.COM

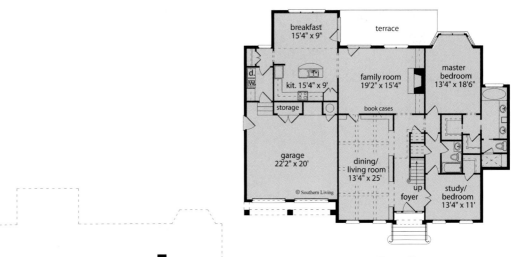

FIRST FLOOR

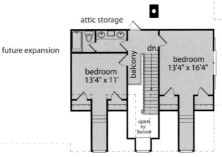

SECOND FLOOR

❧ New Cooper's Bluff ❧

2,824 square feet

Designed by John Tee, Architect

breakfast 14'0" x 10'0"

covered back porch

bedroom 14'4" x 12'0"

kitchen 14'0" x 13'0"

family room 20'6" x 15'4"

master bedroom 15'4" x 19'0"

bedroom 11'-6" x 11'4"

W/d

up

dn

dining 14'0" x 14'0"

foyer 6'10 x 13'8

living 13'0" x 14'0"

garage 20'10" x 21'4"

porch

© Southern Living

Plan # HPK3800149

Square Footage: 2,824

Bedrooms: 3

Bathrooms: 3 ½

Width: 73' - 0"

Depth: 63' - 0"

Foundation: Unfinished Basement

Price Code: L1

1-800-850-1491 • EPLANS.COM

ARCHITECTURAL RENDERING: JOHN TEE

Plan# HPK3800150

First Floor: 1,644 sq. ft.

Second Floor: 1,190 sq. ft.

Total: 2,834 sq. ft.

Bonus Space: 216 sq. ft.

Bedrooms: 3

Bathrooms: 2 ½

Width: 71' - 0"

Depth: 47' - 0"

Foundation: Unfinished Basement

Price Code: C3

1-800-850-1491 • eplans.com

DESIGNED BY JOHN TEE, ARCHITECT

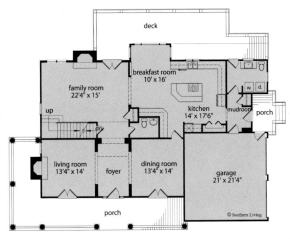

deck

breakfast room
10' x 16'

family room
22'4" x 15'

up

kitchen
14' x 17'6"

mudroom

porch

w. d.

living room
13'4" x 14'

foyer

dining room
13'4" x 14'

garage
21' x 21'4"

© Southern Living

porch

FIRST FLOOR

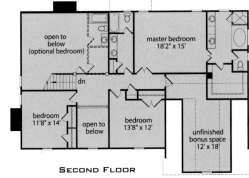

open to below
(optional bedroom)

master bedroom
18'2" x 15'

dn

bedroom
11'8" x 14'

open to below

bedroom
13'8" x 12'

unfinished bonus space
12' x 18'

SECOND FLOOR

2,835
square feet

ARCHITECTURAL RENDERING: ROD DENT

DESIGNED BY STEPHEN FULLER, INC.

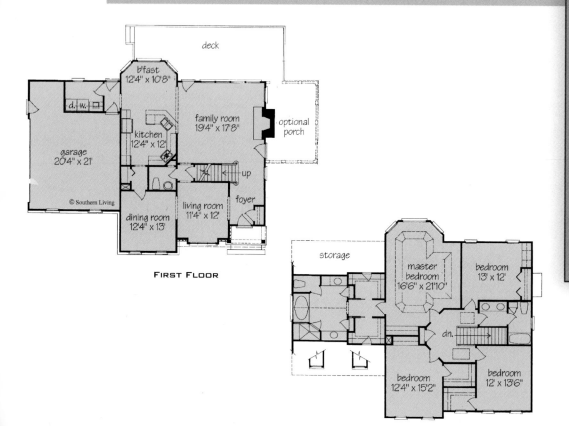

deck

b'fast
12'4" x 10'8"

d. w.

garage
20'4" x 21'

kitchen
12'4" x 12'

family room
19'4" x 17'8"

optional porch

© Southern Living

dining room
12'4" x 13'

living room
11'4" x 12'

foyer

up

FIRST FLOOR

storage

master bedroom
16'6" x 21'10"

bedroom
13' x 12'

dn.

bedroom
12'4" x 15'2"

bedroom
12' x 13'6"

SECOND FLOOR

Plan# HPK3800151

First Floor: 1,290 sq. ft.

Second Floor: 1,545 sq. ft.

Total: 2,835 sq. ft.

Bedrooms: 4

Bathrooms: 2 ½

Width: 65' - 0"

Depth: 50' - 0"

Foundation: Unfinished Basement

Price Code: L1

1-800-850-1491 • EPLANS.COM

·KILBURNE·

2,839 square feet

ARCHITECTURAL RENDERING: MILES MELTON

DESIGNED BY FRUSTERIO AND ASSOCIATES, INC.

Plan# HPK3800152

First Floor: 1,887 sq. ft.

Second Floor: 952 sq. ft.

Total: 2,839 sq. ft.

Bedrooms: 4

Bathrooms: 3 ½

Width: 54' - 0"

Depth: 46' - 0"

Foundation: Unfinished Basement

Price Code: C3

1-800-850-1491 • EPLANS.COM

FIRST FLOOR

SECOND FLOOR

~MAYESVILLE~

2,849 square feet

ARCHITECTURAL RENDERING: MILES MELTON

DESIGNED BY MOSER DESIGN GROUP

Plan # HPK3800153

First Floor: 1,793 sq. ft.

Second Floor: 1,056 sq. ft.

Total: 2,849 sq. ft.

Bedrooms: 4

Bathrooms: 3 ½

Width: 45' - 0"

Depth: 64' - 0"

Foundation: Crawlspace

Price Code: C3

1-800-850-1491 • EPLANS.COM

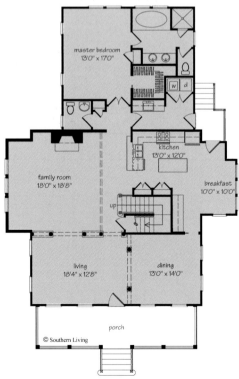

FIRST FLOOR

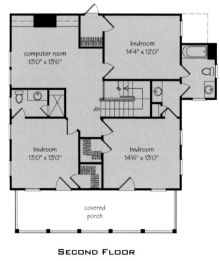

SECOND FLOOR

❧ NEW HOLLY SPRINGS ❧

2,858
square feet

MILES MELTON

Plan# HPK3800154

First Floor: 2,058 sq. ft.

Second Floor: 800 sq. ft.

Total: 2,858 sq. ft.

Bonus Space: 300 sq. ft.

Bedrooms: 3

Bathrooms: 3 ½

Width: 66' - 0"

Depth: 66' - 0"

Foundation: Crawlspace

Price Code: L1

1-800-850-1491 • EPLANS.COM

DESIGNED BY JOHN TEE, ARCHITECT

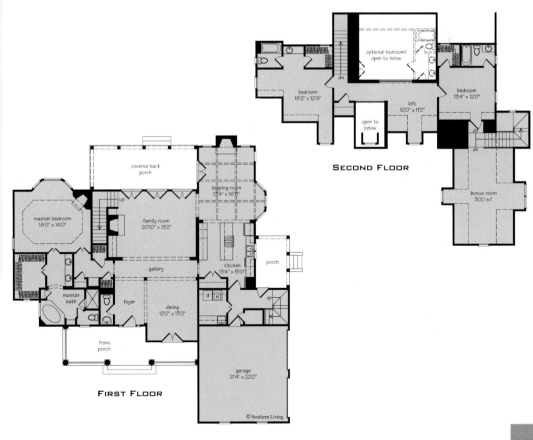

SECOND FLOOR

optional bedroom/
open to below

bedroom
18'2" x 12'6"

bedroom
13'4" x 12'0"

loft
12'0" x 11'2"

open to
below

bonus room
300 s.f.

FIRST FLOOR

covered back
porch

keeping room
12'4" x 16'8"

master bedroom
18'0" x 14'0"

family room
20'10" x 15'2"

gallery

kitchen
13'4" x 15'0"

porch

master
bath

foyer

dining
12'0" x 13'2"

front
porch

garage
21'4" x 22'0"

© Southern Living

2,858 square feet

ARCHITECTURAL RENDERING: ROD DENT

DESIGNED BY STEPHEN FULLER, INC.

Plan # HPK3800155

First Floor: 1,382 sq. ft.

Second Floor: 1,476 sq. ft.

Total: 2,858 sq. ft.

Bedrooms: 4

Bathrooms: 3 ½

Width: 60' - 0"

Depth: 53' - 0"

Foundation: Unfinished Basement

Price Code: L1

1-800-850-1491 • EPLANS.COM

First Floor

deck

kitchen
14'4" x 14'8"

breakfast
12'8" x 12'8"

family room
15'6" x 18'8"

dining room
11'6" x 13'6"

w. d.

living room
12' x 14'10"

foyer

dn.

garage
21'4" x 21'4"

up

porch

© Southern Living

Second Floor

bedroom
12' x 14'6"

master bedroom
15'4" x 18'8"

bedroom
11'4" x 12'4"

bedroom
12' x 12'

open to below

dn.

~NEW SHANNON~

2,864
square feet

Plan# HPK3800156

First Floor: 1,952 sq. ft.

Second Floor: 912 sq. ft.

Total: 2,864 sq. ft.

Bonus Space: 476 sq. ft.

Bedrooms: 4

Bathrooms: 3 full + 2 half

Width: 66' - 0"

Depth: 50' - 0"

Foundation: Crawlspace

Price Code: C3

1-800-850-1491 • EPLANS.COM

DESIGNED BY JOHN TEE, ARCHITECT

FIRST FLOOR

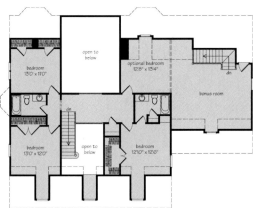

SECOND FLOOR

CRABAPPLE COTTAGE ALTERNATE

2,865 square feet

ARCHITECTURAL RENDERING: MILES MELTON

DESIGNED BY JOHN TEE, ARCHITECT

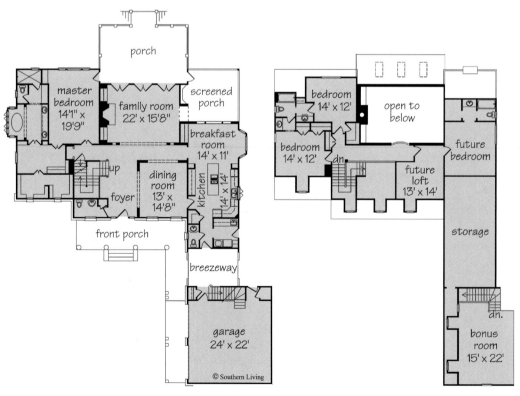

FIRST FLOOR

SECOND FLOOR

Plan # **HPK3800352**

First Floor: 2,280 sq. ft.

Second Floor: 585 sq. ft.

Total: 2,865 sq. ft.

Bonus Space: 504 sq. ft.

Bedrooms: 3

Bathrooms: 2 full + 2 half

Width: 76' - 0"

Depth: 91' - 0"

Foundation: Unfinished Basement

Price Code: L4

1-800-850-1491 • EPLANS.COM

2,875 square feet

ARCHITECTURAL RENDERING: ROD DENT

DESIGNED BY STEPHEN FULLER, INC.

Plan # HPK3800159

First Floor: 1,390 sq. ft.

Second Floor: 1,485 sq. ft.

Total: 2,875 sq. ft.

Bedrooms: 4

Bathrooms: 3 ½

Width: 54' - 0"

Depth: 58' - 0"

Foundation: Unfinished Basement

Price Code: L1

1-800-850-1491 • EPLANS.COM

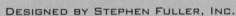

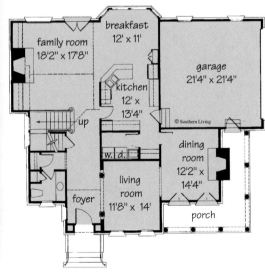

family room 18'2" x 17'8"

breakfast 12' x 11'

garage 21'4" x 21'4"

kitchen 12' x 13'4"

up

© Southern Living

w. d.

dining room 12'2" x 14'4"

living room 11'8" x 14'

foyer

porch

FIRST FLOOR

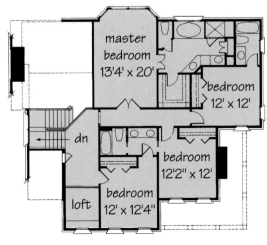

master bedroom 13'4' x 20'

bedroom 12' x 12'

dn

bedroom 12'2" x 12'

loft

bedroom 12' x 12'4"

SECOND FLOOR

2,876 square feet

ARCHITECTURAL RENDERING: LOIS WATSON

DESIGNED BY SULLIVAN DESIGN COMPANY

FIRST FLOOR

SECOND FLOOR

© Southern Living

Plan # HPK3800160

First Floor: 1,969 sq. ft.

Second Floor: 907 sq. ft.

Total: 2,876 sq. ft.

Bonus Space: 346 sq. ft.

Bedrooms: 4

Bathrooms: 3 ½

Width: 70' - 0"

Depth: 79' - 0"

Foundation: Crawlspace

Price Code: C3

1-800-850-1491 • EPLANS.COM

❧ IBERVILLE ❧

2,880
square feet

DESIGNED BY JOHN TEE, ARCHITECT

Plan# HPK3800161

Square Footage: 2,880

Bedrooms: 3

Bathrooms: 3 ½

Width: 75' - 0"

Depth: 69' - 0"

Foundation: Unfinished Basement

Price Code: L1

1-800-850-1491 • EPLANS.COM

breakfast 14'0" x 10'0"

covered back porch

bedroom 14'4" x 12'0"

kitchen 14'0" x 13'0"

family room 20'6" x 15'4"

master bedroom 15'4" x 19'0"

bedroom 11'-6" x 11'4"

w d

dining 14'0" x 14'0"

dn

foyer 6'10 x 13'8

living 13'0" x 14'0"

up

garage 20'10" x 21'4"

covered porch

© Southern Living

SOUTHBERRY FARM

2,888 square feet

ARCHITECTURAL RENDERING: ROD DENT

DESIGNED BY STEPHEN FULLER, INC.

Plan # **HPK3800162**

First Floor: 1,953 sq. ft.

Second Floor: 935 sq. ft.

Total: 2,888 sq. ft.

Bedrooms: 4

Bathrooms: 3 ½

Width: 77' - 0"

Depth: 57' - 0"

Foundation: Unfinished Basement

Price Code: L1

1-800-850-1491 • EPLANS.COM

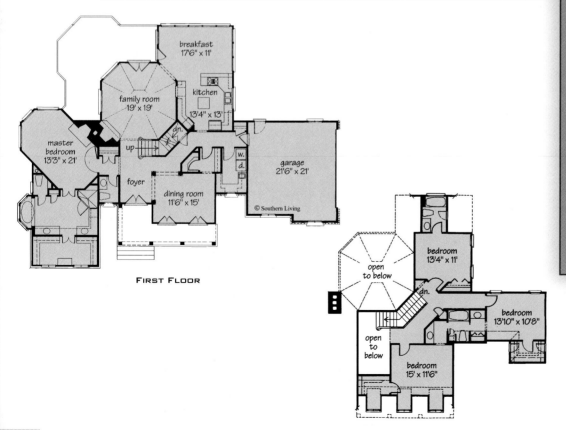

breakfast 17'6" x 11'

family room 19' x 19'

kitchen 13'4" x 13'

master bedroom 13'3" x 21'

up

dn.

w. d.

foyer

dining room 11'6" x 15'

garage 21'6" x 21'

© Southern Living

FIRST FLOOR

open to below

bedroom 13'4" x 11'

dn.

bedroom 13'10" x 10'8"

open to below

bedroom 15' x 11'6"

SECOND FLOOR

~ FAIRFIELD PLACE ~

2,889 square feet

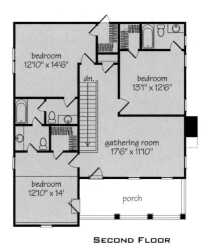

DESIGNED BY SULLIVAN DESIGN COMPANY

Plan # HPK3800163

First Floor: 1,156 sq. ft.

Second Floor: 1,733 sq. ft.

Total: 2,889 sq. ft.

Bedrooms: 4

Bathrooms: 3 ½

Width: 40' - 0"

Depth: 77' - 0"

Foundation: Crawlspace

Price Code: C3

1-800-850-1491 • EPLANS.COM

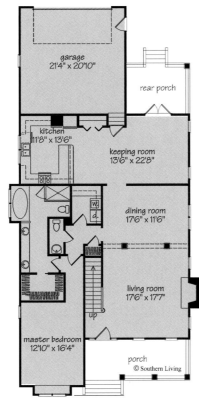

garage
21'4" x 20'10"

rear porch

kitchen
11'8" x 13'6"

keeping room
13'6" x 22'8"

dining room
17'6" x 11'6"

living room
17'6" x 17'7"

master bedroom
12'10" x 16'4"

up

porch

© Southern Living

FIRST FLOOR

bedroom
12'10" x 14'6"

bedroom
13'1" x 12'6"

dn.

gathering room
17'6" x 11'10"

bedroom
12'10" x 14'

porch

SECOND FLOOR

WESLEY

ARCHITECTURAL RENDERING: MILES MELTON

DESIGNED BY GARY/RAGSDALE, INC.

FIRST FLOOR

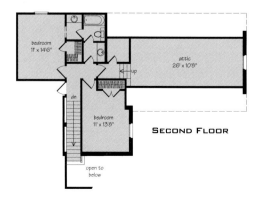

SECOND FLOOR

Plan# **HPK3800164**

First Floor: 2,375 sq. ft.

Second Floor: 520 sq. ft.

Total: 2,895 sq. ft.

Bedrooms: 3

Bathrooms: 2 ½

Width: 51' - 0"

Depth: 89' - 6"

Foundation: Crawlspace

Price Code: C3

1-800-850-1491 • EPLANS.COM

2,897 square feet

ARCHITECTURAL RENDERING: ROD DENT

DESIGNED BY STEPHEN FULLER, INC.

Plan# HPK3800165

First Floor: 1,915 sq. ft.

Second Floor: 982 sq. ft.

Total: 2,897 sq. ft.

Bedrooms: 4

Bathrooms: 3 ½

Width: 63' - 0"

Depth: 71' - 0"

Foundation: Unfinished Basement

Price Code: C3

1-800-850-1491 • EPLANS.COM

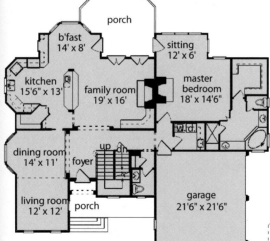

FIRST FLOOR

porch

b'fast
14' x 8'

sitting
12' x 6'

kitchen
15'6" x 13'

family room
19' x 16'

master bedroom
18' x 14'6"

dining room
14' x 11'

foyer

up dn

w. d.

living room
12' x 12'

porch

garage
21'6" x 21'6"

© Southern Living

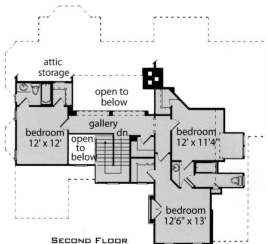

SECOND FLOOR

attic storage

open to below

bedroom
12' x 12'

gallery

dn

open to below

bedroom
12' x 11'4"

bedroom
12'6" x 13'

2,924 square feet

ARCHITECTURAL RENDERING: MUIR STEWART

DESIGNED BY CALDWELL-CLINE ARCHITECTS AND DESIGNERS
FOR COASTAL LIVING MAGAZINE

Plan# HPK3800166

First Floor: 1,424 sq. ft.

Second Floor: 1,376 sq. ft.

Third Floor: 124 sq. ft.

Total: 2,924 sq. ft.

Bedrooms: 4

Bathrooms: 4

Width: 35' - 0"

Depth: 59' - 0"

Foundation: Crawlspace

Price Code: C3

1-800-850-1491 • EPLANS.COM

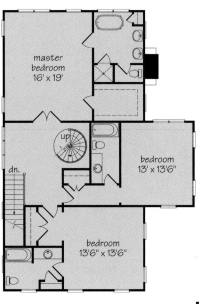

FIRST FLOOR

family room 25'6" x 20'

dining area

kitchen 14'9" x 9'6"

bedroom/study 14'6" x 14'6"

foyer

up

porch

© Southern Living

SECOND FLOOR

master bedroom 16' x 19'

up

dn.

bedroom 13' x 13'6"

bedroom 13'6" x 13'6"

THIRD FLOOR

dn.

lookout 7'6" x 16'6"

2,909
square feet

ARCHITECTURAL RENDERING: RICK HERR

Plan# HPK3800167

First Floor: 2,336 sq. ft.

Optional Second Floor: 573 sq. ft.

Total: 2,909 sq. ft.

Bedrooms: 3

Bathrooms: 2 ½

Width: 81' - 0"

Depth: 64' - 0"

Foundation: Unfinished Basement

Price Code: C3

1-800-850-1491 • EPLANS.COM

DESIGNED BY BRYAN & CONTRERAS, LLC

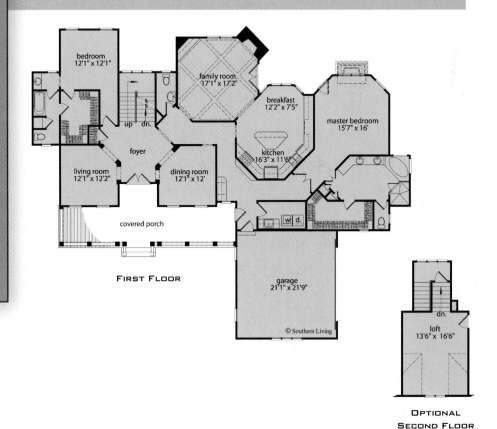

bedroom
12'1" x 12'1"

family room
17'1" x 17'2"

breakfast
12'2" x 7'5"

master bedroom
15'7" x 16'

kitchen
16'3" x 11'6"

up dn.

foyer

living room
12'1" x 12'2"

dining room
12'1" x 12'

w d.

covered porch

garage
21'1" x 21'9"

© Southern Living

FIRST FLOOR

dn.

loft
13'6" x 16'6"

**OPTIONAL
SECOND FLOOR**

2,909
square feet

ARCHITECTURAL RENDERING: RICK HERR

DESIGNED BY BRYAN & CONTRERAS, LLC

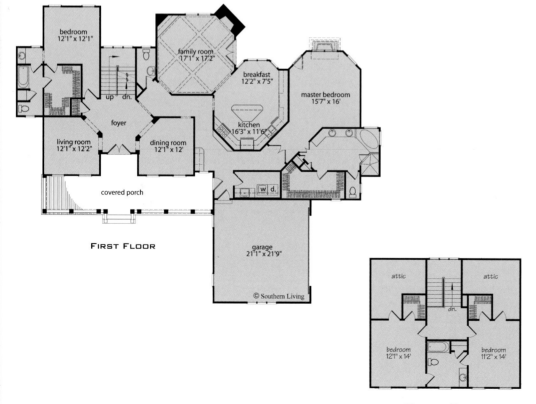

FIRST FLOOR

bedroom
12'1" x 12'1"

family room
17'1" x 17'2"

breakfast
12'2" x 7'5"

master bedroom
15'7" x 16'

kitchen
16'3" x 11'6"

foyer

up   dn.

living room
12'1" x 12'2"

dining room
12'1" x 12'

covered porch

w. d.

garage
21'1" x 21'9"

© Southern Living

SECOND FLOOR

attic

attic

dn.

bedroom
12'1" x 14'

bedroom
11'2" x 14'

Plan # HPK3800168

First Floor: 2,336 sq. ft.

Second Floor: 573 sq. ft.

Total: 2,909 sq. ft.

Bedrooms: 4

Bathrooms: 3 ½

Width: 81' - 0"

Depth: 64' - 0"

Foundation: Unfinished Basement

Price Code: C3

1-800-850-1491 • EPLANS.COM

ARCHITECTURAL RENDERING: MILES MELTON

2,910 square feet

Plan # HPK3800169

First Floor: 1,984 sq. ft.

Second Floor: 926 sq. ft.

Total: 2,910 sq. ft.

Bonus Space: 341 sq. ft.

Bedrooms: 4

Bathrooms: 3 ½

Width: 82' - 0"

Depth: 58' - 0"

Foundation: Crawlspace

Price Code: L4

1-800-850-1491 • EPLANS.COM

DESIGNED BY MOUZON DESIGN

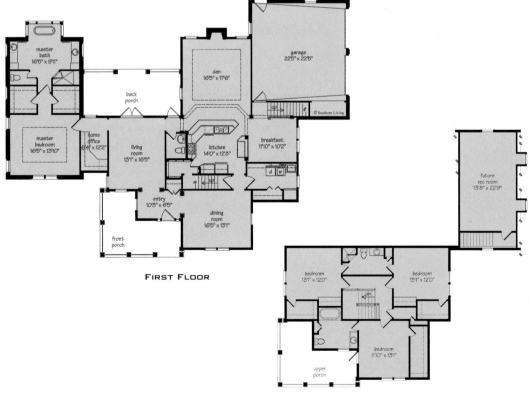

FIRST FLOOR

SECOND FLOOR

New Brookhaven

ARCHITECTURAL RENDERING: MILES MELTON

2,920 square feet

DESIGNED BY JOHN TEE, ARCHITECT

covered back porch

master bedroom
16'0" x 18'0"

family dining
17'0" x 8'2"

kitchen
8'6" x 17'0"

family room
19'4" x 150"

keeping room
17'0" x 14'4"

bedroom
14'0" x 11'8"

up

bedroom/study
12'4" x 11'0"

foyer
7'0" x 15'4"

dining room
12'0" x 15'4"

porch

garage
21'4" x 21'10"

© Southern Living

Plan# **HPK3800170**

Square Footage: 2,920

Bedrooms: 3

Bathrooms: 2 full + 2 half

Width: 79' - 0"

Depth: 64' - 0"

Foundation: Unfinished Basement

Price Code: C3

1-800-850-1491 • EPLANS.COM

2,922
square feet

ARCHITECTURAL RENDERING: MILES MELTON

DESIGNED BY MOUZON DESIGN FOR BILTMORE ESTATE

Plan# HPK3800171

First Floor: 2,179 sq. ft.

Second Floor: 743 sq. ft.

Total: 2,922 sq. ft.

Bedrooms: 3

Bathrooms: 4

Width: 61' - 0"

Depth: 89' - 0"

Foundation: Crawlspace

Price Code: L2

1-800-850-1491 • EPLANS.COM

BILTMORE™
For Your Home

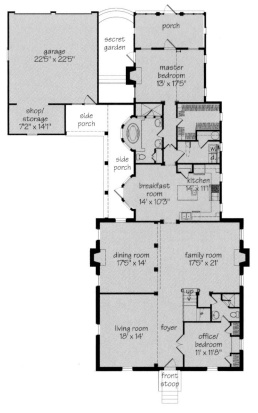

FIRST FLOOR

SECOND FLOOR

~◈~ ALLENDALE ~◈~

ARCHITECTURAL RENDERING: MILES MELTON

DESIGNED BY JOHN TEE, ARCHITECT

Plan # HPK3800172

First Floor: 2,053 sq. ft.

Second Floor: 872 sq. ft.

Total: 2,925 sq. ft.

Bonus Space: 426 sq. ft.

Bedrooms: 3

Bathrooms: 3 ½

Width: 58' - 0"

Depth: 69' - 0"

Foundation: Crawlspace

Price Code: L1

1-800-850-1491 • EPLANS.COM

FIRST FLOOR

dining 13'6" x 11'8"

living room 18'4" x 18'8"

master bedroom 13'2" x 19'2"

kitchen 15'6" x 13'10"

media room 13'4" x 15'

foyer
up

garage 23' x 26'8"

covered porch

© Southern Living

SECOND FLOOR

bedroom 13' x 13'4"

balcony
dn

open to below

bedroom 17'2" x 11'

unfinished room 13'4" x 26'8"

❧ Lousiana Garden Cottage ❧

ARCHITECTURAL RENDERING: MILES MELTON

DESIGNED BY JOHN TEE, ARCHITECT

Plan # HPK3800173

First Floor: 1,929 sq. ft.

Second Floor: 966 sq. ft.

Total: 2,895 sq. ft.

Bonus Space: 330 sq. ft.

Bedrooms: 3

Bathrooms: 2 ½

Width: 76' - 0"

Depth: 59' - 0"

Foundation: Crawlspace

Price Code: C3

1-800-850-1491 • EPLANS.COM

deck

b'fast 12' x 10'

porch

up

family room 19' x 15'

kit. 18' x 12'

garage 24' x 26'

© Southern Living

up

dining room 14' x 14'

dn.

master bedroom 18' x 13'

living room 18' x 13'

porch

FIRST FLOOR

dn.

bonus space 15' x 22'

storage

storage

bedroom 14' x 14'

optional bedroom 15' x 11'

dn.

bedroom 15' x 14'

SECOND FLOOR

CUMBERLAND

2,932 square feet

DESIGNED BY JOHN TEE, ARCHITECT

Plan# HPK3800174

First Floor: 1,949 sq. ft.

Second Floor: 983 sq. ft.

Total: 2,932 sq. ft.

Bonus Space: 330 sq. ft.

Bedrooms: 3

Bathrooms: 2 ½

Width: 76' - 0"

Depth: 59' - 0"

Foundation: Crawlspace

Price Code: C3

1-800-850-1491 • EPLANS.COM

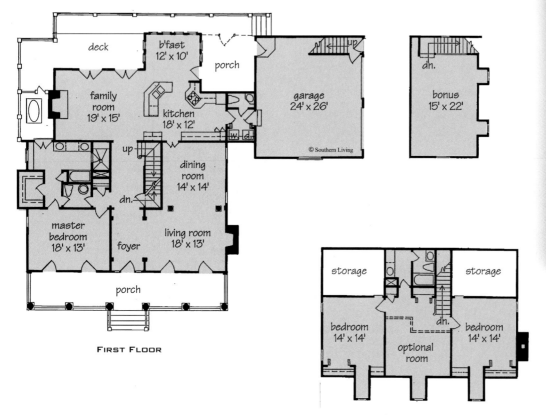

FIRST FLOOR

SECOND FLOOR

2,957 square feet

Plan# **HPK3800177**

First Floor: 1,450 sq. ft.

Second Floor: 1,327 sq. ft.

Total: 2,957 sq. ft.

Bedrooms: 3

Bathrooms: 2 ½

Width: 47' - 0"

Depth: 52' - 0"

Foundation: Unfinished Basement

Price Code: C3

1-800-850-1491 • EPLANS.COM

DESIGNED BY SPITZMILLER AND NORRIS, INC.

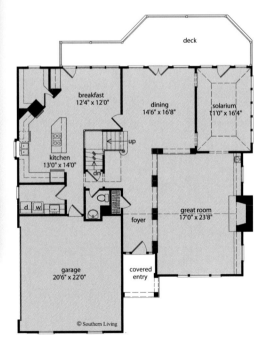

FIRST FLOOR

SECOND FLOOR

2,960 square feet

ARCHITECTURAL RENDERING: ROD DENT

DESIGNED BY STEPHEN FULLER, INC.

Plan# HPK3800178

First Floor: 1,595 sq. ft.

Second Floor: 1,365 sq. ft.

Total: 2,960 sq. ft.

Bedrooms: 4

Bathrooms: 3

Width: 62' - 0"

Depth: 49' - 0"

Foundation: Unfinished Basement

Price Code: L1

1-800-850-1491 • EPLANS.COM

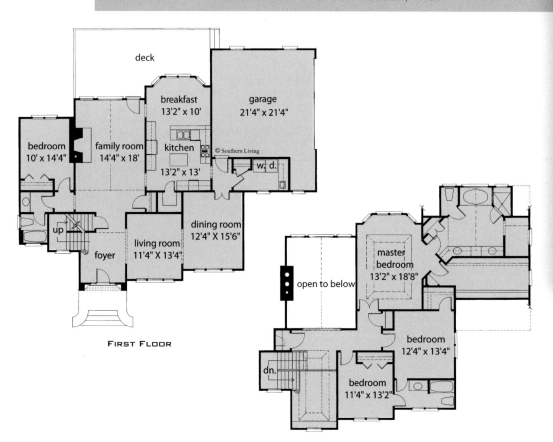

FIRST FLOOR

SECOND FLOOR

✦LANIER✦

2,982
square feet

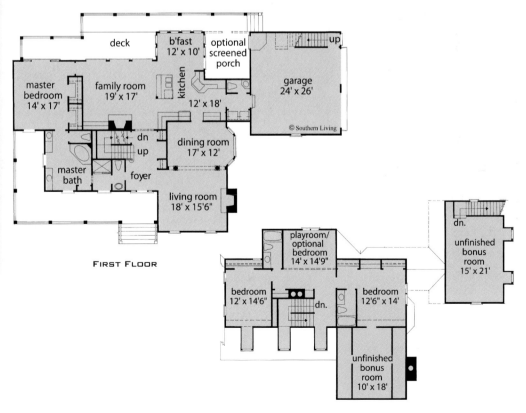

Plan# HPK3800179

First Floor: 2,032 sq. ft.

Second Floor: 950 sq. ft.

Total: 2,982 sq. ft.

Bonus Space: 495 sq. ft.

Bedrooms: 3

Bathrooms: 4 ½

Width: 87' - 0"

Depth: 50' - 0"

Foundation: Crawlspace

Price Code: C3

1-800-850-1491 • EPLANS.COM

DESIGNED BY JOHN TEE, ARCHITECT

First Floor

- deck
- b'fast 12' x 10'
- optional screened porch
- garage 24' x 26'
- master bedroom 14' x 17'
- family room 19' x 17'
- kitchen 12' x 18'
- dining room 17' x 12'
- dn
- up
- master bath
- foyer
- living room 18' x 15'6"
- © Southern Living

Second Floor

- playroom/ optional bedroom 14' x 14'9"
- bedroom 12' x 14'6"
- bedroom 12'6" x 14'
- dn.
- unfinished bonus room 15' x 21'
- unfinished bonus room 10' x 18'

~ROSEHAVEN~

2,989 square feet

ARCHITECTURAL RENDERING: ROD DENT

© Stephen Fuller, Inc.

DESIGNED BY STEPHEN FULLER, INC.

Plan # HPK3800180

First Floor: 1,983 sq. ft.

Second Floor: 1,006 sq. ft.

Total: 2,989 sq. ft.

Bedrooms: 4

Bathrooms: 3 ½

Width: 59' - 0"

Depth: 66' - 0"

Foundation: Unfinished Basement

Price Code: L4

1-800-850-1491 • EPLANS.COM

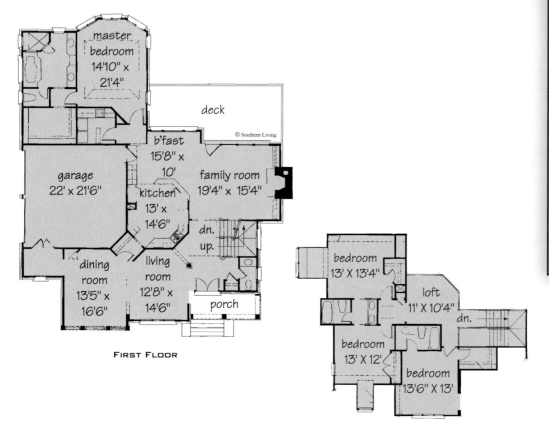

master bedroom 14'10" x 21'4"

deck

© Southern Living

b'fast 15'8" x 10'

family room 19'4" x 15'4"

garage 22' x 21'6"

kitchen 13' x 14'6"

dn. up.

dining room 13'5" x 16'6"

living room 12'8" x 14'6"

porch

FIRST FLOOR

bedroom 13' X 13'4"

loft 11' X 10'4"

dn.

bedroom 13' X 12'

bedroom 13'6" X 13'

SECOND FLOOR

BEDFORD COTTAGE

2,951 square feet

Plan # HPK3800176

First Floor: 1,589 sq. ft.

Second Floor: 1,362 sq. ft.

Total: 2,951 sq. ft.

Bonus Space: 490 sq. ft.

Bedrooms: 3

Bathrooms: 2 ½

Width: 58' - 0"

Depth: 77' - 0"

Foundation: Crawlspace

Price Code: L1

1-800-850-1491 • EPLANS.COM

DESIGNED BY LOONEY RICKS KISS ARCHITECTS, INC., FOR COTTAGE LIVING MAGAZINE

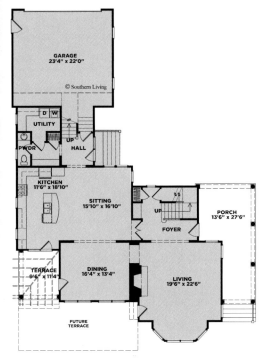

FIRST FLOOR

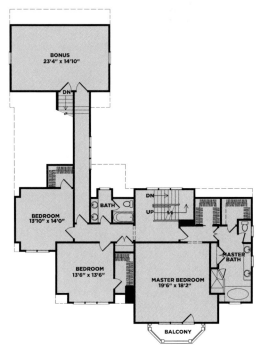

SECOND FLOOR

❧ POPLAR GROVE ❧

3,116
square feet

DESIGNED BY LOONEY RICKS KISS ARCHITECTS, INC.

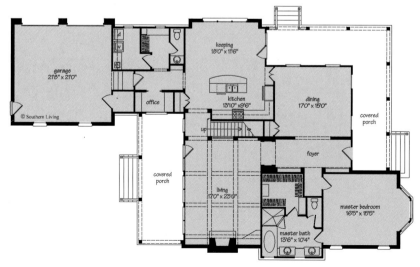

© Southern Living

garage
21'8" x 21'0"

office

keeping
18'0" x 11'6"

kitchen
13'10" x 9'6"

dining
17'0" x 15'0"

covered porch

foyer

covered porch

living
17'0" x 23'0"

master bedroom
16'5" x 15'5"

master bath
13'6" x 10'4"

up

FIRST FLOOR

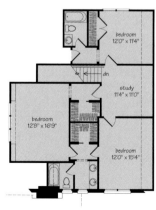

bedroom
12'0" x 11'4"

study
11'4" x 11'0"

bedroom
12'8" x 18'9"

bedroom
12'0" x 15'4"

dn

SECOND FLOOR

THIS HOME'S WRAPAROUND COVERED PORCH invites entry from both ends. In addition, the house plan's L-shaped footprint forms a partial courtyard around the rear deck. French doors all around further enhance the ambiance inside with natural light.

Indoor spaces are equally welcoming. The living room is adorned with a coffered ceiling and bookshelves flanking the fireplace. The dining room assumes a more formal role while the kitchen snack bar handles casual dining.

Plan # HPK3800202

First Floor: 2,133 sq. ft.

Second Floor: 983 sq. ft.

Total: 3,116 sq. ft.

Bedrooms: 4

Bathrooms: 3 ½

Width: 52' - 0"

Depth: 87' - 3"

Foundation: Slab

Price Code: L4

1-800-850-1491 • EPLANS.COM

The kitchen's adjacent keeping room serves equally well as a sunroom or as a breakfast nook.

Off the foyer, the master suite is tucked away from family activity. A bay window welcomes sunlight as it forms a cozy sitting area. Pass through the master bath—with a corner shower, window-side tub, and double vanity—to a spacious walk-in closet. All remaining bedrooms are on the second floor, as is an open study.

A simple office can accommodate a home-based business or quiet studying, with views of the covered rear porch. A mudroom and powder room conveniently located near the garage help make this design perfect for a young family.

~ Poppy Point ~

2,604 square feet

ARCHITECTURAL RENDERING: MILES MELTON

DESIGNED BY GARY/RAGSDALE, INC.

master bedroom
19'6" x 16'0"

covered patio

breakfast
10'0" x 10'10"

family room
17'0" x 20'10"

kitchen
10'6" x 17'8"

study
11'4" x 14'6"

foyer

dining
11'6" x 14'0"

courtyard

up

bedroom
11'0" x 12'0"

porch

bedroom
11'0" x 12'0"

garage
21'0" x 19'0"

© Southern Living

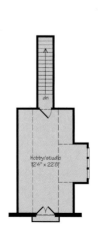

dn

Hobby/studio
12'4" x 22'8"

Plan # HPK3800121

Square Footage: 2,604 sq. ft.

Bonus Space: 350 sq. ft.

Bedrooms: 3

Bathrooms: 2 ½

Width: 49' - 0"

Depth: 89' - 0"

Foundation: Slab

Price Code: C3

1-800-850-1491 • EPLANS.COM

❦JULIETTE❦

2,997
square feet

DESIGNED BY BRYAN & CONTRERAS, LLC

Plan # HPK3800183

First Floor: 2,315 sq. ft.

Second Floor: 682 sq. ft.

Total: 2,997 sq. ft.

Bonus Space: 998 sq. ft.

Bedrooms: 3

Bathrooms: 2 ½

Width: 96' - 0"

Depth: 63' - 0"

Foundation: Unfinished Basement

Price Code: L1

1-800-850-1491 • EPLANS.COM

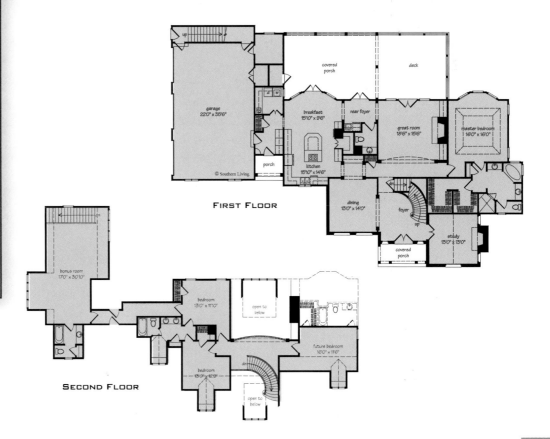

FIRST FLOOR

SECOND FLOOR

2,998 square feet

ARCHITECTURAL RENDERING: BRIAN BARKS

DESIGNED BY JOHN TEE, ARCHITECT

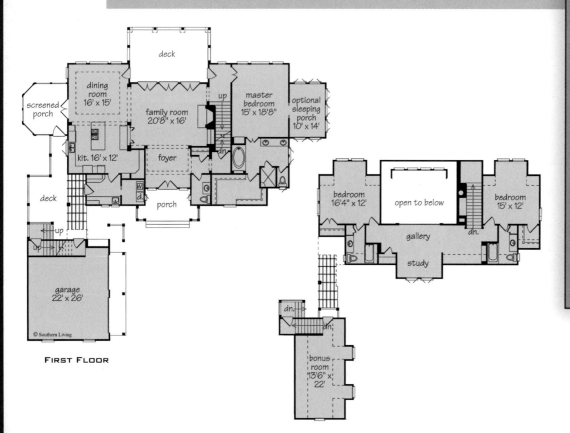

FIRST FLOOR

SECOND FLOOR

Plan# HPK3800184

First Floor: 1,934 sq. ft.

Second Floor: 1,064 sq. ft.

Total: 2,998 sq. ft.

Bonus Space: 297 sq. ft.

Bedrooms: 3

Bathrooms: 3 ½

Width: 81' - 0"

Depth: 72' - 0"

Foundation: Unfinished Basement

Price Code: L4

1-800-850-1491 • EPLANS.COM

❧ BARROW LAKE ❧

3,021
square feet

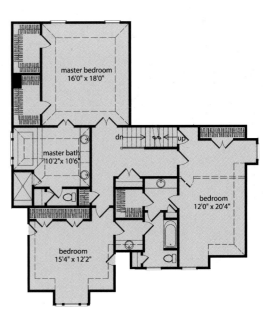

DESIGNED BY SPITZMILLER AND NORRIS, INC.

Plan # HPK3800185

First Floor: 1,496 sq. ft.

Second Floor: 1,525 sq. ft.

Total: 3,021 sq. ft.

Bedrooms: 3

Bathrooms: 2 ½

Width: 45' - 0"

Depth: 50' - 0"

Foundation: Unfinished Basement

Price Code: L1

1-800-850-1491 • EPLANS.COM

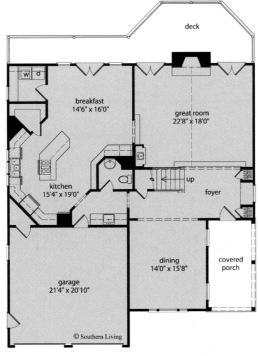

deck

breakfast
14'6" x 16'0"

great room
22'8" x 18'0"

kitchen
15'4" x 19'0"

up

foyer

garage
21'4" x 20'10"

dining
14'0" x 15'8"

covered
porch

© Southern Living

FIRST FLOOR

master bedroom
16'0" x 18'0"

master bath
10'2" x 10'6"

dn

up

bedroom
12'0" x 20'4"

bedroom
15'4" x 12'2"

SECOND FLOOR

⊰GAVINBROOKE⊱

3,022
square feet

ARCHITECTURAL RENDERING: SPITZMILLER AND NORRIS, INC.

DESIGNED BY SPITZMILLER AND NORRIS, INC.

Plan # HPK3800186

First Floor: 1,955 sq. ft.

Second Floor: 1,067 sq. ft.

Total: 3,022 sq. ft.

Bedrooms: 4

Bathrooms: 3 ½

Width: 45' - 0"

Depth: 60' - 0"

Foundation: Crawlspace

Price Code: L1

1-800-850-1491 • EPLANS.COM

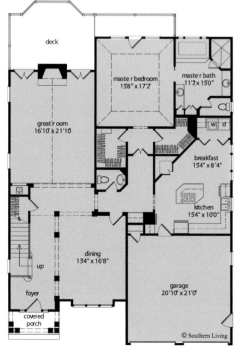

FIRST FLOOR

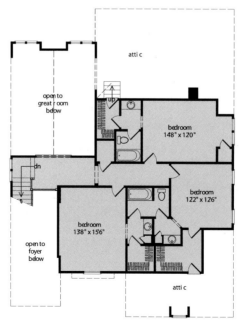

SECOND FLOOR

·INANDA HOUSE·

ARCHITECTURAL RENDERING: MILES MELTON

3,039 square feet

Plan# HPK3800187

First Floor: 2,078 sq. ft.

Second Floor: 961 sq. ft.

Total: 3,039 sq. ft.

Bedrooms: 3

Bathrooms: 3 ½

Width: 74' - 0"

Depth: 71' - 0"

Foundation: Crawlspace

Price Code: L4

1-800-850-1491 • EPLANS.COM

DESIGNED BY MOUZON DESIGN FOR BILTMORE ESTATE

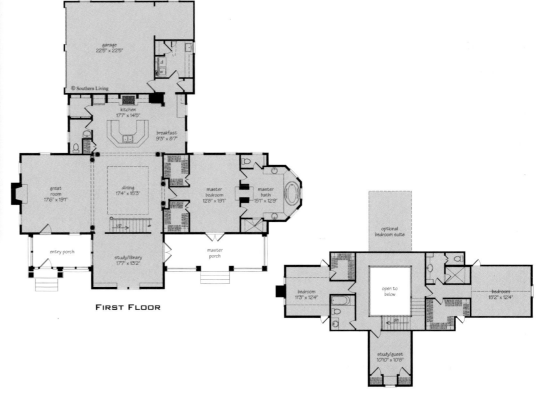

FIRST FLOOR

SECOND FLOOR

BILTMORE™
For Your Home

3,050 square feet

ARCHITECTURAL RENDERING: ROD DENT

DESIGNED BY STEPHEN FULLER, INC.

Plan# HPK3800188

First Floor: 1,935 sq. ft.

Second Floor: 1,115 sq. ft.

Total: 3,050 sq. ft.

Bedrooms: 4

Bathrooms: 3 ½

Width: 69' - 0"

Depth: 60' - 0"

Foundation: Unfinished Basement

Price Code: L1

1-800-850-1491 • EPLANS.COM

First Floor

- deck
- breakfast 13'4" x 10'6"
- sitting 11'4" x 11'4"
- kitchen 13'4" x 10'4"
- family room 18' x 15'
- master bedroom 15'4" x 15'8"
- dining room 13' x 12'
- up
- dn.
- foyer
- w. d.
- living room 11'8" x 14'6"
- porch
- garage 21'4" x 20'6"

© Southern Living

Second Floor

- open to below
- bedroom 13'6" x 14'6"
- dn.
- up
- bedroom 11'8" x 12'2"
- bedroom 14'2" x 12'10"
- storage

· WOODLAWN ·

ARCHITECTURAL RENDERING: RICK HERR

DESIGNED BY BRYAN & CONTRERAS, LLC

Plan # HPK3800189

First Floor: 2,110 sq. ft.

Second Floor: 941 sq. ft.

Total: 3,051 sq. ft.

Bedrooms: 5

Bathrooms: 4

Width: 69' - 0"

Depth: 53' - 0"

Foundation: Unfinished Basement

Price Code: C3

1-800-850-1491 • EPLANS.COM

FIRST FLOOR

SECOND FLOOR

·Andrews·

3,054
square feet

ARCHITECTURAL RENDERING: DON RANKIN

DESIGNED BY JOHN TEE, ARCHITECT

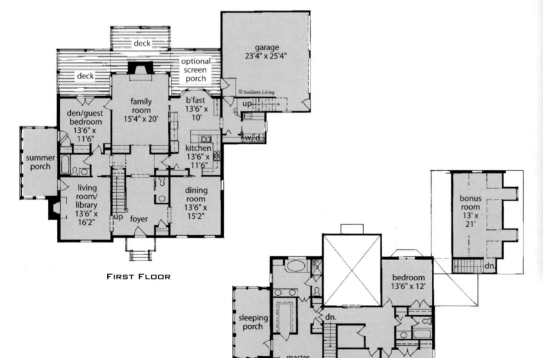

FIRST FLOOR

SECOND FLOOR

deck

deck

optional screen porch

garage
23'4" x 25'4"

© Southern Living

up

family room
15'4" x 20'

b'fast
13'6" x
10'

w. d.

den/guest
bedroom
13'6" x
11'6"

kitchen
13'6" x
11'6"

summer porch

living room/
library
13'6" x
16'2"

up   foyer

dining room
13'6" x 15'2"

bonus room
13' x 21'

dn.

sleeping porch

dn.

bedroom
13'6" x 12'

master
bedroom
13'6" x 17'

bedroom
11'6" x 12'

bedroom
13'6" x 12'

Plan # **HPK3800190**

First Floor: 1,677 sq. ft.

Second Floor: 1,377 sq. ft.

Total: 3,054 sq. ft.

Bonus Space: 273 sq. ft.

Bedrooms: 5

Bathrooms: 3 ½

Width: 68' - 0"

Depth: 59' - 0"

Foundation: Crawlspace

Price Code: C3

1-800-850-1491 • EPLANS.COM

SUMMERFIELD CHASE

3,064
square feet

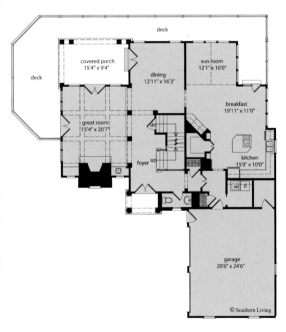

DESIGNED BY SPITZMILLER AND NORRIS, INC.

Plan# HPK3800191

First Floor: 1,553 sq. ft.

Second Floor: 1,511 sq. ft.

Total: 3,064 sq. ft.

Bonus Space: 132 sq. ft.

Bedrooms: 3

Bathrooms: 2 ½

Width: 63' - 0"

Depth: 70' - 0"

Foundation: Unfinished Basement

Price Code: L1

1-800-850-1491 • EPLANS.COM

FIRST FLOOR

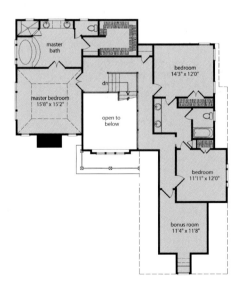

SECOND FLOOR

CAPE MAY

3,069
square feet

ARCHITECTURAL RENDERING: MILES MELTON

DESIGNED BY SPITZMILLER AND NORRIS, INC.

Plan# HPK3800192

First Floor: 2,012 sq. ft.

Second Floor: 1,057 sq. ft.

Total: 3,069 sq. ft.

Bedrooms: 4

Bathrooms: 4 ½

Width: 61' - 0"

Depth: 84' - 0"

Foundation: Unfinished Basement

Price Code: L1

1-800-850-1491 • EPLANS.COM

First Floor

garage
21' x 21'4"

© Southern Living

d.
w.

breakfast room
14'4" x 10'1"

family room
18' x 16'8"

master bedroom
15'4" x 16'8"

kitchen
14'6" x 14'9"

dn. up

foyer

dining room
12'4" x 16'6"

living room
12'2" x 12'6"

covered porch

FIRST FLOOR

Second Floor

bedroom
14'4" x 12

open to below

dn.

computer nook

bedroom
14'4" x 12'4"

open to below

bedroom
12'8" x 12'6"

SECOND FLOOR

CLAYFIELD PLACE

3,070 square feet

ARCHITECTURAL RENDERING: MILES MELTON

DESIGNED BY LOONEY RICKS KISS ARCHITECTS, INC.

Plan# HPK3800193

First Floor: 2,252 sq. ft.

Second Floor: 818 sq. ft.

Total: 3,070 sq. ft.

Bedrooms: 3

Bathrooms: 2 ½

Width: 99' - 0"

Depth: 44' - 0"

Foundation: Slab

Price Code: L1

1-800-850-1491 • EPLANS.COM

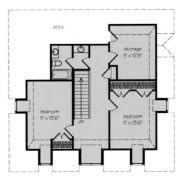

FIRST FLOOR

garage 20' x 9'4"

garage 25'7 x 22

© Southern Living

master bedroom 15'4" x 17'

screened porch

breakfast room 11' x 9'10"

kitchen 10'6" x 15'

family room 18' x 15'4"

up

dining 13'2" x 16'

foyer

living 13'2" x 13'10"

SECOND FLOOR

attic

storage 11' x 12'8"

bedroom 11' x 13'6"

dn

bedroom 11' x 13'6"

3,074 square feet

ARCHITECTURAL RENDERING: MILES MELTON

DESIGNED BY JOHN TEE, ARCHITECT

© Southern Living

OPTIONAL SECOND FLOOR

Plan # **HPK3800194**

Square Footage: 3,074

Optional Second Floor: 1,168 sq. ft.

Bedrooms: 3

Bathrooms: 3 ½

Width: 86' - 4"

Depth: 70' - 0"

Foundation: Crawlspace

Price Code: L1

1-800-850-1491 • EPLANS.COM

⊷ THE ORCHARD HOUSE ⊶

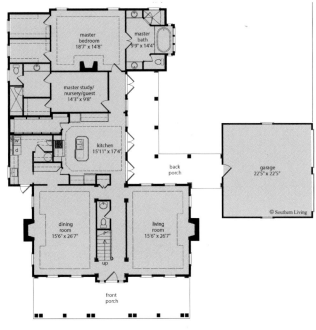

3,084
square feet

DESIGNED BY MOUZON DESIGN FOR BILTMORE ESTATE

FIRST FLOOR

SECOND FLOOR

Plan # HPK3800195

First Floor: 2,240 sq. ft.

Second Floor: 844 sq. ft.

Total: 3,084 sq. ft.

Bonus Space: 381 sq. ft.

Bedrooms: 4 or 5

Bathrooms: 4 ½ or 5 ½

Width: 77' - 0"

Depth: 74' - 6"

Foundation: Crawlspace

Price Code: L4

1-800-850-1491 • EPLANS.COM

BILTMORE™
For Your Home

GRAND AND GRACIOUS

3,087
square feet

DESIGNED BY STEPHEN FULLER, INC.

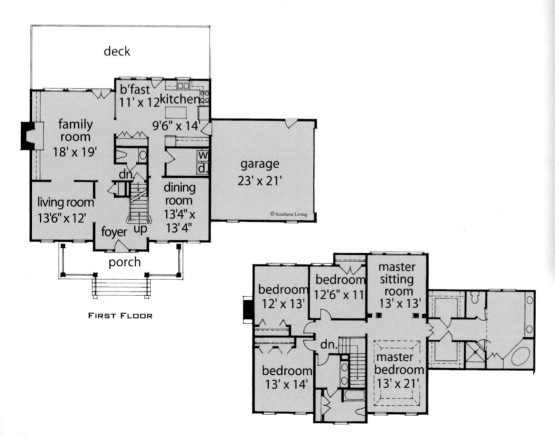

FIRST FLOOR

SECOND FLOOR

Plan # **HPK3800196**

First Floor: 1,344 sq. ft.

Second Floor: 1,743 sq. ft.

Total: 3,087 sq. ft.

Bedrooms: 4

Bathrooms: 2 ½

Width: 62' - 0"

Depth: 54' - 0"

Foundation: Unfinished Basement

Price Code: C3

1-800-850-1491 • EPLANS.COM

3,087 square feet

ARCHITECTURAL RENDERING: DON RANKIN

DESIGNED BY JOHN TEE, ARCHITECT

Plan# HPK3800197

First Floor: 1,642 sq. ft.

Second Floor: 1,445 sq. ft.

Total: 3,087 sq. ft.

Bonus Space: 304 sq. ft.

Bedrooms: 4

Bathrooms: 3

Width: 80' - 9"

Depth: 45' - 4"

Foundation: Crawlspace

Price Code: C3

1-800-850-1491 • EPLANS.COM

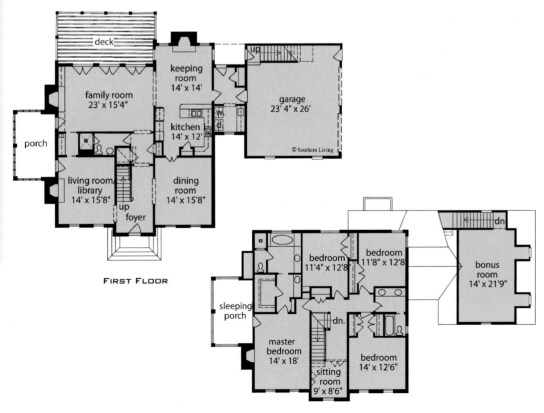

FIRST FLOOR

SECOND FLOOR

A COURTYARD HOME

3,269
square feet

DESIGNED BY MOUZON DESIGN

Plan# **HPK3800198**

Square Footage: 3,269

Bedrooms: 3 or 4

Bathrooms: 3

Width: 71' - 0"

Depth: 111' - 0"

Foundation: Crawlspace

Price Code: L2

1-800-850-1491 • EPLANS.COM

⁌ KENNESAW COUNTRY HOUSE ⁌

ARCHITECTURAL RENDERING: ROD DENT

DESIGNED BY STEPHEN FULLER, INC.

Plan # HPK3800199

First Floor: 1,602 sq. ft.

Second Floor: 1,493 sq. ft.

Total: 3,095 sq. ft.

Bonus Space: 336 sq. ft.

Bedrooms: 4

Bathrooms: 3

Width: 60' - 6"

Depth: 69' - 0"

Foundation: Crawlspace

Price Code: C3

1-800-850-1491 • EPLANS.COM

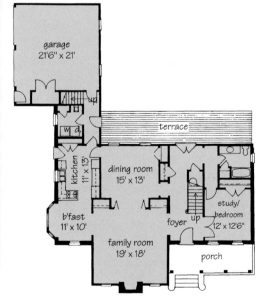

FIRST FLOOR

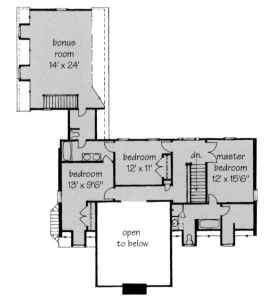

SECOND FLOOR

BROOKWOOD COTTAGE

3,100 square feet

ARCHITECTURAL RENDERING: MILES MELTON

DESIGNED BY JOHN TEE, ARCHITECT

FIRST FLOOR

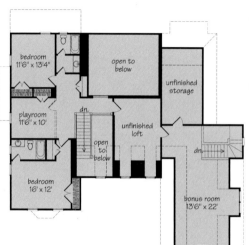

SECOND FLOOR

Plan# **HPK3800200**

First Floor: 2,272 sq. ft.

Second Floor: 828 sq. ft.

Total: 3,100 sq. ft.

Bonus Space: 886 sq. ft.

Bedrooms: 4

Bathrooms: 4

Width: 65' - 0"

Depth: 60' - 0"

Foundation: Unfinished Basement

Price Code: L1

1-800-850-1491 • EPLANS.COM

⊰ PRESQUE ISLE ⊱

ARCHITECTURAL RENDERING: MILES MELTON

3,113 square feet

DESIGNED BY GARY/RAGSDALE, INC.

Plan# HPK3800201

Square Footage: 3,113

Bedrooms: 4 or 5

Bathrooms: 3 ½

Width: 68' - 0"

Depth: 74' - 5"

Foundation: Crawlspace

Price Code: C3

1-800-850-1491 • EPLANS.COM

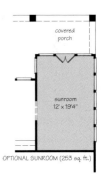

OPTIONAL SUNROOM (253 sq. ft.)

OPTIONAL LAYOUT

BLOUNT SPRINGS RETREAT

2,996 square feet

DESIGNED BY STEPHEN FULLER, INC.

Plan # HPK3800182

First Floor: 1,780 sq. ft.

Second Floor: 1,216 sq. ft.

Total: 2,996 sq. ft.

Bedrooms: 3

Bathrooms: 2 ½

Width: 50' - 0"

Depth: 48' - 0"

Foundation: Crawlspace

Price Code: L4

1-800-850-1491 • EPLANS.COM

kitchen
15' x 16'

sunporch

breakfast room
12' x 16'6"

family room
15' x 26'6"

dining room
15' x 14'

up

foyer

porch

© Southern Living

FIRST FLOOR

dn.

bedroom
12'6" x 11'6"

w. d.

master bedroom
15' x 13'

bedroom
12'6" x 11'6"

porch

SECOND FLOOR

3,420 square feet

ARCHITECTURAL RENDERING: MILES MELTON

Plan # HPK3800203

First Floor: 2,329 sq. ft.

Second Floor: 1,091 sq. ft.

Total: 3,420 sq. ft.

Bedrooms: 4

Bathrooms: 3 ½

Width: 66' - 8"

Depth: 60' - 2"

Foundation: Crawlspace, Unfinished Basement

Price Code: C3

1-800-850-1491 • EPLANS.COM

DESIGNED BY SPITZMILLER & NORRIS, INC.

deck

b'fast room 10'6" x 8'

family room 18'8" x 17'6"

kitchen 16'10" x 17'6"

master bedroom 15'6" x 16'6"

living room/ study 12' x 15'6"

up

foyer

13

w. d.

garage 21'10" x 21'4"

porch

© Southern Living

FIRST FLOOR

open to below

bedroom 11'6" x 13'8"

dn.

attic

open to below

bedroom 15'6" x 16'6"

bedroom 13'7" x 12'6"

attic

attic

SECOND FLOOR

MYRTLE GROVE

3,125 square feet

DESIGNED BY GARY/RAGSDALE, INC.

master bedroom
15' x 20'

bedroom
14'8' x 11'

bedroom
11' x 13'

bedroom
11' x 13'

study/bedroom
12'6' x 12'8'

foyer

dining room
15' x 12'

family room
18' x 22'

breakfast
12'6' x 12'6'

kitchen
12'2" x 14'

tandem garage
12' x 19'8"

garage
21' x 21'

porch

porch

up

up

© Southern Living

Plan# **HPK3800204**

Square Footage: 3,125

Bedrooms: 4

Bathrooms: 2 ½

Width: 68' - 11"

Depth: 78' - 1"

Foundation: Crawlspace

Price Code: C3

1-800-850-1491 • EPLANS.COM

3,150 square feet

ARCHITECTURAL RENDERING: SPITZMILLER AND NORRIS, INC.

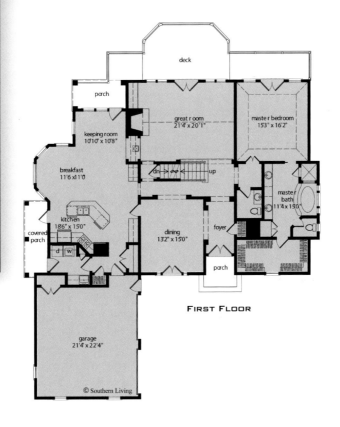

DESIGNED BY SPITZMILLER AND NORRIS, INC.

Plan# HPK3800205

First Floor: 2,127 sq. ft.

Second Floor: 1,023 sq. ft.

Total: 3,150 sq. ft.

Bedrooms: 4

Bathrooms: 3 ½

Width: 61' - 0"

Depth: 66' - 0"

Foundation: Unfinished Basement

Price Code: L1

1-800-850-1491 • EPLANS.COM

FIRST FLOOR

- deck
- porch
- keeping room 10'10" x 10'8"
- great room 21'4" x 20'1"
- master bedroom 15'3" x 16'2"
- breakfast 11'6" x 11'0"
- dn / up
- master bath 11'4" x 15'0"
- kitchen 18'6" x 15'0"
- covered porch
- d / w
- dining 13'2" x 15'0"
- foyer
- porch
- garage 21'4" x 22'4"
- © Southern Living

SECOND FLOOR

- bedroom 12'2" x 14'2"
- dn
- bedroom 13'2" x 12'6"
- bedroom 12'4" x 12'9"

ᴥLIVE OAK COTTAGEᴥ

3,153
square feet

ARCHITECTURAL RENDERING: GREG HAVENS

DESIGNED BY LOONEY RICKS KISS ARCHITECTS, INC.
FOR ST. JOE LAND COMPANY

Plan# HPK3800206

Square Footage: 3,153

Bedrooms: 3

Bathrooms: 3 ½

Width: 79' - 4"

Depth: 91' - 0"

Foundation: Slab

Price Code: L4

1-800-850-1491 • EPLANS.COM

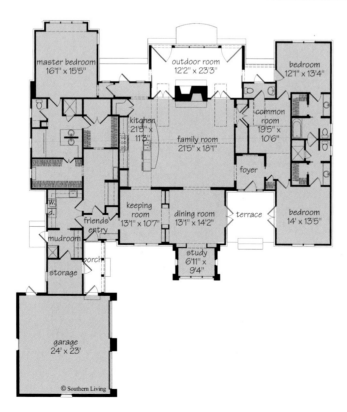

THE JEFFERSON

3,165 square feet

DESIGNED BY GARY/RAGSDALE, INC.

Plan# HPK3800207

Square Footage: 3,165

Bedrooms: 4

Bathrooms: 3 ½

Width: 68' - 11"

Depth: 78' - 1"

Foundation: Crawlspace

Price Code: C3

1-800-850-1491 • EPLANS.COM

OPTIONAL LAYOUT

RIVER BLUFF

3,173 square feet

ARCHITECTURAL RENDERING: MILES MELTON

DESIGNED BY MOUZON DESIGN

Plan# HPK3800208

First Floor: 2,315 sq. ft.

Second Floor: 858 sq. ft.

Total: 3,173 sq. ft.

Bedrooms: 4

Bathrooms: 2 ½

Width: 44' - 4"

Depth: 91' - 8"

Foundation: Crawlspace

Price Code: L2

1-800-850-1491 • EPLANS.COM

FIRST FLOOR

- garage 23'2" x 23'2"
- storage
- breakfast 7'3" x 9'3"
- kitchen 14'5" x 15'7"
- sunroom 15'10" x 14'1"
- w. d.
- dining room 16'4" x 12'7"
- family room 24'2" x 15'7"
- porch
- up
- entry
- master bedroom 15'7" x 23'1"
- porch
- © Southern Living

SECOND FLOOR

- open to below
- dn.
- bedroom 12'1" x 10'3"
- bedroom 15'7" x 10'3"
- porch
- bedroom 11'2" x 10'11"

3,180 square feet

ARCHITECTURAL RENDERING: MILES MELTON

DESIGNED BY JOHN TEE, ARCHITECT, FOR COOKING LIGHT MAGAZINE

Plan # HPK3800209

First Floor: 1,992 sq. ft.

Second Floor: 1,188 sq. ft.

Total: 3,180 sq. ft.

Bonus Space: 362 sq. ft.

Bedrooms: 4

Bathrooms: 4 ½

Width: 60' - 0"

Depth: 99' - 0"

Foundation: Unfinished Basement

Price Code: L2

1-800-850-1491 • EPLANS.COM

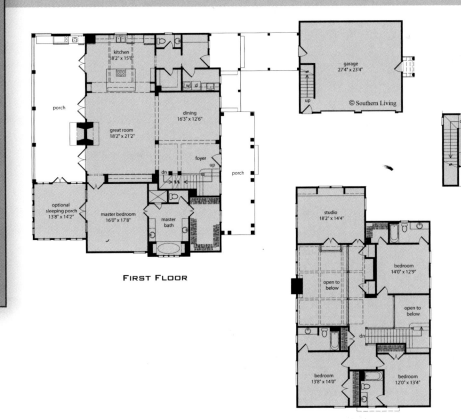

FIRST FLOOR

SECOND FLOOR

❧ WALKER RIDGE ❧

3,180 square feet

DESIGNED BY JOHN TEE, ARCHITECT

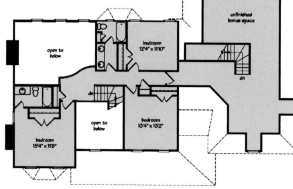

deck

family room
21'0" x 15'4"

breakfast
10'0" x 15'0"

kitchen
11'4" x 15'6"

master bedroom
16'0" x 18'4"

up

living
15'4" x 14'0"

foyer
12'0" x 12'0"

up

dining
13'0" x 15'6"

garage
21'4" x 21'8"

porch

© Southern Living

FIRST FLOOR

open to below

bedroom
12'4" x 11'10"

unfinished bonus space

open to below

bedroom
13'4" x 13'2"

dn

bedroom
15'4" x 11'8"

dn

SECOND FLOOR

Plan# HPK3800210

First Floor: 2,268 sq. ft.

Second Floor: 912 sq. ft.

Total: 3,180 sq. ft.

Bonus Space: 654 sq. ft.

Bedrooms: 4

Bathrooms: 4 ½

Width: 74' - 0"

Depth: 58' - 0"

Foundation: Unfinished Basement

Price Code: C3

1-800-850-1491 • EPLANS.COM

3,221 square feet

ARCHITECTURAL RENDERING: MILES MELTON

DESIGNED BY GARY/RAGSDALE, INC.

Plan# HPK3800211

Square Footage: 3,221

Bedrooms: 4 or 5

Bathrooms: 3 ½

Width: 59' - 0"

Depth: 89' - 10"

Foundation: Slab

Price Code: C3

1-800-850-1491 • EPLANS.COM

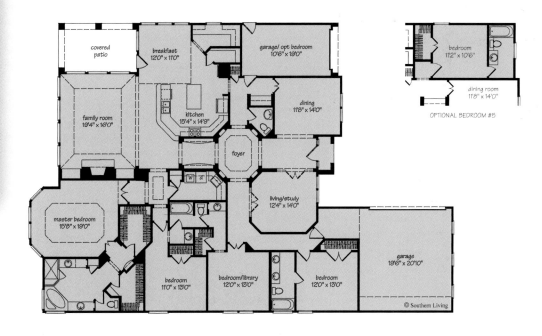

covered patio

breakfast 12'0" x 11'0"

garage/ opt bedroom 10'6" x 19'0"

family room 19'4" x 16'0"

kitchen 15'4" x 14'9"

dining 11'8" x 14'0"

foyer

master bedroom 15'8" x 19'0"

W D

living/study 12'4" x 14'0"

garage 19'6" x 20'10"

bedroom 11'0" x 13'0"

bedroom/library 12'0" x 13'0"

bedroom 12'0" x 13'0"

© Southern Living

bedroom 11'2" x 10'6"

dining room 11'8" x 14'0"

OPTIONAL BEDROOM #5

·LAMBERTH WAY·

3,241 square feet

ARCHITECTURAL RENDERING: LOIS WATSON

DESIGNED BY SULLIVAN DESIGN COMPANY

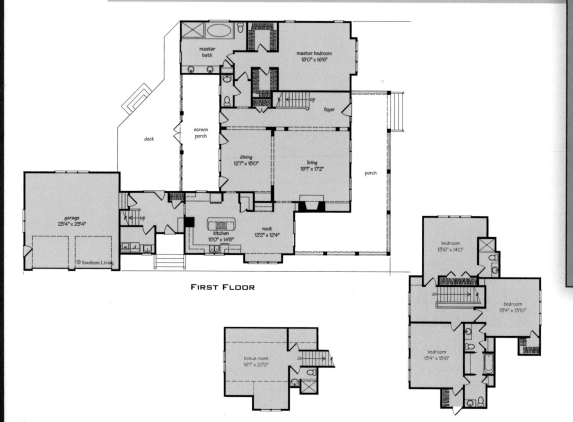

FIRST FLOOR

SECOND FLOOR

Plan# HPK3800212

First Floor: 2,224 sq. ft.

Second Floor: 1,017 sq. ft.

Total: 3,241 sq. ft.

Bonus Space: 436 sq. ft.

Bedrooms: 4

Bathrooms: 3 ½

Width: 60' - 8"

Depth: 92' - 0"

Foundation: Crawlspace

Price Code: C3

1-800-850-1491 • EPLANS.COM

~ THE SHOALS ~

ARCHITECTURAL RENDERING: MILES MELTON

3,248 square feet

DESIGNED BY MITCHELL GINN

Plan # HPK3800213

First Floor: 2,128 sq. ft.

Second Floor: 1,120 sq. ft.

Total: 3,248 sq. ft.

Bedrooms: 3

Bathrooms: 3 ½

Width: 54' - 0"

Depth: 60' - 0"

Foundation: Unfinished Basement

Price Code: C3

1-800-850-1491 • EPLANS.COM

FIRST FLOOR

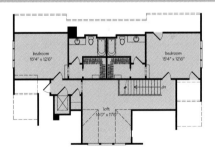

SECOND FLOOR

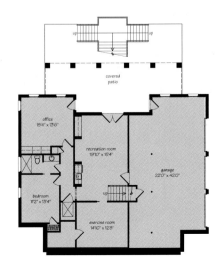

·SHOOK HILL·

3,257 square feet

DESIGNED BY MITCHELL GINN

FIRST FLOOR

SECOND FLOOR

Plan # HPK3800214

First Floor: 2,210 sq. ft.

Second Floor: 1,047 sq. ft.

Total: 3,257 sq. ft.

Bedrooms: 4

Bathrooms: 3 ½

Width: 74' - 0"

Depth: 88' - 6"

Foundation: Unfinished Basement

Price Code: L1

1·800·850·1491 • EPLANS.COM

ARCHITECTURAL RENDERING: MILES MELTON

3,154
square feet

DESIGNED BY GARY/RAGSDALE, INC.

Plan# HPK3800215

Square Footage: 3,154

Bedrooms: 4

Bathrooms: 2 ½

Width: 69' - 0"

Depth: 81 ' - 0"

Foundation: Slab

Price Code: C3

1-800-850-1491 • EPLANS.COM

- exercise room
- master bedroom 15'2" x 22'6"
- patio
- breakfast room 11' x 13'6"
- family room 19'6" x 18'
- bedroom 12' x 13'
- bonus room 12' x 16'3"
- kitchen 17'4" x 15'6"
- bedroom 11' x 14'
- study/living room 13' x 15'
- garage 19'10" x 21'6"
- bedroom 14'8" x 12'
- © Southern Living
- d. w
- dining room 12' x 14'
- foyer

3,301 square feet

ARCHITECTURAL RENDERING: MUIR STEWART

MUIR STEWART '03

DESIGNED BY MOUZON DESIGN FOR COASTAL LIVING MAGAZINE

Plan # HPK3800217

First Floor: 1,566 sq. ft.

Second Floor: 884 sq. ft.

Third Floor: 851 sq. ft.

Total: 3,301 sq. ft.

Bedrooms: 3

Bathrooms: 2 ½

Width: 44' - 6"

Depth: 47' - 6"

Foundation: Crawlspace

Price Code: L2

1-800-850-1491 • EPLANS.COM

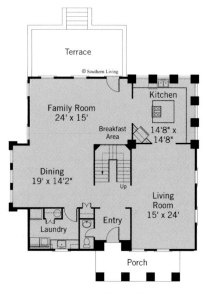

Terrace

© Southern Living

Kitchen

Family Room
24' x 15'

Breakfast Area

14'8" x 14'8"

Dining
19' x 14'2"

Living Room
15' x 24'

Laundry

Entry

Porch

FIRST FLOOR

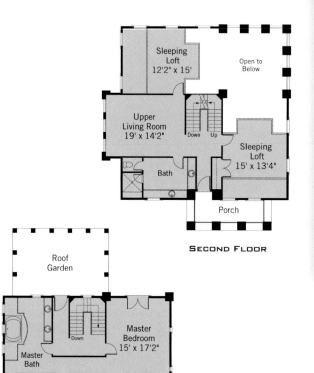

Sleeping Loft
12'2" x 15'

Open to Below

Upper Living Room
19' x 14'2"

Down Up

Sleeping Loft
15' x 13'4"

Bath

Porch

SECOND FLOOR

Roof Garden

Down

Master Bedroom
15' x 17'2"

Master Bath

Closet   Closet

Study
15' x 6'4"

THIRD FLOOR

❧ KENSINGTON PLACE ❧

ARCHITECTURAL RENDERING: MILES MELTON

3,925
square feet

DESIGNED BY SPITZMILLER AND NORRIS, INC.

Plan # HPK3800291

First Floor: 2,355 sq. ft.

Second Floor: 1,570 sq. ft.

Total: 3,925 sq. ft.

Bedrooms: 4

Bathrooms: 4

Width: 55' - 2"

Depth: 66' - 8"

Foundation: Unfinished Basement

Price Code: L1

1-800-850-1491 • EPLANS.COM

FIRST FLOOR

SECOND FLOOR

3,273
square feet

ARCHITECTURAL RENDERING: MILES MELTON

DESIGNED BY MITCHELL GINN

Plan # HPK3800216

First Floor: 2,303 sq. ft.

Second Floor: 970 sq. ft.

Total: 3,273 sq. ft.

Bonus Space: 442 sq. ft.

Bedrooms: 4

Bathrooms: 3 ½

Width: 62' - 0"

Depth: 47' - 6"

Foundation: Basement/Slab

Price Code: L1

1-800-850-1491 • EPLANS.COM

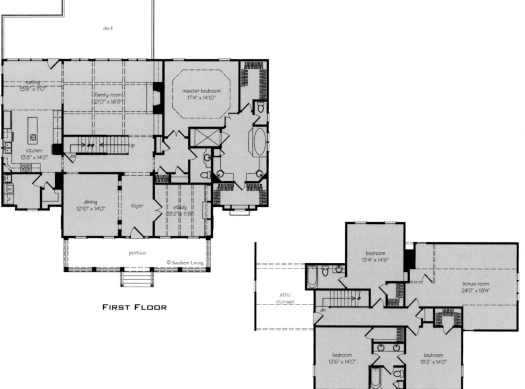

FIRST FLOOR

SECOND FLOOR

New Willow Grove

3,412 square feet

Plan# HPK3800218

First Floor: 2,368 sq. ft.

Second Floor: 948 sq. ft.

Total: 3,412 sq. ft.

Bonus Space: 480 sq. ft.

Bedrooms: 5

Bathrooms: 4 ½

Width: 70' - 4"

Depth: 56' - 8"

Foundation: Crawlspace

Price Code: L1

1-800-850-1491 • EPLANS.COM

DESIGNED BY JOHN TEE, ARCHITECT

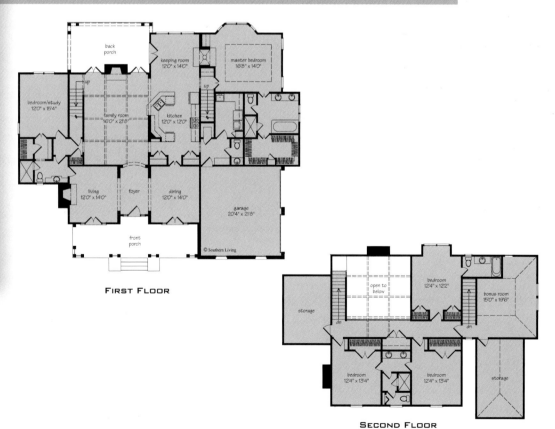

FIRST FLOOR

SECOND FLOOR

⤺ PLANTERS RETREAT ⤻

3,321 square feet

DESIGNED BY ESKEW+DUMEZ+RIPPLE ARCHITECTS
FOR ST. JOE LAND COMPANY

ARCHITECTURAL RENDERING: MILES MELTON

garage
22'1" x 30'1"

© Southern Living

study

mudroom

SECOND FLOOR

master bed-room
11'8" x 22'2"

dn.

library

open to below

boy's room
11'2" x 12'1"

girl's room
11'6" x 12'1"

FIRST FLOOR

kitchen
13' x 18'1"

dining room
12' x 18'1"

family room
16'6" x 18'1"

screened porch

up

guest room
23'5" x 13'6"

Plan# HPK3800219

First Floor: 1,930 sq. ft.

Second Floor: 1,391 sq. ft.

Total: 3,321 sq. ft.

Bedrooms: 4

Bathrooms: 3 ½

Width: 79' - 0"

Depth: 24' - 0"

Foundation: Crawlspace

Price Code: L4

1-800-850-1491 • EPLANS.COM

CRESCENT HILL

3,335
square feet

DESIGNED BY GARY/RAGSDALE, INC.

Plan# HPK3800220

First Floor: 2,450 sq. ft.

Second Floor: 885 sq. ft.

Total: 3,335 sq. ft.

Bonus Space: 254 sq. ft.

Bedrooms: 4

Bathrooms: 3 ½

Width: 65' - 11"

Depth: 72' - 5"

Foundation: Crawlspace

Price Code: C3

1-800-850-1491 • EPLANS.COM

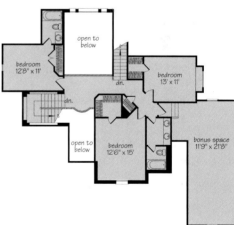

SECOND FLOOR

FIRST FLOOR

VAN BUREN

3,335 square feet

ARCHITECTURAL RENDERING: MILES MELTON

DESIGNED BY GARY/RAGSDALE, INC.

FIRST FLOOR

master bedroom
17 x 14'

living room
12' x 14'10

family room
17 x 19'

kitchen
12'8" x 13'6"

breakfast room
9' x 13'6

covered porch

study
11' x 15'

entry

dining room
12' x 15'

garage
20' x 29'6

© Southern Living

SECOND FLOOR

bedroom
15'6 x 11'

open to below

bedroom
14' x 10'10"

open to below

bedroom
12'6 x 15'

Plan# HPK3800222

First Floor: 2,450 sq. ft.

Second Floor: 885 sq. ft.

Total: 3,335 sq. ft.

Bedrooms: 4

Bathrooms: 3 ½

Width: 65' - 0"

Depth: 66' - 0"

Foundation: Crawlspace

Price Code: C3

1-800-850-1491 • EPLANS.COM

BELLWOODE

3,346 square feet

DESIGNED BY SPITZMILLER AND NORRIS, INC.

Plan# HPK3800223

Square Footage: 3,346

Bedrooms: 3

Bathrooms: 3 ½

Width: 104' - 2"

Depth: 58' - 6"

Foundation: Daylight Walkout Basement

Price Code: L1

1-800-850-1491 • EPLANS.COM

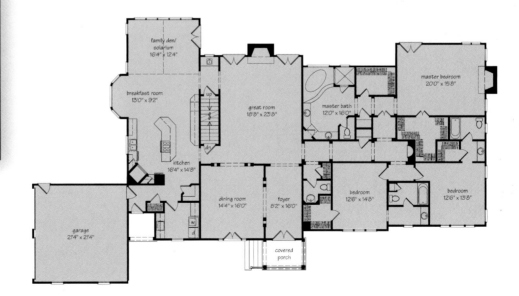

THE HAMPTONS

3,355
square feet

ARCHITECTURAL RENDERING: ROLAND DAVIS

DESIGNED BY STEPHEN FULLER, INC.

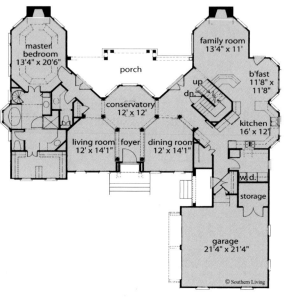

FIRST FLOOR

- master bedroom 13'4" x 20'6"
- porch
- family room 13'4" x 11'
- up
- dn.
- b'fast 11'8" x 11'8"
- conservatory 12' x 12'
- kitchen 16' x 12'
- living room 12' x 14'1"
- foyer
- dining room 12' x 14'1"
- w. d.
- storage
- garage 21'4" x 21'4"
- © Southern Living

Plan# HPK3800224

First Floor: 2,130 sq. ft.

Second Floor: 1,225 sq. ft.

Total: 3,355 sq. ft.

Bedrooms: 4

Bathrooms: 3 ½

Width: 66' - 0"

Depth: 73' - 0"

Foundation: Unfinished Basement

Price Code: L1

1-800-850-1491 • EPLANS.COM

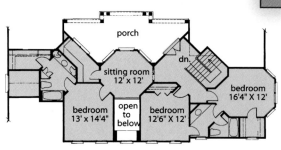

SECOND FLOOR

- porch
- sitting room 12' x 12'
- dn.
- bedroom 16'4" X 12'
- bedroom 13' x 14'4"
- open to below
- bedroom 12'6" x 12'

MONET HOUSE

3,375
square feet

DESIGNED BY BRYAN & CONTRERAS, LLC

Plan# HPK3800225

First Floor: 1,732 sq. ft.

Second Floor: 1,643 sq. ft.

Total: 3,375 sq. ft.

Bedrooms: 4

Bathrooms: 4

Width: 50' - 0"

Depth: 41' - 0"

Foundation: Slab

Price Code: C3

1-800-850-1491 • EPLANS.COM

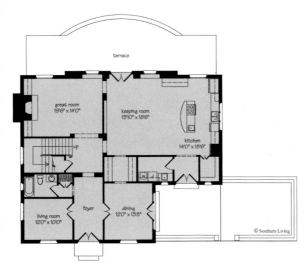

FIRST FLOOR

SECOND FLOOR

THE ASHEVILLE

3,376 square feet

DESIGNED BY STEPHEN FULLER, INC.

Plan# **HPK3800226**

First Floor: 1,707 sq. ft.

Second Floor: 1,669 sq. ft.

Total: 3,376 sq. ft.

Bedrooms: 4

Bathrooms: 4 ½

Width: 69' - 0"

Depth: 73' - 0"

Foundation: Unfinished Basement

Price Code: L1

1-800-850-1491 • EPLANS.COM

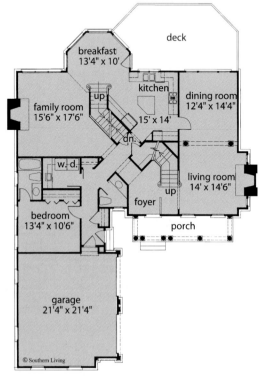

FIRST FLOOR

deck

breakfast
13'4" x 10'

kitchen
15' x 14'

dining room
12'4" x 14'4"

family room
15'6" x 17'6"

up

dn.

living room
14' x 14'6"

up

foyer

w. d.

bedroom
13'4" x 10'6"

porch

garage
21'4" x 21'4"

© Southern Living

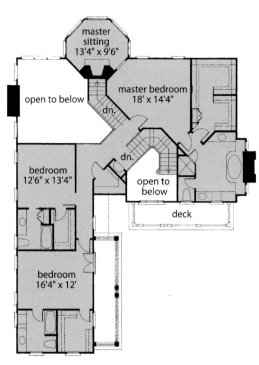

SECOND FLOOR

master sitting
13'4" x 9'6"

open to below

master bedroom
18' x 14'4"

dn.

dn.

bedroom
12'6" x 13'4"

open to below

bedroom
16'4" x 12'

deck

DENHAM SPRINGS

3,412
square feet

Plan # HPK3800227

First Floor: 2,414 sq. ft.

Second Floor: 998 sq. ft.

Total: 3,412 sq. ft.

Bonus Space: 292 sq. ft.

Bedrooms: 5

Bathrooms: 4 ½

Width: 71' - 0"

Depth: 57' - 0"

Foundation: Crawlspace

Price Code: L2

1-800-850-1491 • EPLANS.COM

DESIGNED BY JOHN TEE, ARCHITECT

FIRST FLOOR

SECOND FLOOR

MULBERRY ALTERNATE

3,899 square feet

DESIGNED BY LOONEY RICKS KISS ARCHITECTS, INC.

Plan# HPK3800228

First Floor: 2,073 sq. ft.

Second Floor: 1,826 sq. ft.

Total: 3,899 sq. ft.

Bedrooms: 4

Bathrooms: 4 full + 2 half

Width: 57' - 5"

Depth: 85' - 2"

Foundation: Slab

Price Code: L4

1-800-850-1491 • EPLANS.COM

First Floor

terrace

porch

family room 19' x 17'

master bedroom 16' x 18'1"

garden parlor 15'6" x 14'3"

breakfast 11'6" x 14'3"

kitchen 18' x 10'6"

office

porch

study/guestroom 12'1" x 14'2"

foyer

dining/library hall 22' x 14'2"

butlers pantry

porch

up

garage 21' x 21'6"

FIRST FLOOR

Second Floor

future expansion 12'6" x 14'3"

dn.

bedroom 12'4" x 13'

study 7'6" x 9'10"

bedroom 11'8" x 14'2"

dn.

optional guest suite 17'4" x 17'

SECOND FLOOR

❧ OLD FIELD HOUSE ❧

3,420 square feet

DESIGNED BY SPITZMILLER AND NORRIS, INC.

Plan# HPK3800229

First Floor: 2,329 sq. ft.

Second Floor: 1,091 sq. ft.

Total: 3,420 sq. ft.

Bedrooms: 4

Bathrooms: 3 ½

Width: 67' - 0"

Depth: 61' - 0"

Foundation: Unfinished Basement

Price Code: L1

1-800-850-1491 • EPLANS.COM

FIRST FLOOR

© Southern Living

SECOND FLOOR

~CLENNEY POINT~

3,426
square feet

ARCHITECTURAL RENDERING: MILES MELTON

DESIGNED BY MITCHELL GINN

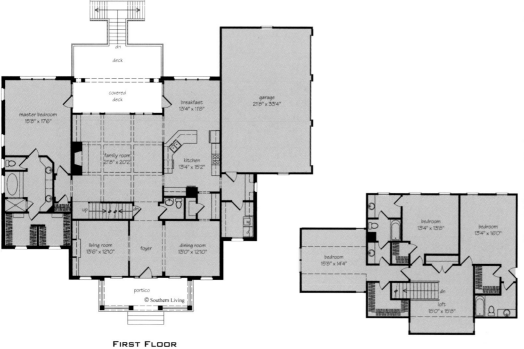

FIRST FLOOR

SECOND FLOOR

Plan# **HPK3800230**

First Floor: 2,088 sq. ft.

Second Floor: 1,338 sq. ft.

Total: 3,426 sq. ft.

Bedrooms: 4

Bathrooms: 3 ½

Width: 75' - 0"

Depth: 66' - 0"

Foundation: Unfinished Basement

Price Code: L1

1-800-850-1491 • EPLANS.COM

3,429
square feet

ARCHITECTURAL RENDERING: MILES MELTON

DESIGNED BY GARY/RAGSDALE, INC.

Plan# HPK3800231

First Floor: 2,626 sq. ft.

Second Floor: 803 sq. ft.

Total: 3,429 sq. ft.

Bedrooms: 3

Bathrooms: 3

Width: 55' - 0"

Depth: 102' - 0"

Foundation: Slab

Price Code: C3

1-800-850-1491 • EPLANS.COM

© Southern Living

FIRST FLOOR

SECOND FLOOR

MADISON PLACE

3,440
square feet

DESIGNED BY STEPHEN FULLER, INC.

Plan# HPK3800232

First Floor: 2,420 sq. ft.

Second Floor: 1,020 sq. ft.

Total: 3,440 sq. ft.

Bedrooms: 4

Bathrooms: 3 ½

Width: 84' - 0"

Depth: 73' - 0"

Foundation: Unfinished Basement

Price Code: L1

1-800-850-1491 • EPLANS.COM

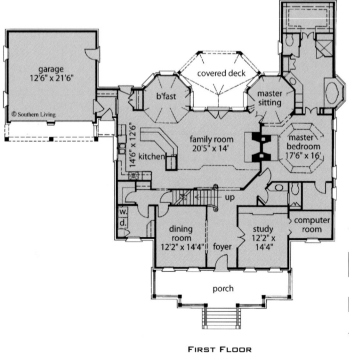

FIRST FLOOR

SECOND FLOOR

NEW HAVEN COTTAGE

3,441
square feet

DESIGNED BY SPITZMILLER AND NORRIS, INC.

Plan # HPK3800233

First Floor: 1,568 sq. ft.

Second Floor: 1,873 sq. ft.

Total: 3,441 sq. ft.

Bedrooms: 4

Bathrooms: 3 ½

Width: 45' - 0"

Depth: 58' - 10"

Foundation: Crawlspace

Price Code: L1

1-800-850-1491 • EPLANS.COM

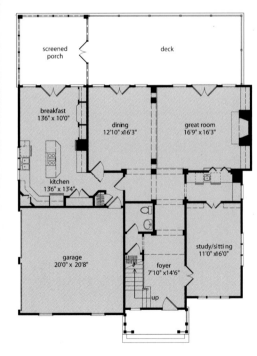

FIRST FLOOR

SECOND FLOOR

3,337
square feet

ARCHITECTURAL RENDERING: BRIAN BARKS

DESIGNED BY SOUTHERN AVENUES, INC.

Plan # HPK3800234

First Floor: 2,270 sq. ft.

Second Floor: 1,067 sq. ft.

Total: 3,337 sq. ft.

Bedrooms: 4

Bathrooms: 3 full + 1 half

Width: 63' - 0"

Depth: 61' - 0"

Foundation: Unfinished Walkout Basement

Price Code: L1

1-800-850-1491 • EPLANS.COM

FIRST FLOOR

breakfast
13'0" x 11'0"

master bedroom
15'2" x 16'2"

family room
22'0" x 16'0"

kitchen
13'0" x 16'0"

dining
13'0" x 15'0"

living
12'8" x 16'8"

foyer

garage
22'0" x 24'0"

entry

© Southern Living

SECOND FLOOR

bedroom
13'0" x 13'8"

open to below

bedroom
13'0" x 12'6"

open to below

bedroom
12'8" x 14'4"

ARCHITECTURAL RENDERING: MILES MELTON

3,452 square feet

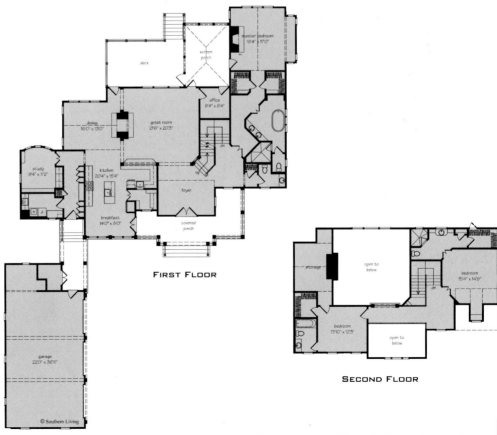

DESIGNED BY BRYAN & CONTRERAS, LLC

Plan # HPK3800235

First Floor: 2,612 sq. ft.

Second Floor: 840 sq. ft.

Total: 3,452 sq. ft.

Bedrooms: 3

Bathrooms: 3 ½

Width: 82' - 10"

Depth: 114' - 8"

Foundation: Unfinished Basement

Price Code: L1

1-800-850-1491 • EPLANS.COM

FIRST FLOOR

SECOND FLOOR

THE TWIN GABLES

3,617
square feet

DESIGNED BY STEPHEN FULLER, INC.

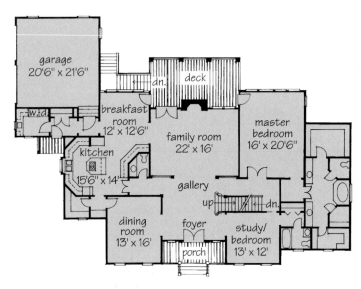

FIRST FLOOR

garage 20'6" x 21'6"

w. d.

breakfast room 12' x 12'6"

dn. deck

kitchen 15'6" x 14'

family room 22' x 16'

master bedroom 16' x 20'6"

gallery

up / dn.

dining room 13' x 16'

foyer

porch

study/ bedroom 13' x 12'

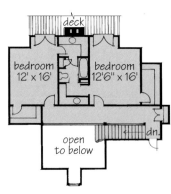

SECOND FLOOR

deck

bedroom 12' x 16'

bedroom 12'6" x 16'

open to below

dn.

Plan # HPK3800346

First Floor: 2,620 sq. ft.

Second Floor: 997 sq. ft.

Total: 3,617 sq. ft.

Bedrooms: 3

Bathrooms: 3 ½

Width: 84' - 0"

Depth: 59' - 6"

Foundation: Unfinished Basement

Price Code: L2

1-800-850-1491 • EPLANS.COM

‹·NEW LONDON·›

3,474
square feet

DESIGNED BY SPITZMILLER AND NORRIS, INC.

Plan # HPK3800237

First Floor: 2,792 sq. ft.

Second Floor: 682 sq. ft.

Total: 3,474 sq. ft.

Bedrooms: 3

Bathrooms: 3

Width: 74' - 0"

Depth: 69' - 0"

Foundation: Unfinished
Basement

Price Code: L1

1-800-850-1491 • EPLANS.COM

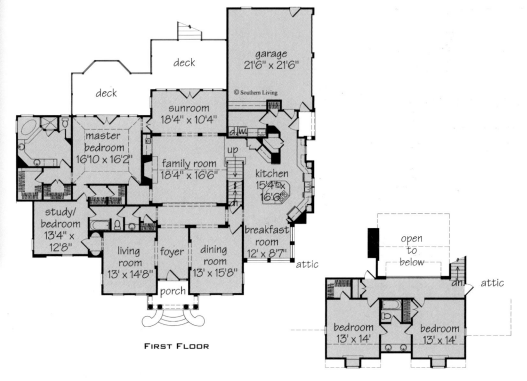

FIRST FLOOR

SECOND FLOOR

OAK HILL LANE

3,487
square feet

ARCHITECTURAL RENDERING: MILES MELTON

DESIGNED BY SPITZMILLER AND NORRIS, INC.

Plan# HPK3800238

Square Footage: 3,487

Bonus Space: 1,428 sq. ft.

Bedrooms: 3

Bathrooms: 2 full + 2 half

Width: 82' - 8"

Depth: 78' - 4"

Foundation: Unfinished Basement

Price Code: L2

1-800-850-1491 • EPLANS.COM

3,491 square feet

ARCHITECTURAL RENDERING: SPITZMILLER AND NORRIS, INC.

DESIGNED BY SPITZMILLER AND NORRIS, INC.

Plan # HPK3800240

First Floor: 2,292 sq. ft.

Second Floor: 1,199 sq. ft.

Total: 3,491 sq. ft.

Bedrooms: 4

Bathrooms: 3 full + 2 half

Width: 97' - 8"

Depth: 48' - 0"

Foundation: Unfinished Basement

Price Code: L1

1-800-850-1491 • EPLANS.COM

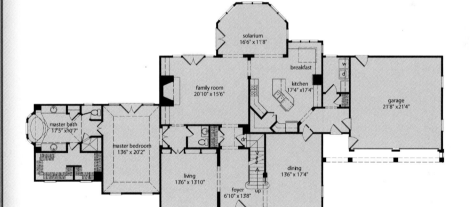

FIRST FLOOR

SECOND FLOOR

3,497
square feet

ARCHITECTURAL RENDERING: MILES MELTON

DESIGNED BY CALDWELL-CLINE ARCHITECTS AND DESIGNERS

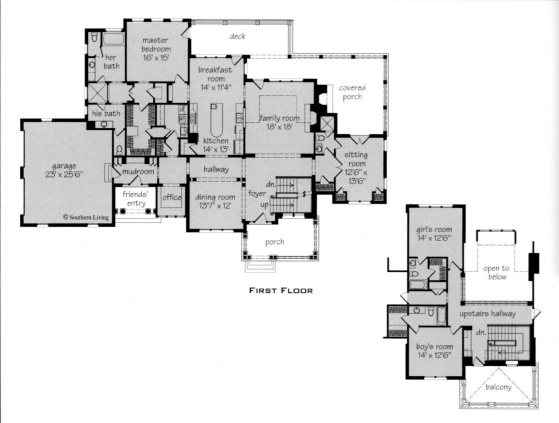

FIRST FLOOR

SECOND FLOOR

Plan# HPK3800241

First Floor: 2,645 sq. ft.

Second Floor: 852 sq. ft.

Total: 3,497 sq. ft.

Bedrooms: 4

Bathrooms: 4

Width: 94' - 0"

Depth: 60' - 0"

Foundation: Crawlspace,
Unfinished Basement, Slab

Price Code: L4

1-800-850-1491 • EPLANS.COM

SOUTHRIDGE

3,014
square feet

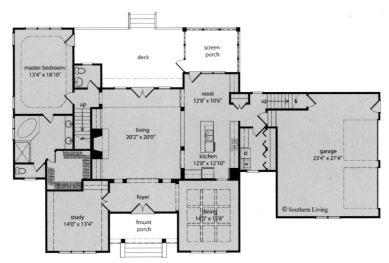

Plan# HPK3800242

First Floor: 2,092 sq. ft.

Second Floor: 922 sq. ft.

Total: 3,014 sq. ft.

Bonus Space: 490 sq. ft.

Bedrooms: 4

Bathrooms: 3 ½

Width: 85' - 0"

Depth: 50' - 0"

Foundation: Crawlspace

Price Code: C3

1-800-850-1491 • EPLANS.COM

DESIGNED BY SULLIVAN DESIGN COMPANY

FIRST FLOOR

master bedroom
13'4" x 18'10"

deck

screen porch

nook
12'8" x 10'6"

living
20'2" x 20'0"

kitchen
12'8" x 12'10"

garage
23'4" x 27'4"

© Southern Living

study
14'0" x 13'4"

foyer

dining
14'0" x 15'8"

frount porch

SECOND FLOOR

bedroom
13'4" x 13'0"

bedroom
15'6" x 11'4"

bedroom
12'0" x 15'0"

bonus room
16'0" x 27'4"

3,510
square feet

DESIGNED BY MOUZON DESIGN FOR BILTMORE ESTATE

shop or storage 5'11" x 20'8"

garage 24'3" x 22'5"

© Southern Living

grilling porch

breakfast/ sunroom 11'8" x 11'8"

kitchen 18'0" x 11'10"

dining 14'8" x 12'3"

back porch

entry hall 19'8" x 7'8"

great room 18'0" x 21'0"

living/ guest 14'8" x 12'3"

master bath 8'6" x 15'9"

master bedroom 15'9" x 15'9"

nursery/ master study 18'3" x 9'6"

FIRST FLOOR

Plan# HPK3800243

First Floor: 2,410 sq. ft.

Second Floor: 1,100 sq. ft.

Total: 3,510 sq. ft.

Bedrooms: 4

Bathrooms: 4

Width: 71' - 0"

Depth: 79' - 0"

Foundation: Crawlspace

Price Code: L4

1-800-850-1491 • EPLANS.COM

bedroom 12'7" x 12'3"

bedroom 14'0" x 12'3"

loft 16'6 x 7'4

down

open to great room below

bedroom 14'2" x 12'3"

SECOND FLOOR

BILTMORE™
For Your Home

KINSLEY PLACE

3,575 square feet

DESIGNED BY LOONEY RICKS KISS ARCHITECTS, INC., FOR ST. JOE LAND COMPANY

Plan # HPK3800244

First Floor: 2,757 sq. ft.

Second Floor: 818 sq. ft.

Total: 3,575 sq. ft.

Bonus Space: 206 sq. ft.

Bedrooms: 4

Bathrooms: 5 ½

Width: 64' - 0"

Depth: 122' - 0"

Foundation: Slab

Price Code: SQ3

1-800-850-1491 • EPLANS.COM

FIRST FLOOR

SECOND FLOOR

·DANBURY OAKS·

3,538 square feet

DESIGNED BY GARY/RAGSDALE, INC.

FIRST FLOOR

Plan# HPK3800246

First Floor: 2,712 sq. ft.

Second Floor: 826 sq. ft.

Total: 3,538 sq. ft.

Bedrooms: 3

Bathrooms: 3 ½

Width: 54' - 0"

Depth: 101' - 0"

Foundation: Slab

Price Code: L1

1-800-850-1491 • EPLANS.COM

SECOND FLOOR

ARCHITECTURAL RENDERING: MILES MELTON

3,584 square feet

DESIGNED BY GARY/RAGSDALE, INC.

Plan # HPK3800247

First Floor: 2,053 sq. ft.

Second Floor: 1,531 sq. ft.

Total: 3,584 sq. ft.

Bedrooms: 5

Bathrooms: 4 ½

Width: 69' - 0"

Depth: 54' - 0"

Foundation: Slab, Basement, Crawlspace

Price Code: L1

1-800-850-1491 • EPLANS.COM

FIRST FLOOR

SECOND FLOOR

Luxury Homes

SEE PAGE 298 TO
VIEW THIS PLAN.

The epitome of elegance, these plans capture all that is refined and graceful in Southern home design. All more than 3,600 square feet, these designs have far more to offer than generous dimensions: they are also packed with luxury amenities and details.

The Arborview Alternate on page 274 features a family room warmed by a massive hearth, an extended media room upstairs, and a floor plan that allows for options that you won't find in smaller house plans.

Whatever your preferences, on each page you will find luxury and comfort.

SEE PAGE 316 TO VIEW THIS PLAN.

© SOUTHERN LIVING.

SEE PAGE 298 TO VIEW THIS PLAN.

© SOUTHERN LIVING.

3,624
square feet

DESIGNED BY LOONEY RICKS KISS ARCHITECTS, INC.

Plan # HPK3800245

First Floor: 2,351 sq. ft.

Second Floor: 1,273 sq. ft.

Total: 3,624 sq. ft.

Bedrooms: 4

Bathrooms: 3 ½

Width: 83' - 0"

Depth: 54' - 0"

Foundation: Crawlspace,
Pier (same as Piling)

Price Code: L1

1-800-850-1491 • EPLANS.COM

FIRST FLOOR

SECOND FLOOR

ROCKWELL HOUSE

3,783
square feet

DESIGNED BY MITCHELL GINN

Plan# HPK3800275

First Floor: 2,347 sq. ft.

Second Floor: 1,436 sq. ft.

Total: 3,783 sq. ft.

Bedrooms: 4

Bathrooms: 3 ½

Width: 72' - 0"

Depth: 82' - 0"

Foundation: Unfinished Basement

Price Code: L1

1-800-850-1491 • EPLANS.COM

FIRST FLOOR

SECOND FLOOR

❧ NEWBERRY PARK ❧

3,625
square feet

DESIGNED BY ALLISON-RAMSEY ARCHITECTS, INC.

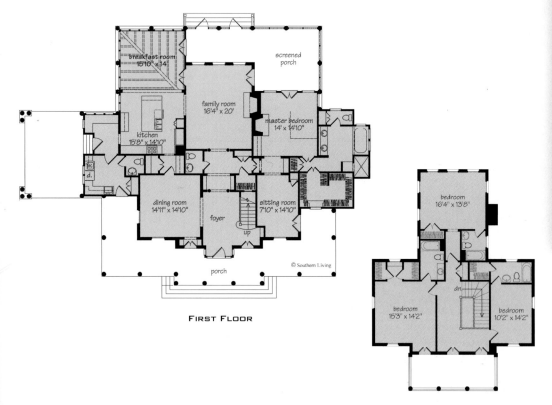

First Floor

breakfast room
15'10" x 14'

screened
porch

family room
16'4" x 20'

kitchen
15'8" x 14'10"

master bedroom
14' x 14'10"

dining room
14'11" x 14'10"

foyer

sitting room
7'10" x 14'10"

up

porch

© Southern Living

Second Floor

bedroom
16'4" x 13'8"

bedroom
15'3" x 14'2"

dn

bedroom
10'2" x 14'2"

Plan# HPK3800248

First Floor: 2,490 sq. ft.

Second Floor: 1,135 sq. ft.

Total: 3,625 sq. ft.

Bedrooms: 4

Bathrooms: 4 full + 2 half

Width: 87' - 0"

Depth: 62' - 0"

Foundation: Crawlspace

Price Code: L4

1-800-850-1491 • EPLANS.COM

⚬ AVINGTON PLACE ⚬

3,629
square feet

MILES MELTON

DESIGNED BY JOHN TEE, ARCHITECT

Plan # HPK3800249

First Floor: 2,516 sq. ft.

Second Floor: 1,113 sq. ft.

Total: 3,629 sq. ft.

Bonus Space: 247 sq. ft.

Bedrooms: 4

Bathrooms: 3 full + 2 half

Width: 80' - 0"

Depth: 59' - 0"

Foundation: Crawlspace

Price Code: L1

1-800-850-1491 • EPLANS.COM

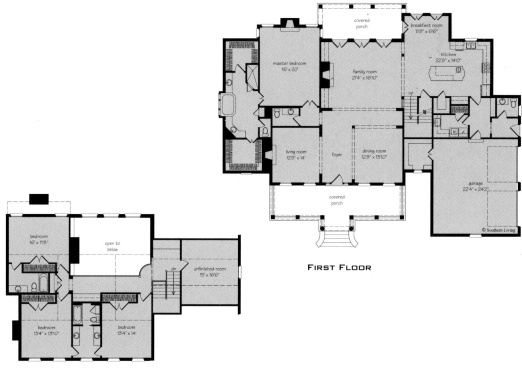

FIRST FLOOR

SECOND FLOOR

ARBORVIEW ALTERNATE

3,633 square feet

DESIGNED BY GARY/RAGSDALE, INC.

FIRST FLOOR

- master bedroom 18'0" x 15'0"
- garage 26'0" x 20'4"
- kitchen 13'10" x 17'4"
- dining 11'0" x 16'0"
- family room 23'6" x 18'4"
- © Southern Living
- porch
- breakfast 10'2" x 15'10"
- study 11'4" x 11'0"
- up   foyer   porch

SECOND FLOOR

- bedroom 17'2" x 11'2"
- media room 24'4" x 12'8"
- bedroom 11'0" x 13'6"
- bedroom 13'6 1/2" x 12'9 1/2"
- open to below
- dn   up

Plan # HPK3800250

First Floor: 2,260 sq. ft.

Second Floor: 1,373 sq. ft.

Total: 3,633 sq. ft.

Bedrooms: 4

Bathrooms: 3 ½

Width: 51' - 0"

Depth: 82' - 0"

Foundation: Slab

Price Code: L2

1-800-850-1491 • EPLANS.COM

CUMBERLAND RIVER COTTAGE

ARCHITECTURAL RENDERING: DON RANKIN

3,640 square feet

DESIGNED BY STEPHEN FULLER, INC.

Plan # HPK3800251

First Floor: 2,565 sq. ft.

Second Floor: 1,075 sq. ft.

Total: 3,640 sq. ft.

Bedrooms: 3

Bathrooms: 3 ½

Width: 81' - 0"

Depth: 85' - 0"

Foundation: Unfinished Basement

Price Code: L4

1-800-850-1491 • EPLANS.COM

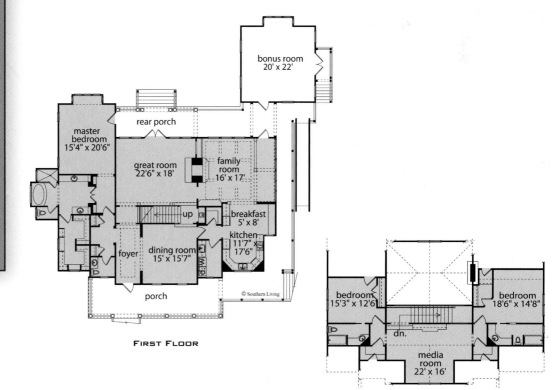

FIRST FLOOR

bonus room 20' x 22'

rear porch

master bedroom 15'4" x 20'6"

great room 22'6" x 18'

family room 16' x 17'

up

breakfast 5' x 8'

kitchen 11'7" x 17'6"

foyer

dining room 15' x 15'7"

porch

© Southern Living

SECOND FLOOR

bedroom 15'3" x 12'6"

dn.

bedroom 18'6" x 14'8"

media room 22' x 16'

❧CYPRESS GARDEN❧

3,641 square feet

ARCHITECTURAL RENDERING: BRIAN BARKS

DESIGNED BY LOONEY RICKS KISS ARCHITECTS, INC.

Plan # **HPK3800252**

First Floor: 2,507 sq. ft.

Second Floor: 1,134 sq. ft.

Total: 3,641 sq. ft.

Bonus Space: 496 sq. ft.

Bedrooms: 4

Bathrooms: 4 ½

Width: 70' - 0"

Depth: 55' - 0"

Foundation: Crawlspace

Price Code: L1

1-800-850-1491 • EPLANS.COM

garage
24' x 24'2"

© Southern Living

FIRST FLOOR

office

breakfast/
kitchen
15' x 20'8"

covered porch

family room
19' x 16'

master
bedroom
15'4" x 17'

covered
walk to
garage

gallery

dining room
13' x 15'4"

living room
13' x 15'4"

foyer

up

covered porch

bonus
room

dn.

SECOND FLOOR

storage

bedroom
13'4" x 17'8"

storage

bedroom
13'8" x 15'4"

dn.

open to
below

bedroom
13'8" x 15'4"

3,651 square feet

DESIGNED BY MITCHELL GINN

Plan # HPK3800253

First Floor: 2,113 sq. ft.

Second Floor: 1,538 sq. ft.

Total: 3,651 sq. ft.

Bedrooms: 4

Bathrooms: 3 ½

Width: 54' - 0"

Depth: 62' - 0"

Foundation: Unfinished Basement

Price Code: L1

1-800-850-1491 • EPLANS.COM

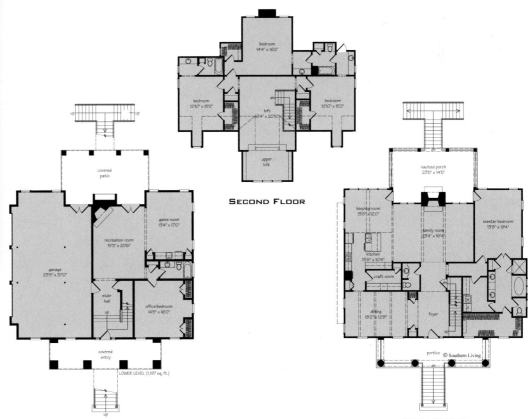

SECOND FLOOR

FIRST FLOOR

SMYTHE PARK HOUSE

3,655 square feet

DESIGNED BY MITCHELL GINN

Plan # HPK3800254

First Floor: 1,884 sq. ft.

Second Floor: 1,627 sq. ft.

Third Floor: 144 sq. ft.

Total: 3,655 sq. ft.

Bonus Space: 763 sq. ft.

Bedrooms: 4

Bathrooms: 4 ½

Width: 60' - 0"

Depth: 105' - 0"

Foundation: Crawlspace

Price Code: L4

1-800-850-1491 • EPLANS.COM

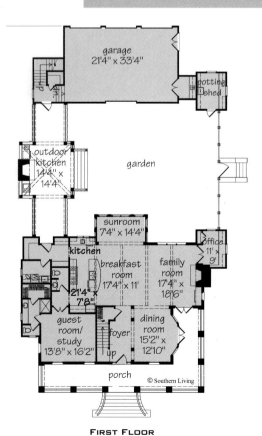

garage
21'4" x 33'4"

potting shed

outdoor kitchen
14'4" x 14'4"

garden

sunroom
7'4" x 14'4"

office
11' x 9'

kitchen

breakfast room
17'4" x 11'

family room
17'4" x 18'6"

21'4" x 7'8"

guest room/study
13'8" x 16'2"

foyer

up

dining room
15'2" x 12'10"

porch

© Southern Living

FIRST FLOOR

bonus room
21'4" x 23'2"

dn.

girl's room
14'8" x 12'4"

master bedroom
17'4" x 19'10"

up

boy's room
12'4" x 16'4"

open to below

dn.

study
15'8" x 10'8"

porch

SECOND FLOOR

dn.
observation tower
11'4" x 11'4"

THIRD FLOOR

~AMELIA PLACE~

3,659 square feet

ARCHITECTURAL RENDERING: MILES MELTON

DESIGNED BY JOHN TEE, ARCHITECT

Plan # HPK3800255

First Floor: 2,617 sq. ft.

Second Floor: 1,042 sq. ft.

Total: 3,659 sq. ft.

Bonus Space: 896 sq. ft.

Bedrooms: 5

Bathrooms: 4

Width: 79' - 0"

Depth: 66' - 0"

Foundation: Crawlspace

Price Code: L4

1-800-850-1491 • EPLANS.COM

FIRST FLOOR

SECOND FLOOR

~BELFIELD BEND~

3,660 square feet

DESIGNED BY JOHN TEE, ARCHITECT

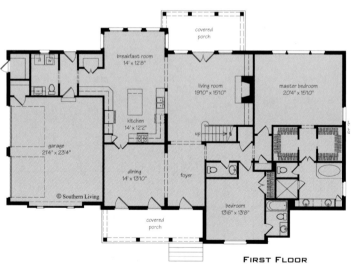

FIRST FLOOR

SECOND FLOOR

Plan # HPK3800256

First Floor: 2,321 sq. ft.

Second Floor: 1,339 sq. ft.

Total: 3,660 sq. ft.

Bonus Space: 334 sq. ft.

Bedrooms: 5

Bathrooms: 5 full + 2 half

Width: 78' - 0"

Depth: 52' - 0"

Foundation: Crawlspace

Price Code: L2

1-800-850-1491 • EPLANS.COM

~Chatham Hall~

3,666 square feet

Plan# HPK3800257

First Floor: 2,669 sq. ft.

Second Floor: 997 sq. ft.

Total: 3,666 sq. ft.

Bedrooms: 4

Bathrooms: 3 full + 2 half

Width: 105' - 0"

Depth: 51' - 0"

Foundation: Unfinished Basement

Price Code: L2

1-800-850-1491 • EPLANS.COM

DESIGNED BY BRYAN & CONTRERAS, LLC

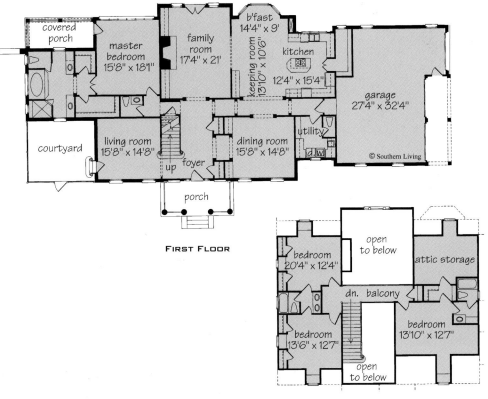

FIRST FLOOR

SECOND FLOOR

·BRENTHAVEN·

3,674
square feet

ARCHITECTURAL RENDERING: RICK HERR

DESIGNED BY LOONEY RICKS KISS ARCHITECTS, INC.

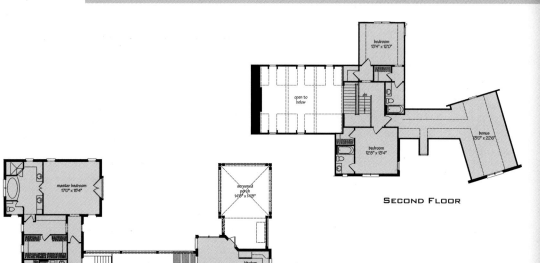

SECOND FLOOR

FIRST FLOOR

Plan# HPK3800258

First Floor: 3,011 sq. ft.

Second Floor: 663 sq. ft.

Total: 3,674 sq. ft.

Bonus Space: 292.5 sq. ft.

Bedrooms: 4

Bathrooms: 4 ½

Width: 111' - 0"

Depth: 83' - 0"

Foundation: Slab, Unfinished Basement

Price Code: L4

1-800-850-1491 • EPLANS.COM

·Belvedere·

3,687 square feet

Plan # HPK3800259

First Floor: 2,285 sq. ft.

Second Floor: 1,402 sq. ft.

Total: 3,687 sq. ft.

Bonus Space: 250 sq. ft.

Bedrooms: 4

Bathrooms: 4

Width: 56' - 0"

Depth: 85' - 0"

Foundation: Slab

Price Code: L1

1-800-850-1491 • EPLANS.COM

DESIGNED BY LOONEY RICKS KISS ARCHITECTS, INC.

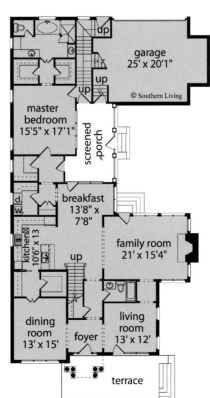

garage 25' x 20'1"

© Southern Living

master bedroom 15'5" x 17'1"

screened porch

breakfast 13'8" x 7'8"

kitchen 10'6" x 13

family room 21' x 15'4"

dining room 13' x 15'

foyer

living room 13' x 12'

terrace

FIRST FLOOR

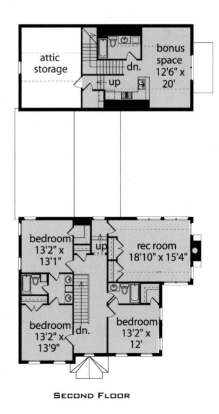

attic storage

bonus space 12'6" x 20'

dn.

up

bedroom 13'2" x 13'1"

rec room 18'10" x 15'4"

bedroom 13'2" x 13'9"

dn.

bedroom 13'2" x 12'

SECOND FLOOR

❧ CENTENNIAL HOUSE ALTERNATE ❧

3,687
square feet

ARCHITECTURAL RENDERING: BRIAN BARKS

DESIGNED BY SPITZMILLER AND NORRIS, INC.

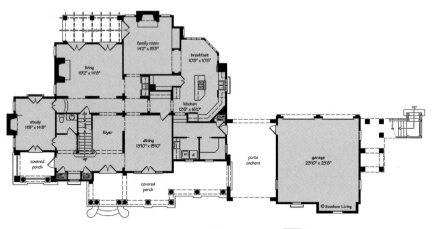

FIRST FLOOR

SECOND FLOOR

Plan # **HPK3800260**

First Floor: 2,102 sq. ft.

Second Floor: 1,585 sq. ft.

Total: 3,687 sq. ft.

Studio: 366 sq. ft.

Bedrooms: 4

Bathrooms: 4 ½

Width: 104' - 0"

Depth: 57' - 0"

Foundation: Daylight Basement

Price Code: L4

1-800-850-1491 • EPLANS.COM

~ANSLEY PARK~

3,689
square feet

Plan # HPK3800261

First Floor: 2,602 sq. ft.

Second Floor: 1,087 sq. ft.

Total: 3,689 sq. ft.

Bonus Space: 413 sq. ft.

Bedrooms: 4

Bathrooms: 3 ½

Width: 97' - 0"

Depth: 64' - 0"

Foundation: Unfinished Basement

Price Code: L1

1-800-850-1491 • EPLANS.COM

DESIGNED BY BRYAN & CONTRERAS, LLC

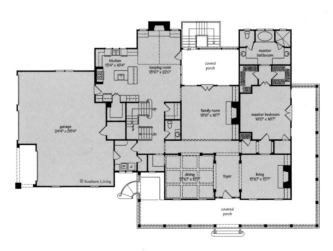

FIRST FLOOR

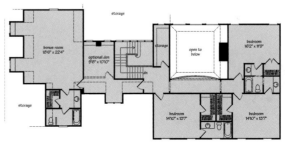

SECOND FLOOR

3,690
square feet

ARCHITECTURAL RENDERING: MILES MELTON

DESIGNED BY MOUZON DESIGN

Plan # HPK3800262

First Floor: 2,746 sq. ft.

Second Floor: 944 sq. ft.

Total: 3,690 sq. ft.

Bedrooms: 3

Bathrooms: 3 ½

Width: 71' - 0"

Depth: 100' - 0"

Foundation: Crawlspace

Price Code: L2

1-800-850-1491 • EPLANS.COM

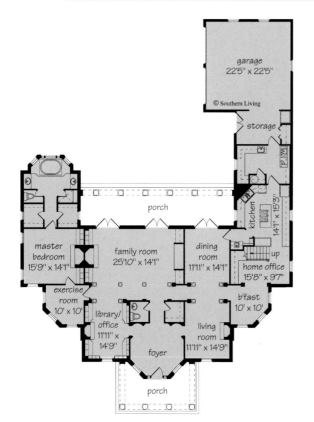

garage
22'5" x 22'5"

© Southern Living

storage

porch

kitchen
14'1" x 15'3"

master
bedroom
15'9" x 14'1"

family room
25'10" x 14'1"

dining
room
11'11" x 14'1"

home office
15'8" x 9'7"

up

exercise
room
10' x 10'

library/
office
11'11" x
14'9"

b'fast
10' x 10'

living
room
11'11" x 14'9"

foyer

porch

FIRST FLOOR

bedroom
16'2" x 14'11"

bedroom
12'8" x 11'5"

playroom
16'2" x
9'2"
dn.

SECOND FLOOR

~HABERSHAM~

3,696 square feet

ARCHITECTURAL RENDERING: DON RANKIN

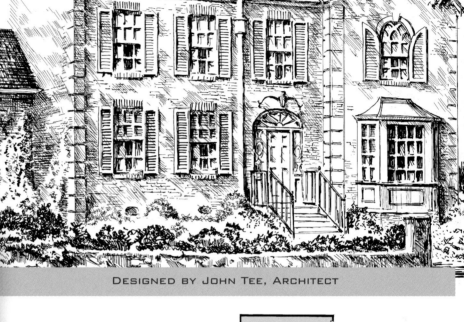

DESIGNED BY JOHN TEE, ARCHITECT

Plan # HPK3800263

First Floor: 2,241 sq. ft.

Second Floor: 1,455 sq. ft.

Total: 3,696 sq. ft.

Bonus Space: 266 sq. ft.

Bedrooms: 3

Bathrooms: 3 ½

Width: 81' - 0"

Depth: 66' - 0"

Foundation: Crawlspace

Price Code: C3

1-800-850-1491 • EPLANS.COM

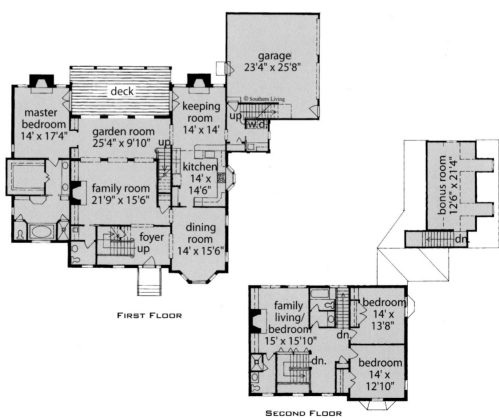

FIRST FLOOR

SECOND FLOOR

❧SWANNANOA RIVER HOUSE❧

3,703 square feet

ARCHITECTURAL RENDERING: MILES MELTON

DESIGNED BY MOUZON DESIGN FOR BILTMORE ESTATE

Plan# **HPK3800264**

First Floor: 2,376 sq. ft.

Second Floor: 1,327 sq. ft.

Total: 3,703 sq. ft.

Bedrooms: 4

Bathrooms: 3 ½

Width: 98' - 0"

Depth: 63' - 0"

Foundation: Crawlspace

Price Code: L4

1-800-850-1491 • EPLANS.COM

master bedroom 15'1" x 15'1"

office/nursery 8'4" x 10'8"

porch

porch

garage 22'5" x 22'5"

family room 15' x 23'2"

kitchen 16'1" x 12'6"

w. d.

© Southern Living

living room 15' x 15'

up

dining room 12' x 22'8"

foyer

porch

library 12' x 12'

FIRST FLOOR

media room 18'3" x 10'2"

bedroom 10'6" x 13'9"

dn.

bedroom 10'6" x 14'2"

bedroom 18'3" x 14'10"

SECOND FLOOR

BILTMORE™
For Your Home

❧ WESTON HOUSE ❧

3,706
square feet

Plan# HPK3800265

First Floor: 2,629 sq. ft.

Second Floor: 1,077 sq. ft.

Total: 3,706 sq. ft.

Bedrooms: 4

Bathrooms: 4

Width: 65' - 0"

Depth: 91' - 0"

Foundation: Crawlspace

Price Code: L4

1-800-850-1491 • EPLANS.COM

DESIGNED BY MOUZON DESIGN FOR BILTMORE ESTATE

FIRST FLOOR

SECOND FLOOR

BILTMORE™
For Your Home

SURREY CREST

3,730 square feet

DESIGNED BY STEPHEN FULLER, INC.

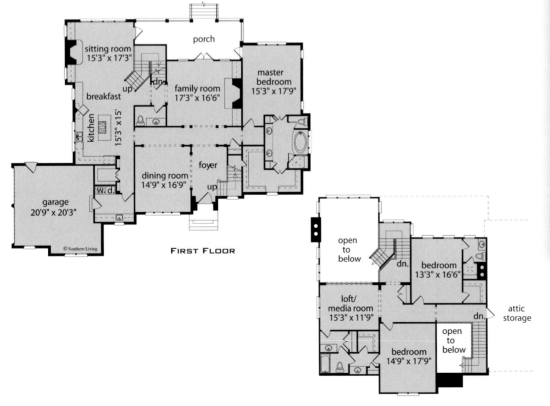

FIRST FLOOR

- sitting room 15'3" x 17'3"
- porch
- breakfast
- up dn.
- family room 17'3" x 16'6"
- master bedroom 15'3" x 17'9"
- kitchen 15'3" x 15'
- dining room 14'9" x 16'9"
- foyer
- up
- garage 20'9" x 20'3"
- w. d.
- © Southern Living

SECOND FLOOR

- open to below
- dn.
- bedroom 13'3" x 16'6"
- loft/ media room 15'3" x 11'9"
- attic storage
- dn.
- bedroom 14'9" x 17'9"
- open to below

Plan # HPK3800266

First Floor: 2,502 sq. ft.

Second Floor: 1,228 sq. ft.

Total: 3,730 sq. ft.

Bedrooms: 3

Bathrooms: 3 ½

Width: 78' - 0"

Depth: 60' - 0"

Foundation: Unfinished Basement

Price Code: L1

1-800-850-1491 • EPLANS.COM

3,747 square feet

Plan# HPK3800267

First Floor: 2,511 sq. ft.

Second Floor: 1,236 sq. ft.

Total: 3,747 sq. ft.

Bedrooms: 4

Bathrooms: 3 ½

Width: 72' - 0"

Depth: 76' - 0"

Foundation: Unfinished Basement

Price Code: C3

1-800-850-1491 • EPLANS.COM

DESIGNED BY SPITZMILLER AND NORRIS, INC.

FIRST FLOOR

solarium 14'5" x 16'2"

great room 20'0" x 15'8"

master bedroom 17'2" x 15'2"

breakfast 13'4" x 10'4"

kitchen 15'5" x 14'2"

dining 13'6" x 16'0"

porch

study 11'10" x 13'4"

foyer

covered porch

garage 21'2" x 23'2"

© Southern Living

SECOND FLOOR

storage

open to below

attic storage

bedroom 13'11" x 13'9"

open to below

bedroom 12'0" x 12'7"

bedroom 15'8" x 13'8"

CRABAPPLE COTTAGE

3,757 square feet

DESIGNED BY JOHN TEE, ARCHITECT

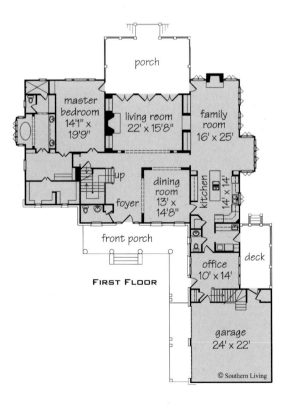

porch

master bedroom 14'1" x 19'9"

living room 22' x 15'8"

family room 16' x 25'

up

dining room 13' x 14'8"

kitchen 14' x 14'

foyer

front porch

office 10' x 14'

deck

garage 24' x 22'

© Southern Living

FIRST FLOOR

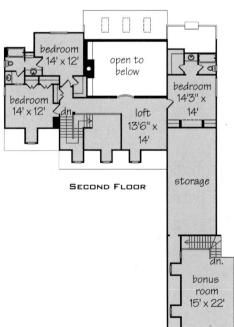

bedroom 14' x 12'

open to below

bedroom 14' x 12'

dn

loft 13'6" x 14'

bedroom 14'3" x 14'

storage

dn.

bonus room 15' x 22'

SECOND FLOOR

Plan# HPK3800268

First Floor: 2,674 sq. ft.

Second Floor: 1,083 sq. ft.

Total: 3,757 sq. ft.

Bonus Space: 330 sq. ft.

Bedrooms: 4

Bathrooms: 3 full + 2 half

Width: 76' - 0"

Depth: 90' - 0"

Foundation: Unfinished Basement

Price Code: L4

1-800-850-1491 • EPLANS.COM

STERETT SPRINGS

3,758
square feet

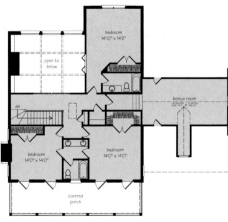

DESIGNED BY JOHN TEE, ARCHITECT

Plan # HPK3800269

First Floor: 2,674 sq. ft.

Second Floor: 1,084 sq. ft.

Total: 3,758 sq. ft.

Bonus Space: 274 sq. ft.

Bedrooms: 5

Bathrooms: 4 ½

Width: 77' - 0"

Depth: 73' - 0"

Foundation: Crawlspace

Price Code: L1

1-800-850-1491 • EPLANS.COM

FIRST FLOOR

SECOND FLOOR

~CHICKERING COUNTRY HOUSE~

3,761
square feet

ARCHITECTURAL RENDERING: ROD DENT

DESIGNED BY STEPHEN FULLER, INC.

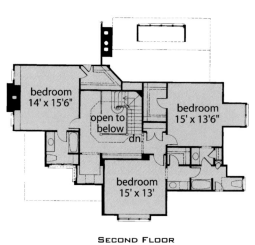

FIRST FLOOR

- master bedroom 15' x 18'6"
- dn. porch
- b'fast area
- family room 15'6" x 26'
- office
- study 15'6" x 13'6"
- up
- kitchen 12' x 16'6"
- w.d.
- foyer
- dn.
- porch
- dining room 13'6" x 15'3"
- garage 22'6" x 21'6"
- up

© Southern Living

SECOND FLOOR

- bedroom 14' x 15'6"
- open to below
- bedroom 15' x 13'6"
- dn
- bedroom 15' x 13'

Plan# HPK3800270

First Floor: 2,452 sq. ft.

Second Floor: 1,309 sq. ft.

Total: 3,761 sq. ft.

Bedrooms: 4

Bathrooms: 3 ½

Width: 61' - 0"

Depth: 82' - 0"

Foundation: Unfinished Basement

Price Code: SQ3

1-800-850-1491 • EPLANS.COM

BRITTINGHAM

3,770
square feet

DESIGNED BY MITCHELL GINN

Plan# HPK3800271

First Floor: 2,462 sq. ft.

Second Floor: 1,308 sq. ft.

Total: 3,770 sq. ft.

Bedrooms: 5

Bathrooms: 4

Width: 68' - 0"

Depth: 57' - 0"

Foundation: Unfinished Basement

Price Code: L1

1-800-850-1491 • EPLANS.COM

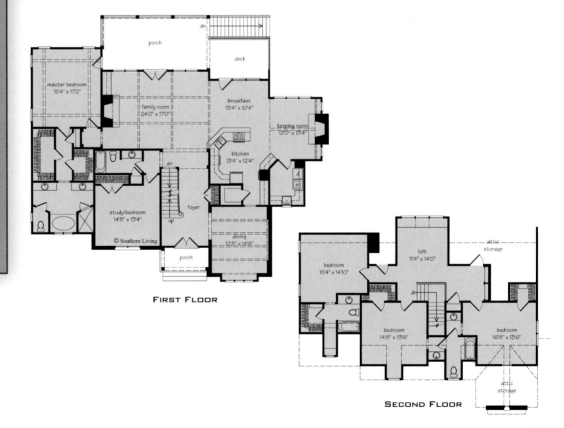

FIRST FLOOR

SECOND FLOOR

3,775
square feet

ARCHITECTURAL RENDERING: ROD DENT

DESIGNED BY STEPHEN FULLER, INC.

Plan# HPK3800272

First Floor: 2,000 sq. ft.

Second Floor: 1,775 sq. ft.

Total: 3,775 sq. ft.

Bonus Space: 210 sq. ft.

Bedrooms: 4

Bathrooms: 3 ½

Width: 69' - 0"

Depth: 67' - 0"

Foundation: Crawlspace

Price Code: L1

1-800-850-1491 • EPLANS.COM

First Floor

- deck
- garage 21'6" x 21'6"
- kitchen 15' x 16'6"
- breakfast/den 15' x 15'6"
- porch
- w.d.
- dining room 18'6" x 13'
- living room 16'8" x 15'4"
- foyer
- family room 18' x 15'4"
- © Southern Living
- porch
- entry

Second Floor

- bonus space 10'6" x 20'
- master bedroom 18'6" x 15'6"
- bedroom 13'6" x 13'6"
- bedroom 12' x 12'
- bedroom 13' x 14'
- roof
- roof

3,776 square feet

ARCHITECTURAL RENDERING: SPITZMILLER AND NORRIS, INC.

DESIGNED BY SPITZMILLER AND NORRIS, INC.

Plan # HPK3800273

First Floor: 1,961 sq. ft.

Second Floor: 1,815 sq. ft.

Total: 3,776 sq. ft.

Bedrooms: 4

Bathrooms: 3 ½

Width: 107' - 0"

Depth: 34' - 0"

Foundation: Unfinished Basement

Price Code: L1

1-800-850-1491 • EPLANS.COM

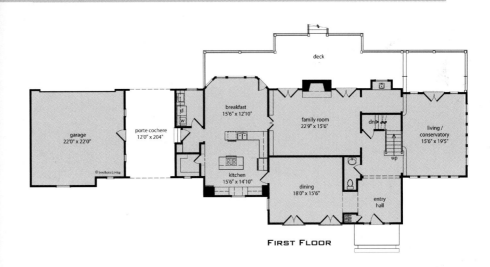

FIRST FLOOR

SECOND FLOOR

GREYWELL COTTAGE

3,781
square feet

DESIGNED BY FRUSTERIO AND ASSOCIATES

terrace

master bedroom
13'10" x 22'

covered deck

© Southern Living

deck

dn.

breakfast room
10'6" x 16'2"

kitchen
14'6" x 14'4"

up

dn.

study
9'10" x 14'2"

living room
24'8" x 15'4"

w. d.

dining room
13'4" x 15'4"

foyer

FIRST FLOOR

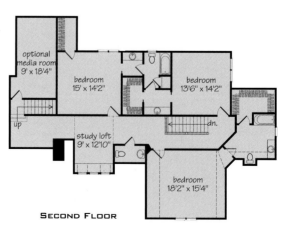

optional media room
9' x 18'4"

bedroom
15' x 14'2"

bedroom
13'6" x 14'2"

up

dn.

study loft
9' x 12'10"

bedroom
18'2" x 15'4"

SECOND FLOOR

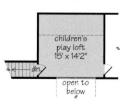

children's play loft
15' x 14'2"

dn.

open to below

THIRD FLOOR

THIS ELEGANT HOME offers a European-inspired exterior.

Inside, a large living room serves as the hub of the home. On one side of the living room, the formal dining room has a pretty bay window and offers easy passage to the large kitchen. A breakfast area with space for a large table creates a more casual dining space for the family. On the opposite side of the living room, arches frame the fireplace and the entrance to a study, which in turn leads to a master suite with a private terrace for views of the backyard. A luxurious master bath offers dual vanities and direct access to a walk-in closet.

REAR EXTERIOR

© SOUTHERN LIVING

Plan# HPK3800274

First Floor: 2,051 sq. ft.

Second Floor: 1,517 sq. ft.

Third Floor: 213 sq. ft.

Total: 3,781 sq. ft.

Bedrooms: 4

Bathrooms: 3 full + 2 half

Width: 66' - 0"

Depth: 48' - 0"

Foundation: Unfinished Basement

Price Code: L4

1-800-850-1491 • EPLANS.COM

© SOUTHERN LIVING.

On the upper floor, the bedroom at the front of the home boasts a large private bath and a walk-in closet. The other two bedrooms share a split bath.

A study loft and a media room complete the grand upper floor. An optional third-floor children's play loft is the perfect hideaway for youngsters.

WENTWORTH HEIGHTS

3,792 square feet

ARCHITECTURAL RENDERING: MILES MELTON

DESIGNED BY GARY/RAGSDALE, INC.

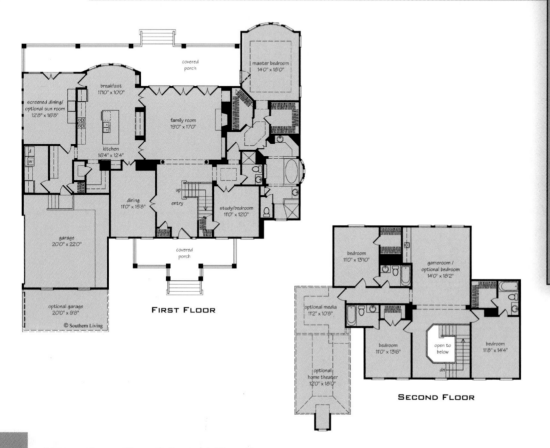

FIRST FLOOR

- screened dining/ optional sun room 12'8" x 16'8"
- breakfast 11'10" x 10'0"
- kitchen 16'4" x 12'4"
- covered porch
- master bedroom 14'0" x 18'0"
- family room 19'0" x 17'0"
- dining 11'0" x 15'8"
- entry
- up
- study/bedroom 11'0" x 12'0"
- garage 20'0" x 22'0"
- optional garage 20'0" x 9'8"
- covered porch

© Southern Living

SECOND FLOOR

- bedroom 11'0" x 13'10"
- gameroom / optional bedroom 14'0" x 18'2"
- optional media 11'2" x 10'8"
- bedroom 11'0" x 13'6"
- open to below
- bedroom 11'8" x 14'4"
- dn
- optional home theater 12'0" x 18'0"

Plan # HPK3800276

First Floor: 2,513 sq. ft.

Second Floor: 1,279 sq. ft.

Total: 3,792 sq. ft.

Bonus Space: 411 sq. ft.

Bedrooms: 5

Bathrooms: 5

Width: 68' - 0"

Depth: 73' - 0"

Foundation: Crawlspace

Price Code: L1

1-800-850-1491 • EPLANS.COM

~Braden House~

ARCHITECTURAL RENDERING: GREG HAVENS

3,802
square feet

Plan # HPK3800277

First Floor: 2,366 sq. ft.

Second Floor: 1,436 sq. ft.

Total: 3,802 sq. ft.

Bonus Space: 480 sq. ft.

Bedrooms: 3

Bathrooms: 4 ½

Width: 86' - 0"

Depth: 63' - 0"

Foundation: Unfinished Basement

Price Code: L4

1-800-850-1491 • EPLANS.COM

DESIGNED BY CALDWELL-CLINE ARCHITECTS AND DESIGNERS
FOR COOKING LIGHT MAGAZINE

FIRST FLOOR

SECOND FLOOR

MARTHA'S VINEYARD

3,806
square feet

ARCHITECTURAL RENDERING: SPITZMILLER AND NORRIS, INC.

DESIGNED BY SPITZMILLER AND NORRIS, INC.

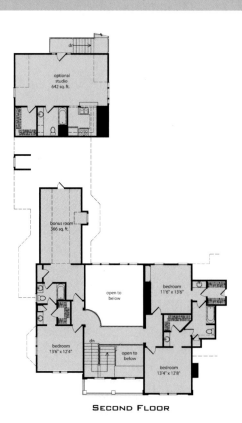

FIRST FLOOR

SECOND FLOOR

Plan # HPK3800278

First Floor: 2,697 sq. ft.

Second Floor: 1,109 sq. ft.

Total: 3,806 sq. ft.

Bonus Space: 366 sq. ft.

Bedrooms: 4

Bathrooms: 4

Width: 67' - 0"

Depth: 95' - 0"

Foundation: Unfinished Basement

Price Code: L1

1-800-850-1491 • EPLANS.COM

3,810 square feet

Plan# HPK3800279

First Floor: 2,380 sq. ft.

Second Floor: 1,430 sq. ft.

Total: 3,810 sq. ft.

Bedrooms: 4

Bathrooms: 4 ½

Width: 65' - 0"

Depth: 27' - 0"

Foundation: Unfinished Basement

Price Code: L1

1-800-850-1491 • EPLANS.COM

DESIGNED BY MITCHELL GINN

SECOND FLOOR

FIRST FLOOR

3,812
square feet

ARCHITECTURAL RENDERING: MILES MELTON

DESIGNED BY GARY/RAGSDALE, INC.

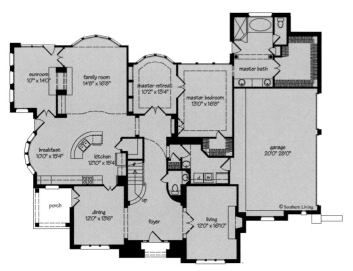

FIRST FLOOR

- sunroom 10" x 14'0"
- family room 14'8" x 16'8"
- master retreat 10'2" x 13'4"
- master bedroom 13'0" x 16'8"
- master bath
- breakfast 10'0" x 15'4"
- kitchen 12'0" x 15'4"
- garage 20'0" x 28'0"
- porch
- dining 12'0" x 13'6"
- foyer
- living 12'0" x 16'0"
- up

© Southern Living

SECOND FLOOR

- gameroom 14'6" x 15'10"
- bedroom 12'6" x 10'0"
- bedroom 12'6" x 17'0"
- bedroom 10'10" x 15'0"
- open to below
- dn

Plan # **HPK3800280**

First Floor: 2,485 sq. ft.

Second Floor: 1,327 sq. ft.

Total: 3,812 sq. ft.

Bedrooms: 4

Bathrooms: 3 ½

Width: 74' - 0"

Depth: 58' - 0"

Foundation: Slab

Price Code: L1

1-800-850-1491 • EPLANS.COM

❧ABBERLEY LANE❧

3,816
square feet

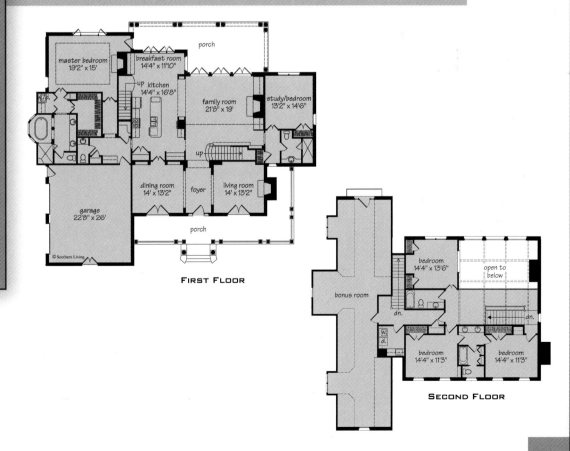

DESIGNED BY JOHN TEE, ARCHITECT

Plan # HPK3800281

First Floor: 2,686 sq. ft.

Second Floor: 1,130 sq. ft.

Total: 3,816 sq. ft.

Bonus Space: 1,000 sq. ft.

Bedrooms: 5

Bathrooms: 4 ½

Width: 78' - 0"

Depth: 62' - 0"

Foundation: Crawlspace

Price Code: L4

1-800-850-1491 • EPLANS.COM

First Floor

master bedroom
19'2" x 15'

breakfast room
14'4" x 11'10"

porch

up kitchen
14'4" x 16'8"

family room
21'8" x 19'

study/bedroom
13'2" x 14'6"

up

dining room
14' x 13'2"

foyer

living room
14' x 13'2"

garage
22'8" x 26'

© Southern Living

porch

Second Floor

bonus room

bedroom
14'4" x 13'6"

open to
below

dn.

dn.

W. d.

bedroom
14'4" x 11'3"

bedroom
14'4" x 11'3"

ST. ANNE GEORGIAN

3,825 square feet

ARCHITECTURAL RENDERING: SPITZMILLER AND NORRIS, INC.

DESIGNED BY SPITZMILLER AND NORRIS, INC.

FIRST FLOOR

deck

covered porch

keeping room
19'1" x 15'9"

dining
12'11" x 16'4"

breakfast
19'1" x 11'9"

great room
15'6" x 20'7"

foyer

up

dn

kitchen
17'3" x 8'8"

w | d

garage
20'6" x 28'6"

© Southern Living

SECOND FLOOR

balcony

master bedroom
15'8" x 22'0"

bedroom
15'3" x 13'4"

dn

open to below

bedroom
12'5" x 14'0"

bedroom
12'0" x 15'8"

Plan # HPK3800282

First Floor: 1,833 sq. ft.

Second Floor: 1,992 sq. ft.

Total: 3,825 sq. ft.

Bedrooms: 4

Bathrooms: 3 ½

Width: 52' - 0"

Depth: 86' - 0"

Foundation: Unfinished Basement

Price Code: L1

1-800-850-1491 • EPLANS.COM

NORMANDY MANOR

ARCHITECTURAL RENDERING: SPITZMILLER AND NORRIS, INC.

3,833
square feet

DESIGNED BY SPITZMILLER AND NORRIS, INC.

Plan # HPK3800283

First Floor: 2,696 sq. ft.

Second Floor: 1,137 sq. ft.

Total: 3,833 sq. ft.

Bonus Space: 215 sq. ft.

Bedrooms: 4

Bathrooms: 3 ½

Width: 73' - 0"

Depth: 83' - 0"

Foundation: Unfinished Basement

Price Code: L1

1-800-850-1491 • EPLANS.COM

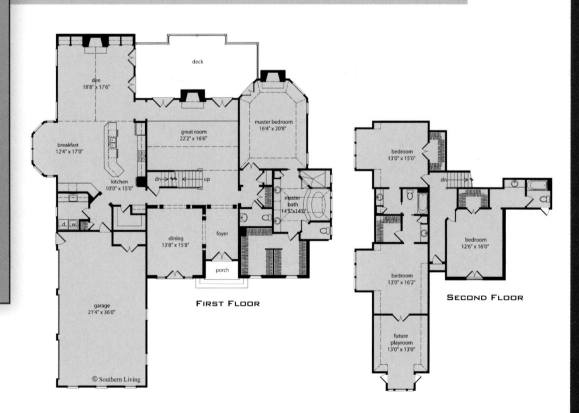

FIRST FLOOR

SECOND FLOOR

3,854 square feet

ARCHITECTURAL RENDERING: MILES MELTON

DESIGNED BY BRYAN & CONTRERAS, LLC

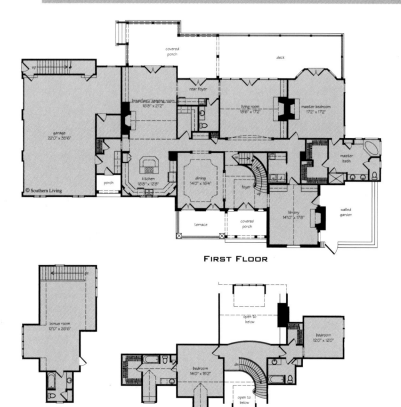

FIRST FLOOR

SECOND FLOOR

Plan# HPK3800284

First Floor: 3,000 sq. ft.

Second Floor: 854 sq. ft.

Total: 3,854 sq. ft.

Bonus Space: 664 sq. ft.

Bedrooms: 3

Bathrooms: 3 ½

Width: 110' - 0"

Depth: 67' - 0"

Foundation: Unfinished Basement

Price Code: L1

1-800-850-1491 • EPLANS.COM

3,858 square feet

DESIGNED BY CALDWELL-CLINE ARCHITECTS AND DESIGNERS

Plan# HPK3800285

First Floor: 1,875 sq. ft.

Second Floor: 1,983 sq. ft.

Total: 3,858 sq. ft.

Bedrooms: 4

Bathrooms: 3 ½

Width: 60' - 0"

Depth: 74' - 7"

Foundation: Crawlspace

Price Code: L1

1-800-850-1491 • EPLANS.COM

FIRST FLOOR

SECOND FLOOR

~AMSTERDAM AVENUE~

3,861
square feet

ARCHITECTURAL RENDERING: SPITZMILLER AND NORRIS, INC.

DESIGNED BY SPITZMILLER AND NORRIS, INC.

Plan# HPK3800286

First Floor: 2,624 sq. ft.

Second Floor: 1,237 sq. ft.

Total: 3,861 sq. ft.

Bedrooms: 4

Bathrooms: 3 ½

Width: 63' - 0"

Depth: 71' - 0"

Foundation: Unfinished Basement

Price Code: L1

1-800-850-1491 • EPLANS.COM

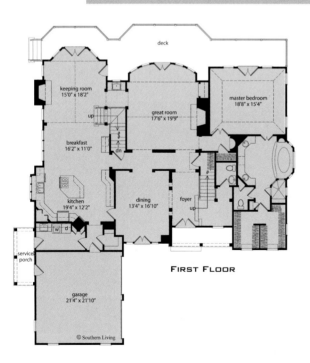

FIRST FLOOR

keeping room 15'0" x 18'2"

great room 17'6" x 19'9"

master bedroom 18'8" x 15'4"

breakfast 16'2" x 11'0"

kitchen 19'4" x 12'2"

dining 13'4" x 16'10"

foyer

deck

service porch

garage 21'4" x 21'10"

© Southern Living

SECOND FLOOR

open to below

open to below

open to below

open to below

bedroom 12'10" x 16'0"

bedroom 13'4" x 16'9"

bedroom 14'8" x 13'11"

312   SOUTHERN LIVING *Classic Collection of House Plans*

~ WEATHERFORD ~

3,864
square feet

Plan # HPK3800287

First Floor: 1,828 sq. ft.

Second Floor: 2,036 sq. ft.

Total: 3,864 sq. ft.

Bedrooms: 4

Bathrooms: 3 ½

Width: 68' - 8"

Depth: 44' - 11"

Foundation: Unfinished Basement

Price Code: L1

1-800-850-1491 • EPLANS.COM

DESIGNED BY SPITZMILLER AND NORRIS, INC.

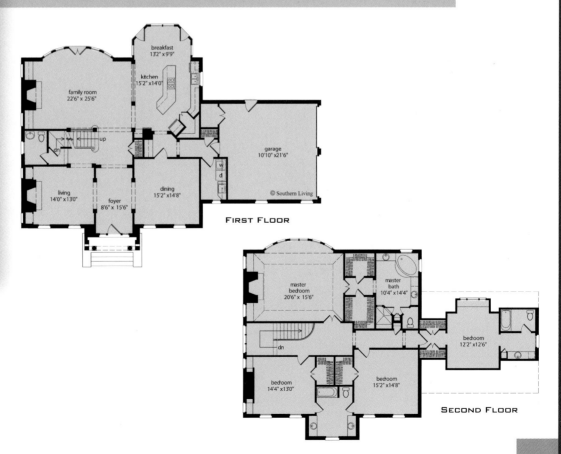

FIRST FLOOR

- breakfast 13'2" x 9'9"
- kitchen 15'2" x 14'0"
- family room 22'6" x 25'6"
- garage 10'10" x 21'6"
- living 14'0" x 13'0"
- foyer 8'6" x 15'6"
- dining 15'2" x 14'8"
- © Southern Living

SECOND FLOOR

- master bedroom 20'6" x 15'6"
- master bath 10'4" x 14'4"
- bedroom 12'2" x 12'6"
- bedroom 14'4" x 13'0"
- bedroom 15'2" x 14'8"

~MULBERRY PARK~

3,899
square feet

DESIGNED BY LOONEY RICKS KISS ARCHITECTS, INC.

Plan# HPK3800288

First Floor: 2,013 sq. ft.

Second Floor: 1,826 sq. ft.

Total: 3,899 sq. ft.

Bedrooms: 4

Bathrooms: 4 ½

Width: 57' - 5"

Depth: 85' - 2"

Foundation: Slab

Price Code: L4

1-800-850-1491 • EPLANS.COM

First Floor

office/studio 15'2" x 20'8"

garden

pergola

garden courtyard

potting room

garage 20'7" x 23'10"

© Southern Living

w. d.

up

porch

family room 15' x 20'

office 8'9" x 7'4"

side entry

sunroom 15'4" x 14'3"

b'fast 10'6" x 14'

kitchen 10' x 18'

office 8'9" x 7'4"

study/ guestroom 14'2" x 12'1"

foyer/dining hall 14'2" x 22'

butler's pantry

portico

FIRST FLOOR

Second Floor

guest apartment 17'7" x 17'4"

dn.

balcony

master bedroom 16'9" x 16'10"

morning bar

dn.

up

nursery 12'4" x 13'5"

comp. nook 7'6" x 10'1"

boy's bedroom 11'8" x 14'2"

SECOND FLOOR

BRENTWOOD COTTAGE

3,915 square feet

DESIGNED BY SPITZMILLER AND NORRIS, INC.

Plan# **HPK3800289**

First Floor: 2,083 sq. ft.

Second Floor: 1,832 sq. ft.

Total: 3,915 sq. ft.

Bedrooms: 4

Bathrooms: 3 ½

Width: 70' - 0"

Depth: 75' - 0"

Foundation: Unfinished Basement

Price Code: L1

1-800-850-1491 • EPLANS.COM

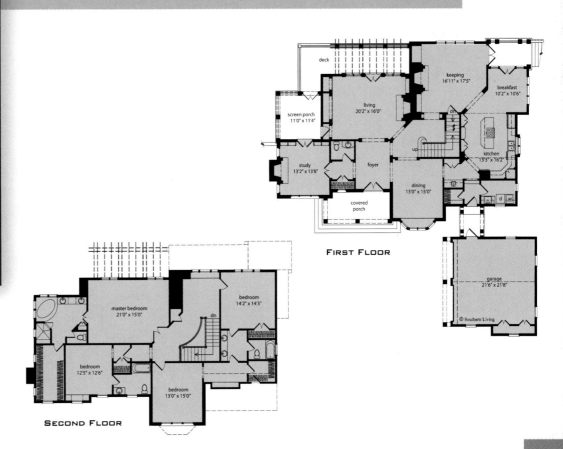

FIRST FLOOR

SECOND FLOOR

STONES RIVER FARM

3,916 square feet

DESIGNED BY LOONEY RICKS KISS ARCHITECTS, INC. FOR THE PROGRESSIVE FARMER

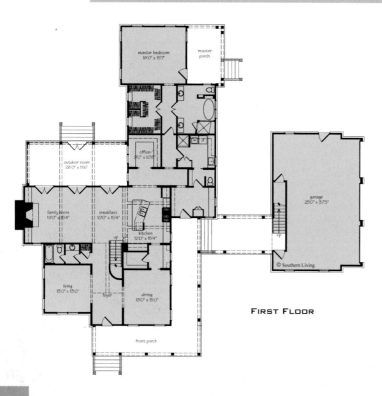

FIRST FLOOR

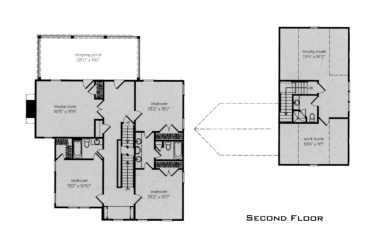

SECOND FLOOR

JUST INSIDE this quaint country charmer, a

foyer flanked by the dining and living rooms leads directly to the combined family room and breakfast room, where three French doors open to the outdoor patio. At the rear of the house an office is tucked away with the master suite, featuring a private porch and his and hers walk-in closets. Three bedrooms are located upstairs with a media room and sleeping porch.

Plan # HPK3800290

First Floor: 2,548 sq. ft.

Second Floor: 1,368 sq. ft.

Total: 3,916 sq. ft.

Bedrooms: 4

Bathrooms: 5

Width: 97' - 0"

Depth: 87' - 0"

Foundation: Crawlspace

Price Code: L4

1-800-850-1491 • EPLANS.COM

CRABAPPLE GROVE

ARCHITECTURAL RENDERING: SPITZMILLER AND NORRIS, INC.

DESIGNED BY SPITZMILLER AND NORRIS, INC.

Plan # HPK3800292

First Floor: 2,782 sq. ft.

Second Floor: 1,148 sq. ft.

Total: 3,930 sq. ft.

Bonus Space: 588 sq. ft.

Bedrooms: 4

Bathrooms: 4 ½

Width: 81' - 0"

Depth: 84' - 0"

Foundation: Unfinished Basement

Price Code: L1

1-800-850-1491 • EPLANS.COM

First Floor

breakfast 10'0" x 8'0"

deck

keeping room 13'6" x 15'8"

great room 19'0" x 15'10"

master bedroom 19'2" x 16'2"

kitchen 15'0" x 18'0"

up

W d

porch

foyer up

dining 13'1" x 16'0"

dn

porch

study/guest room 12'11" x 14'4"

garage 21'7" x 33'10"

© Southern Living

attic

open to below

balcony

dn

future study

dn

bedroom 13'5" x 13'8"

open to below

bedroom 14'7" x 14'4"

future bedroom 17'3" x 13'6"

Second Floor

AVALON ALTERNATE

3,931 square feet

DESIGNED BY SPITZMILLER AND NORRIS, INC.

Plan# HPK3800293

First Floor: 2,478 sq. ft.

Second Floor: 1,453 sq. ft.

Total: 3,931 sq. ft.

Bonus Space: 781 sq. ft.

Bedrooms: 4

Bathrooms: 4 ½

Width: 68' - 0"

Depth: 86' - 0"

Foundation: Crawlspace

Price Code: L4

1-800-850-1491 • EPLANS.COM

FIRST FLOOR

master bedroom 15'4" x 25'1"

family room 25'10" x 19'10"

sunroom 15'2" x 22'2"

kitchen 17'4" x 16'6"

foyer

dining 14'0" x 18'9"

garage 21'4" x 21'8"

© Southern Living

SECOND FLOOR

bedroom 15'4" x 12'10"

t.v. room 15'2" x 15'0"

bedroom 16'0" x 15'2"

bedroom 15'4" x 12'2"

optional exercise 13'5" x 13'2"

optional playroom 13'2" x 19'8"

SABINE RIVER COTTAGE

3,940
square feet

ARCHITECTURAL RENDERING: MILES MELTON

DESIGNED BY JOHN TEE, ARCHITECT

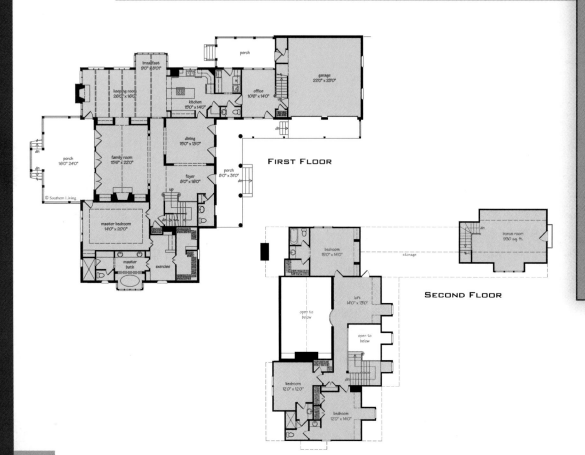

FIRST FLOOR

SECOND FLOOR

Plan# **HPK3800294**

First Floor: 2,722 sq. ft.

Second Floor: 1,218 sq. ft.

Total: 3,940 sq. ft.

Bonus Space: 930 sq. ft.

Bedrooms: 4

Bathrooms: 3 full + 2 half

Width: 74' - 6"

Depth: 85' - 4"

Foundation: Unfinished Basement

Price Code: L2

1-800-850-1491 • EPLANS.COM

KENNESAW RIDGE

3,951 square feet

DESIGNED BY STEPHEN FULLER, INC.

Plan# HPK3800295

First Floor: 2,909 sq. ft.

Second Floor: 1,042 sq. ft.

Total: 3,951 sq. ft.

Bedrooms: 4

Bathrooms: 3 ½

Width: 71' - 0"

Depth: 74' - 0"

Foundation: Unfinished Basement

Price Code: L2

1-800-850-1491 • EPLANS.COM

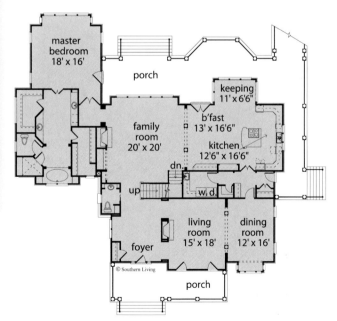

master bedroom 18' x 16'

porch

keeping 11' x 6'6"

b'fast 13' x 16'6"

family room 20' x 20'

kitchen 12'6" x 16'6"

dn.

up

w.d.

living room 15' x 18'

dining room 12' x 16'

foyer

© Southern Living

porch

FIRST FLOOR

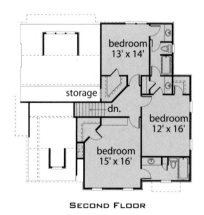

storage

bedroom 13' x 14'

dn.

bedroom 12' x 16'

bedroom 15' x 16'

SECOND FLOOR

~BROOKHOLLOW~

3,951 square feet

DESIGNED BY STEPHEN FULLER, INC.

SECOND FLOOR

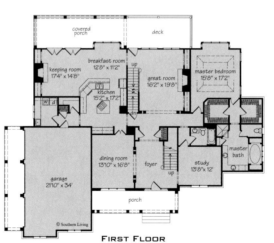

FIRST FLOOR

Plan# HPK3800296

First Floor: 2,727 sq. ft.

Second Floor: 1,224 sq. ft.

Total: 3,951 sq. ft.

Bonus Space: 210 sq. ft.

Bedrooms: 4

Bathrooms: 4

Width: 82' - 0"

Depth: 69' - 0"

Foundation: Unfinished Basement

Price Code: L4

1-800-850-1491 • EPLANS.COM

COLONIAL LAKE COTTAGE

4,029 square feet

Plan# HPK3800297

First Floor: 2,304 sq. ft.

Second Floor: 1,725 sq. ft.

Total: 4,029 sq. ft.

Bonus Space: 884 sq. ft.

Bedrooms: 5

Bathrooms: 5

Width: 57' - 0"

Depth: 117' - 0"

Foundation: Slab

Price Code: L1

1-800-850-1491 • EPLANS.COM

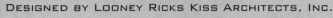

DESIGNED BY LOONEY RICKS KISS ARCHITECTS, INC.

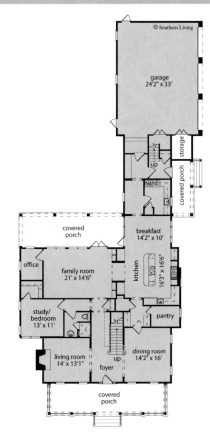

© Southern Living

garage
24'2" x 33'

storage

covered porch

up

w/d.

covered porch

family room
21' x 14'6"

office

breakfast
14'2' x 10'

kitchen
16'3" x 16'6"

study/
bedroom
13' x 11'

pantry

living room
14' x 13'1"

up

dining room
14'2" x 16'

foyer

covered porch

FIRST FLOOR

bedroom
11'3" x 13'

bedroom
11'3" x 13'

living room
16'7" x 19'7"

dn.

optional living area

exercise room
14'2" x 10'

bedroom
12'9" x 14'6"

bedroom
11'6" x 14'

dn.

bedroom
14'6" x 12'

master
bedroom
14'5" x 16'

SECOND FLOOR

❖ WALKER'S BLUFF ❖

4,035
square feet

ARCHITECTURAL RENDERING: GREG HAVENS

DESIGNED BY GARY/RAGSDALE, INC.

Plan # **HPK3800298**

First Floor: 2,570 sq. ft.

Second Floor: 1,465 sq. ft.

Total: 4,035 sq. ft.

Bedrooms: 4

Bathrooms: 3 full + 2 half

Width: 61' - 0"

Depth: 76' - 0"

Foundation: Slab

Price Code: L4

1-800-850-1491 • EPLANS.COM

First Floor

- master bedroom 19' x 14'
- family room 16' x 21'
- covered patio
- breakfast room 10'2" x 10'10"
- kitchen 18'4" x 15'
- garage 20'8" x 36'
- dining room 12' x 15'
- foyer
- study/library 11' x 13'10"
- porch
- © Southern Living

Second Floor

- balcony
- game room 16'6" x 16'4"
- bedroom 12' x 13'4"
- dn
- bedroom 12' x 13'10"
- bedroom 12' x 15'
- open to below
- upper study

ARCHITECTURAL RENDERING: MILES MELTON

4,035
square feet

DESIGNED BY GARY/RAGSDALE, INC.

Plan # **HPK3800299**

First Floor: 2,570 sq. ft.

Second Floor: 1,465 sq. ft.

Total: 4,035 sq. ft.

Bedrooms: 4

Bathrooms: 4 ½

Width: 63' - 0"

Depth: 76' - 0"

Foundation: Slab

Price Code: L1

1-800-850-1491 • EPLANS.COM

FIRST FLOOR

SECOND FLOOR

~ PINE GLEN ~

4,037 square feet

DESIGNED BY LOONEY RICKS KISS ARCHITECTS, INC.

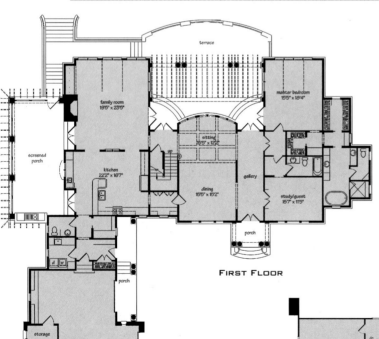

FIRST FLOOR

© Southern Living

SECOND FLOOR

Plan# HPK3800300

First Floor: 2,921 sq. ft.

Second Floor: 1,116 sq. ft.

Total: 4,037 sq. ft.

Bonus Space: 396 sq. ft.

Bedrooms: 3

Bathrooms: 3 full + 2 half

Width: 98' - 0"

Depth: 103' - 0"

Foundation: Crawlspace

Price Code: L2

1-800-850-1491 • EPLANS.COM

SIENNA PARK

4,047
square feet

DESIGNED BY RPGA DESIGN GROUP, INC.

Plan# **HPK3800301**

First Floor: 2,849 sq. ft.

Second Floor: 1,198 sq. ft.

Total: 4,047 sq. ft.

Bedrooms: 5

Bathrooms: 4 ½

Width: 94' - 0"

Depth: 58' - 0"

Foundation: Slab

Price Code: L2

1-800-850-1491 • EPLANS.COM

FIRST FLOOR

SECOND FLOOR

4,059
square feet

ARCHITECTURAL RENDERING: BRIAN BARKS

DESIGNED BY GARY/RAGSDALE, INC.

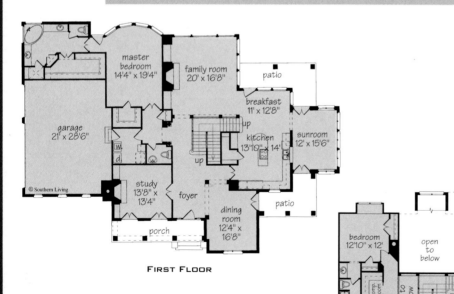

FIRST FLOOR

master bedroom
14'4" x 19'4"

family room
20' x 16'8"

patio

breakfast
11' x 12'8"

garage
21' x 28'6"

up

kitchen
13'10" x 14'

sunroom
12' x 15'6"

up

© Southern Living

study
13'8" x 13'4"

foyer

dining room
12'4" x 16'8"

patio

porch

SECOND FLOOR

bedroom
12'10" x 12'

open to below

balcony

comp. room

open to below

media room
13'6" x 16'4"

dn.

bedroom
14'8" x 11'8"

open to below

bedroom
13' x 14'8"

balcony

balcony

Plan # HPK3800302

First Floor: 2,649 sq. ft.

Second Floor: 1,410 sq. ft.

Total: 4,059 sq. ft.

Bedrooms: 4

Bathrooms: 3 ½

Width: 83' - 0"

Depth: 59' - 0"

Foundation: Slab

Price Code: C4

1-800-850-1491 • EPLANS.COM

~MONTCREST~

ARCHITECTURAL RENDERING: MILES MELTON

DESIGNED BY LOONEY RICKS KISS ARCHITECTS, INC.

Plan# HPK3800303

First Floor: 3,032 sq. ft.

Second Floor: 1,038 sq. ft.

Total: 4,070 sq. ft.

Bedrooms: 4

Bathrooms: 4 full + 2 half

Width: 78' - 0"

Depth: 35' - 0"

Foundation: Slab

Price Code: L2

1-800-850-1491 • EPLANS.COM

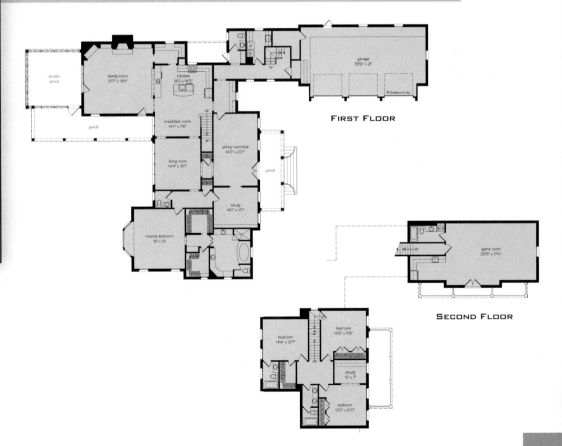

FIRST FLOOR

SECOND FLOOR

❦ LUBERON ❦

4,100 square feet

ARCHITECTURAL RENDERING: MILES MELTON

DESIGNED BY GARY/RAGSDALE, INC.

Plan # HPK3800304

First Floor: 2,518 sq. ft.

Second Floor: 1,582 sq. ft.

Total: 4,100 sq. ft.

Bonus Space: 246 sq. ft.

Bedrooms: 5

Bathrooms: 4

Width: 62' - 0"

Depth: 74' - 0"

Foundation: Slab

Price Code: L1

1-800-850-1491 • EPLANS.COM

FIRST FLOOR

SECOND FLOOR

~TRAVIS RIDGE~

4,101
square feet

DESIGNED BY DESIGN DISCOVERIES II

Plan# HPK3800305

First Floor: 3,296 sq. ft.

Second Floor: 805 sq. ft.

Total: 4,101 sq. ft.

Bonus Space: 447 sq. ft.

Bedrooms: 4

Bathrooms: 4

Width: 85' - 0"

Depth: 111' - 0"

Foundation: Slab

Price Code: L4

1-800-850-1491 • EPLANS.COM

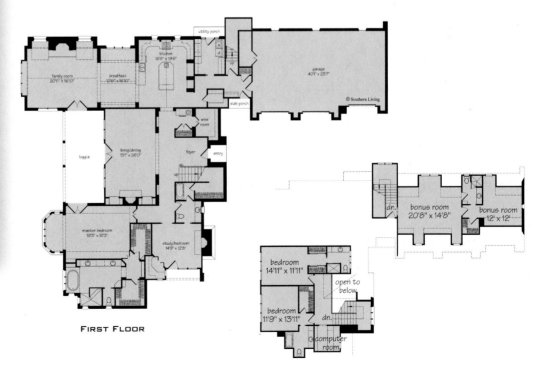

FIRST FLOOR

SECOND FLOOR

4,137 square feet

ARCHITECTURAL RENDERING: MILES MELTON

DESIGNED BY LOONEY RICKS KISS ARCHITECTS, INC.

Plan# HPK3800306

First Floor: 2,767 sq. ft.

Second Floor: 1,370 sq. ft.

Total: 4,137 sq. ft.

Bonus Space: 475 sq. ft.

Bedrooms: 4

Bathrooms: 3 ½

Width: 74' - 0"

Depth: 97' - 0"

Foundation: Crawlspace

Price Code: L2

1-800-850-1491 • EPLANS.COM

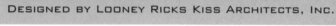

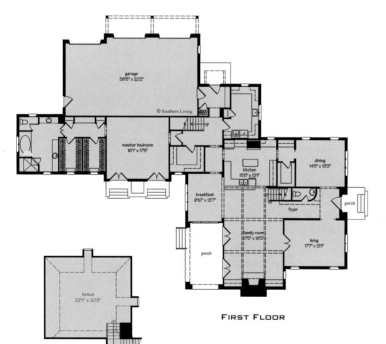

FIRST FLOOR

SECOND FLOOR

4,152 square feet

Plan# HPK3800307

First Floor: 2,740 sq. ft.

Second Floor: 1,412 sq. ft.

Total: 4,152 sq. ft.

Bonus Space: 285 sq. ft.

Bedrooms: 4

Bathrooms: 3 ½

Width: 72' - 0"

Depth: 66' - 0"

Foundation: Unfinished Basement

Price Code: L1

1-800-850-1491 • EPLANS.COM

DESIGNED BY SPITZMILLER AND NORRIS, INC.

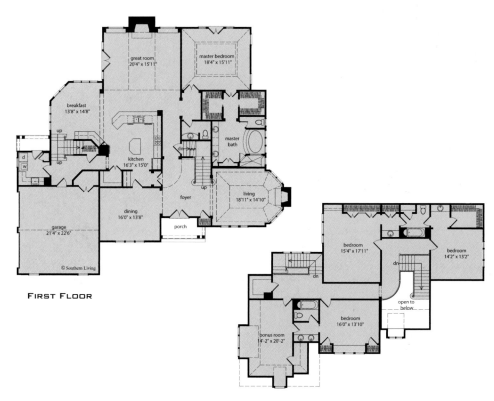

FIRST FLOOR

SECOND FLOOR

4,158
square feet

DESIGNED BY BRYAN & CONTRERAS, LLC

Plan # HPK3800308

First Floor: 3,166 sq. ft.

Second Floor: 992 sq. ft.

Total: 4,158 sq. ft.

Bedrooms: 4

Bathrooms: 4 ½

Width: 107' - 0"

Depth: 76' - 0"

Foundation: Unfinished Basement

Price Code: L1

1-800-850-1491 • EPLANS.COM

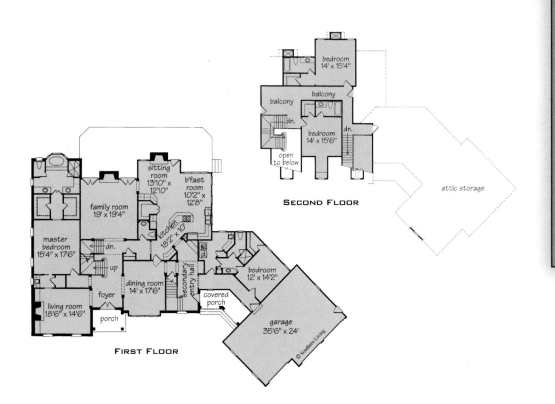

4,171 square feet

ARCHITECTURAL RENDERING: MILES MELTON

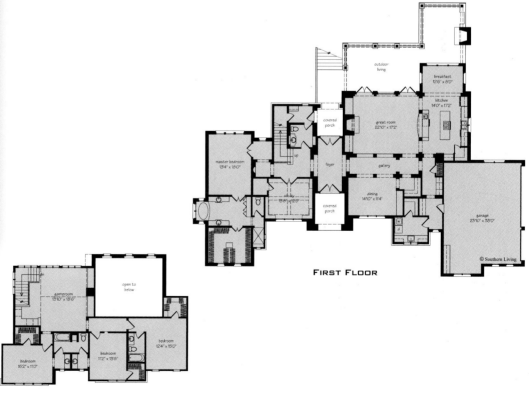

DESIGNED BY CORNERSTONE GROUP ARCHITECTS

Plan# HPK3800309

First Floor: 2,861 sq. ft.

Second Floor: 1,310 sq. ft.

Total: 4,171 sq. ft.

Bedrooms: 4

Bathrooms: 3 ½

Width: 102' - 0"

Depth: 81' - 0"

Foundation: Slab

Price Code: L1

1-800-850-1491 • EPLANS.COM

FIRST FLOOR

SECOND FLOOR

4,177
square feet

ARCHITECTURAL RENDERING: SPITZMILLER AND NORRIS, INC.

DESIGNED BY SPITZMILLER AND NORRIS, INC.

FIRST FLOOR

SECOND FLOOR

Plan # **HPK3800310**

First Floor: 2,764 sq. ft.

Second Floor: 1,413 sq. ft.

Total: 4,177 sq. ft.

Bonus Space: 603 sq. ft.

Bedrooms: 4

Bathrooms: 3 ½

Width: 78' - 0"

Depth: 67' - 0"

Foundation: Unfinished Basement

Price Code: L1

1-800-850-1491 • EPLANS.COM

4,171 square feet

Plan# HPK3800343

First Floor: 2,463 sq. ft.

Second Floor: 1,564 sq. ft.

Third Floor: 144 sq. ft.

Total: 4,171 sq. ft.

Bonus Space: 263 sq. ft.

Bedrooms: 4

Bathrooms: 4 ½

Width: 60' - 0"

Depth: 64' - 0"

Foundation: Unfinished Basement

Price Code: L2

1-800-850-1491 • EPLANS.COM

DESIGNED BY MITCHELL GINN

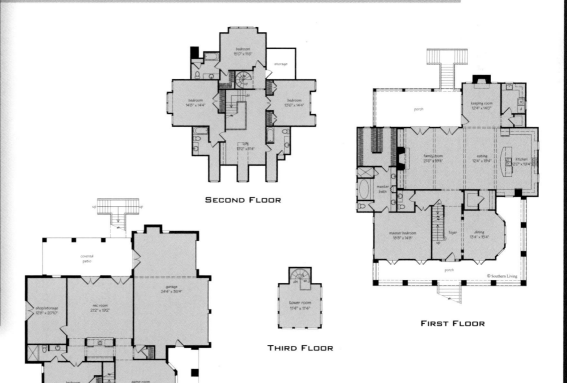

SECOND FLOOR

THIRD FLOOR

FIRST FLOOR

4,918
square feet

ARCHITECTURAL RENDERING: ANITA BICE

DESIGNED BY MITCHELL GINN

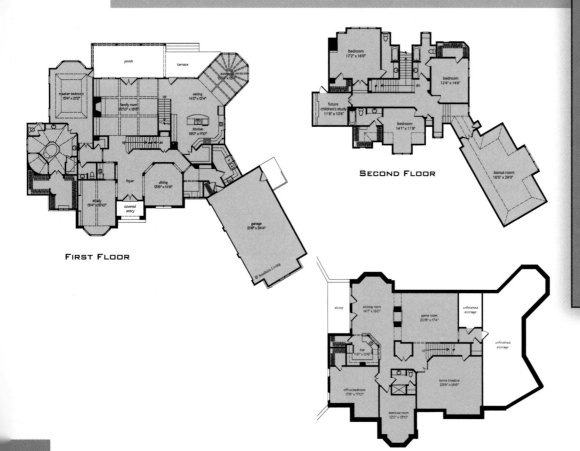

FIRST FLOOR

SECOND FLOOR

Plan # HPK3800340

First Floor: 3,412 sq. ft.

Second Floor: 1,506 sq. ft.

Total: 4,918 sq. ft.

Bonus Space: 682 sq. ft.

Bedrooms: 4

Bathrooms: 4 ½

Width: 100' - 6"

Depth: 84' - 4"

Foundation: Unfinished Basement

Price Code: L2

1-800-850-1491 • EPLANS.COM

ARCHITECTURAL RENDERING: MILES MELTON

4,186
square feet

DESIGNED BY GARY/RAGSDALE, INC.

Plan# **HPK3800311**

First Floor: 2,866 sq. ft.

Second Floor: 1,320 sq. ft.

Total: 4,186 sq. ft.

Bedrooms: 4

Bathrooms: 4 ½

Width: 62' - 0"

Depth: 100' - 0"

Foundation: Slab

Price Code: L1

1-800-850-1491 • EPLANS.COM

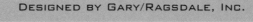

FIRST FLOOR

SECOND FLOOR

❧ STANTON COURT ❧

4,206
square feet

ARCHITECTURAL RENDERING: MILES MELTON

DESIGNED BY BRYAN & CONTRERAS, LLC

FIRST FLOOR

SECOND FLOOR

Plan # HPK3800312

First Floor: 3,000 sq. ft.

Second Floor: 1,206 sq. ft.

Total: 4,206 sq. ft.

Bonus Space: 664 sq. ft.

Bedrooms: 4

Bathrooms: 4 ½

Width: 110' - 0"

Depth: 67' - 0"

Foundation: Unfinished Basement

Price Code: L1

1-800-850-1491 • EPLANS.COM

4,228 square feet

ARCHITECTURAL RENDERING: MILES MELTON

DESIGNED BY GARY/RAGSDALE, INC.

Plan# HPK3800313

First Floor: 2,597 sq. ft.

Second Floor: 1,631 sq. ft.

Total: 4,228 sq. ft.

Bonus Space: 242 sq. ft.

Bedrooms: 5

Bathrooms: 4 ½

Width: 60' - 0"

Depth: 86' - 0"

Foundation: Slab

Price Code: L1

1-800-850-1491 • EPLANS.COM

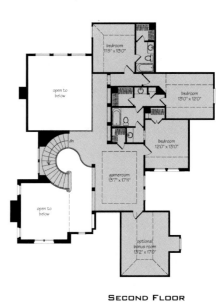

FIRST FLOOR

SECOND FLOOR

~HUNTER'S GLEN~

4,239
square feet

DESIGNED BY SPITZMILLER AND NORRIS, INC.

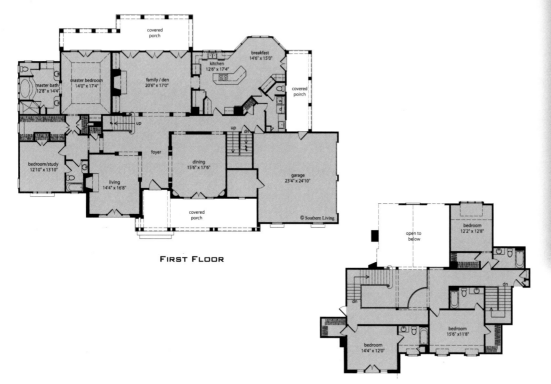

FIRST FLOOR

SECOND FLOOR

Plan # HPK3800314

First Floor: 3,039 sq. ft.

Second Floor: 1,200 sq. ft.

Total: 4,239 sq. ft.

Bedrooms: 5

Bathrooms: 5 ½

Width: 92' - 0"

Depth: 60' - 0"

Foundation: Unfinished Basement

Price Code: L2

1-800-850-1491 • EPLANS.COM

·IVY MANOR·

4,245
square feet

DESIGNED BY SPITZMILLER AND NORRIS, INC.

Plan# HPK3800315

First Floor: 2,958 sq. ft.

Second Floor: 1,287 sq. ft.

Total: 4,245 sq. ft.

Bedrooms: 4

Bathrooms: 3 full + 2 half

Width: 77' - 0"

Depth: 93' - 0"

Foundation: Unfinished Basement

Price Code: L2

1-800-850-1491 • EPLANS.COM

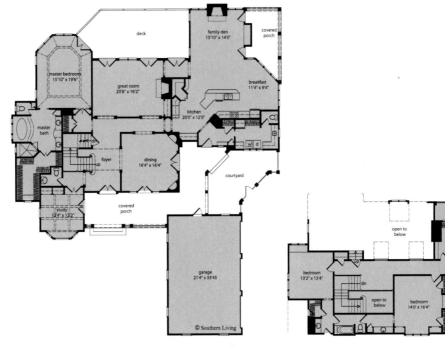

FIRST FLOOR

SECOND FLOOR

4,246 square feet

ARCHITECTURAL RENDERING: MILES MELTON

DESIGNED BY STEPHEN FULLER, INC.

Plan # **HPK3800316**

First Floor: 2,526 sq. ft.

Second Floor: 1,720 sq. ft.

Total: 4,246 sq. ft.

Bedrooms: 4

Bathrooms: 3 ½

Width: 77' - 0"

Depth: 61' - 0"

Foundation: Slab

Price Code: L2

1-800-850-1491 • EPLANS.COM

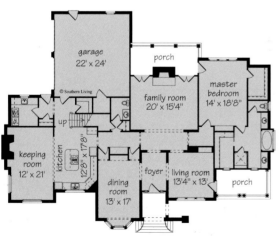

garage 22' x 24'

porch

keeping room 12' x 21'

kitchen 12'8" x 17'8"

family room 20' x 15'4"

master bedroom 14' x 18'8"

dining room 13' x 17'

foyer

living room 13'4" x 13'

porch

up

© Southern Living

FIRST FLOOR

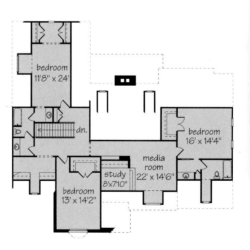

bedroom 11'8" x 24'

dn.

bedroom 16' x 14'4"

study 8'x7'10"

media room 22' x 14'6"

bedroom 13' x 14'2"

SECOND FLOOR

4,290
square feet

Plan# HPK3800317

First Floor: 2,901 sq. ft.

Second Floor: 1,389 sq. ft.

Total: 4,290 sq. ft.

Bonus Space: 326 sq. ft.

Bedrooms: 4

Bathrooms: 4 ½

Width: 73' - 0"

Depth: 80' - 0"

Foundation: Slab

Price Code: L1

1-800-850-1491 • EPLANS.COM

DESIGNED BY GARY/RAGSDALE, INC.

FIRST FLOOR

SECOND FLOOR

4,299 square feet

DESIGNED BY BRYAN & CONTRERAS, LLC

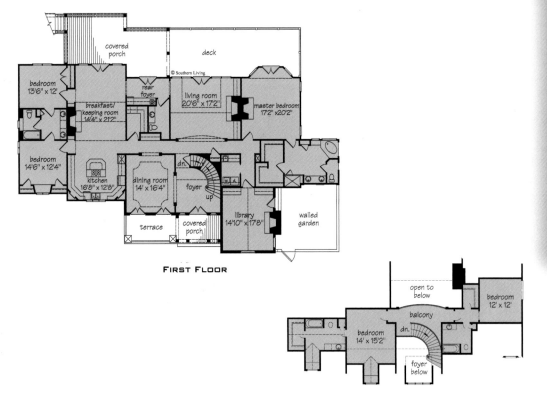

FIRST FLOOR

- covered porch
- deck
- bedroom 13'6" x 12'
- rear foyer
- living room 20'6" x 17'2"
- master bedroom 17'2" x 20'2"
- breakfast/ keeping room 14'4" x 21'2"
- bedroom 14'6" x 12'4"
- kitchen 16'8" x 12'8"
- dining room 14' x 16'4"
- dn.
- foyer up
- library 14'10" x 17'8"
- walled garden
- terrace
- covered porch

SECOND FLOOR

- open to below
- bedroom 12' x 12'
- balcony
- bedroom 14' x 15'2"
- dn.
- foyer below

Plan # HPK3800318

First Floor: 3,445 sq. ft.

Second Floor: 854 sq. ft.

Total: 4,299 sq. ft.

Bedrooms: 5

Bathrooms: 4 ½

Width: 95' - 0"

Depth: 67' - 0"

Foundation: Unfinished Basement

Price Code: L1

1-800-850-1491 • EPLANS.COM

ARCHITECTURAL RENDERING: MILES MELTON

4,302
square feet

Plan # HPK3800319

First Floor: 2,609 sq. ft.

Second Floor: 1,693 sq. ft.

Total: 4,302 sq. ft.

Bedrooms: 4

Bathrooms: 3 ½

Width: 82' - 0"

Depth: 59' - 0"

Foundation: Unfinished Basement

Price Code: L1

1-800-850-1491 • EPLANS.COM

DESIGNED BY MITCHELL GINN

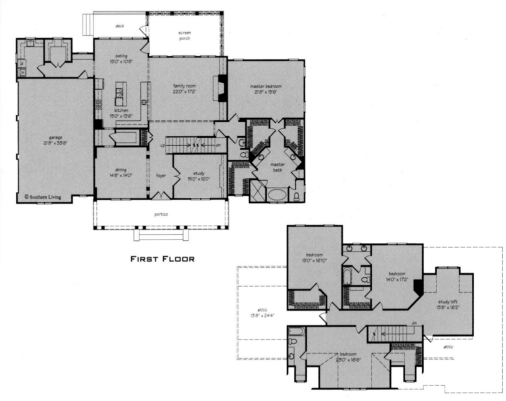

FIRST FLOOR

SECOND FLOOR

4,337
square feet

DESIGNED BY SPITZMILLER AND NORRIS, INC.

FIRST FLOOR

- deck
- breakfast 19'8" x 10'0"
- great room 21'4" x 17'2"
- kitchen 19'8" x 12'4"
- screened porch
- up
- parlour 13'6" x 15'8"
- dn
- foyer
- up
- dining 13'0" x 16'10"
- garage 21'2" x 21'4"
- w d
- © Southern Living

SECOND FLOOR

- master sitting 13'6" x 10'2"
- master bedroom 15'0" x 17'6"
- bedroom 15'8" x 16'6"
- master bath 14'0" x 12'10"
- open to below
- bedroom 13'4" x 14'4"
- bedroom 14'2" x 18'8"
- up
- dn
- dn

Plan # HPK3800320

First Floor: 2,058 sq. ft.

Second Floor: 2,284 sq. ft.

Total: 4,337 sq. ft.

Bedrooms: 4

Bathrooms: 3 ½

Width: 62' - 0"

Depth: 47' - 0"

Foundation: Unfinished Basement

Price Code: L1

1-800-850-1491 • EPLANS.COM

BEACON HILL

4,345 square feet

Plan# HPK3800321

First Floor: 3,418 sq. ft.

Second Floor: 927 sq. ft.

Total: 4,345 sq. ft.

Bonus Space: 408 sq. ft.

Bedrooms: 4

Bathrooms: 4 ½ or 5 ½

Width: 116' - 0"

Depth: 65' - 0"

Foundation: Unfinished Basement

Price Code: L2

1-800-850-1491 • EPLANS.COM

DESIGNED BY BRYAN & CONTRERAS, LLC

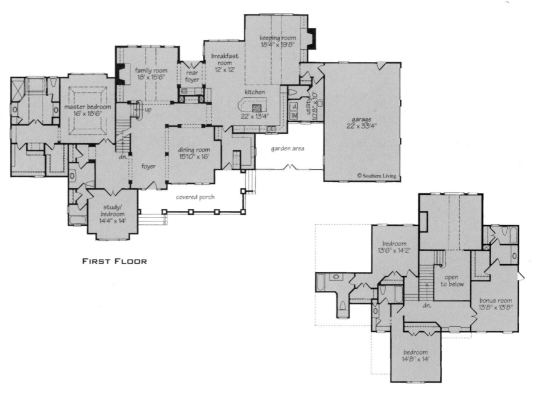

FIRST FLOOR

SECOND FLOOR

OCEAN HOUSE

4,362 square feet

DESIGNED BY GEORGE GRAVES, AIA, FOR COASTAL LIVING MAGAZINE

Plan # HPK3800322

First Floor: 2,127 sq. ft.

Second Floor: 2,235 sq. ft.

Total: 4,362 sq. ft.

Bedrooms: 4

Bathrooms: 5 ½

Width: 70' - 0"

Depth: 54' - 0"

Foundation: Crawlspace

Price Code: SQ3

1-800-850-1491 • EPLANS.COM

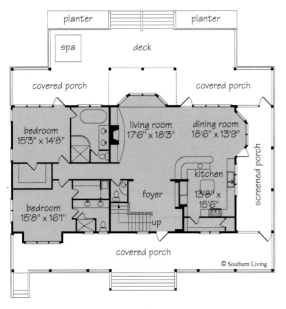

planter | planter
spa | deck
covered porch | covered porch
bedroom 15'3" x 14'8"
living room 17'6" x 18'3"
dining room 18'6" x 13'9"
screened porch
kitchen 13'8" x 15'6"
foyer
bedroom 15'8" x 16'1"
up
covered porch

© Southern Living

FIRST FLOOR

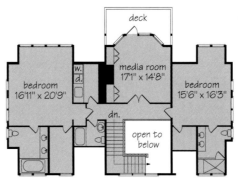

deck
bedroom 16'11" x 20'9"
w. d.
media room 17'1" x 14'8"
bedroom 15'6" x 16'3"
dn.
open to below

SECOND FLOOR

OAK HILL LANE ALTERNATE

4,437
square feet

DESIGNED BY SPITZMILLER AND NORRIS, INC.

Plan# HPK3800323

First Floor: 3,487 sq. ft.

Second Floor: 950 sq. ft.

Total: 4,437 sq. ft.

Bonus Space: 335 sq. ft.

Bedrooms: 5

Bathrooms: 4 full + 2 half

Width: 83' - 0"

Depth: 79' - 0"

Foundation: Unfinished Basement

Price Code: L1

1-800-850-1491 • EPLANS.COM

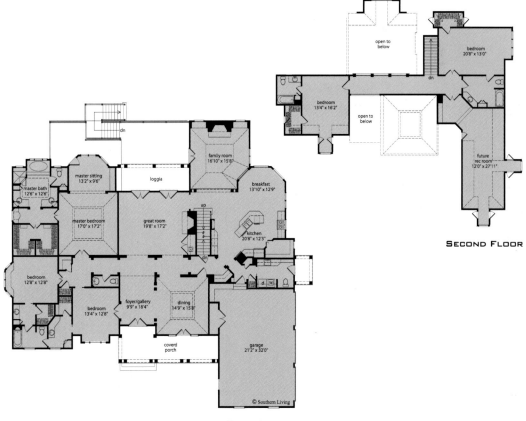

SECOND FLOOR

FIRST FLOOR

4,531 square feet

ARCHITECTURAL RENDERING: SPITZMILLER AND NORRIS, INC.

DESIGNED BY SPITZMILLER AND NORRIS, INC.

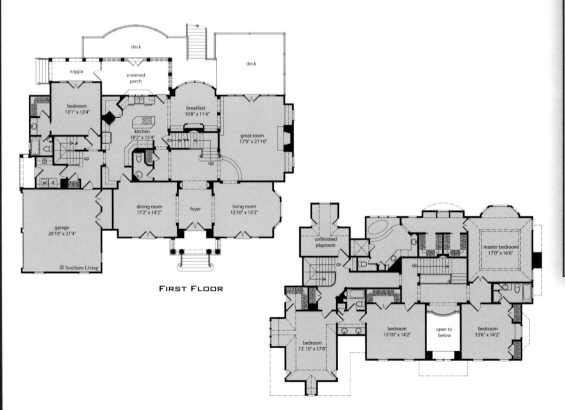

FIRST FLOOR

SECOND FLOOR

Plan # **HPK3800324**

First Floor: 2,345 sq. ft.

Second Floor: 2,186 sq. ft.

Total: 4,531 sq. ft.

Bonus Space: 155 sq. ft.

Bedrooms: 5

Bathrooms: 4 ½

Width: 73' - 0"

Depth: 64' - 0"

Foundation: Unfinished Basement

Price Code: L2

1-800-850-1491 • EPLANS.COM

ARCHITECTURAL RENDERING: RICK HERR

4,537
square feet

Plan # **HPK3800325**

First Floor: 3,270 sq. ft.

Second Floor: 1,267 sq. ft.

Total: 4,537 sq. ft.

Bonus Space: 570 sq. ft.

Bedrooms: 4

Bathrooms: 4 full + 2 half

Width: 91' - 0"

Depth: 71' - 0"

Foundation: Unfinished Basement

Price Code: L1

1-800-850-1491 • EPLANS.COM

DESIGNED BY BRYAN & CONTRERAS, LLC

FIRST FLOOR

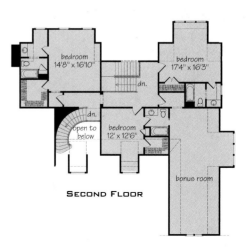

SECOND FLOOR

4,551
square feet

DESIGNED BY CORNERSTONE GROUP ARCHITECTS

Plan # **HPK3800326**

First Floor: 3,781 sq. ft.

Second Floor: 770 sq. ft.

Total: 4,551 sq. ft.

Bedrooms: 5

Bathrooms: 4

Width: 126' - 0"

Depth: 86' - 0"

Foundation: Slab

Price Code: L4

1-800-850-1491 • EPLANS.COM

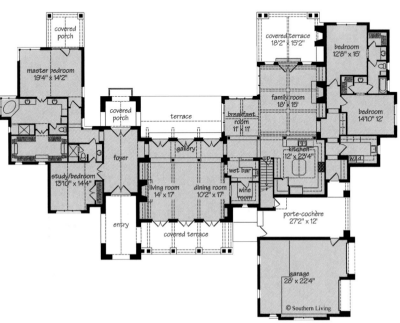

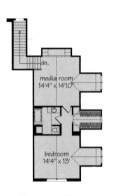

FIRST FLOOR

SECOND FLOOR

~ BEECHAM MANOR ~

4,574 square feet

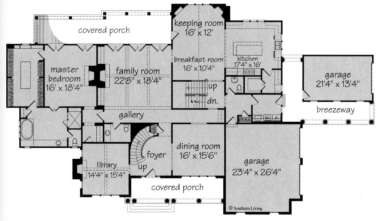

Plan # HPK3800327

First Floor: 3,261 sq. ft.

Second Floor: 1,313 sq. ft.

Total: 4,574 sq. ft.

Bedrooms: 4

Bathrooms: 4 full + 2 half

Width: 114' - 0"

Depth: 63' - 0"

Foundation: Unfinished Basement

Price Code: L2

1-800-850-1491 • EPLANS.COM

DESIGNED BY BRYAN & CONTRERAS, LLC

FIRST FLOOR

covered porch

keeping room 16' x 12'

master bedroom 16' x 18'4"

family room 22'8" x 18'4"

breakfast room 16' x 10'4"

kitchen 17'4" x 16'

garage 21'4" x 13'4"

breezeway

up

dn.

gallery

library 14'4" x 15'4"

foyer

up

dining room 16' x 15'6"

garage 23'4" x 26'4"

covered porch

© Southern Living

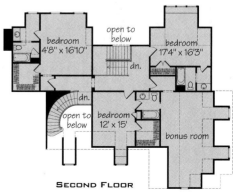

SECOND FLOOR

bedroom 4'8" x 16'10"

open to below

bedroom 17'4" x 16'3"

dn.

dn.

open to below

bedroom 12' x 15'

bonus room

~ALOUETTE~

4,639 square feet

DESIGNED BY BRYAN & CONTRERAS, LLC

Plan # **HPK3800328**

First Floor: 3,051 sq. ft.

Second Floor: 1,588 sq. ft.

Total: 4,639 sq. ft.

Bedrooms: 5

Bathrooms: 5 ½

Width: 102' - 0"

Depth: 87' - 0"

Foundation: Slab

Price Code: L1

1-800-850-1491 • EPLANS.COM

FIRST FLOOR

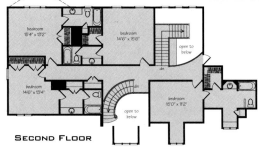

SECOND FLOOR

⊶HYANNIS PORT⊷

4,655 square feet

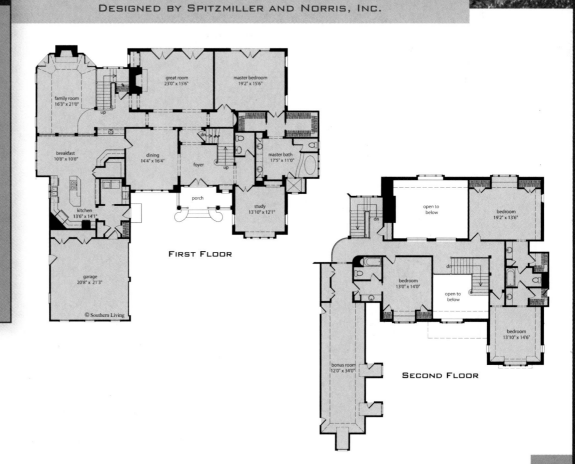

DESIGNED BY SPITZMILLER AND NORRIS, INC.

Plan# HPK3800329

First Floor: 3,213 sq. ft.

Second Floor: 1,442 sq. ft.

Total: 4,655 sq. ft.

Bonus Space: 588 sq. ft.

Bedrooms: 4

Bathrooms: 3 ½

Width: 79' - 0"

Depth: 76' - 0"

Foundation: Unfinished Basement

Price Code: L2

1-800-850-1491 • EPLANS.COM

CUSCOWILLA

4,735
square feet

DESIGNED BY STEPHEN FULLER, INC.

SECOND LEVEL

guestroom
13' x 23'
dn. deck

MAIN LEVEL

covered deck
master bedroom 16'1" x 18'1"
sun deck
screened porch
kitchen
living room 15'2" x 24'7"
dining room 14'11" x 24'7"
15'4" x 15'
dn. grilling deck
foyer
utility room
garage 23' x 34'9"
up
© Southern Living

LOWER LEVEL

covered patio
veranda
patio
lanai
fish prep. area
up
exercise room/ bedroom 16'1" x 19'5"
game room 12' x 24'3"
bar
storage
family room 18'6" x 24'3"
office/ bedroom 12' x 14'7"
bedroom 15'6" x 12'2"
up
storage
mechanical

Plan# **HPK3800330**

Main Level: 2,275 sq. ft.

Second Level: 312 sq. ft.

Lower Level: 2,148 sq. ft.

Total: 4,735 sq. ft.

Bedrooms: 5

Bathrooms: 4 ½

Width: 110' - 0"

Depth: 110' - 0"

Foundation: Daylight Walkout Basement

Price Code: SQ3

1-800-850-1491 • EPLANS.COM

4,933
square feet

ARCHITECTURAL RENDERING: MILES MELTON

DESIGNED BY CORNERSTONE GROUP ARCHITECTS

Plan# HPK3800331

First Floor: 3,845 sq. ft.

Second Floor: 1,088 sq. ft.

Total: 4,933 sq. ft.

Bedrooms: 4

Bathrooms: 4 ½

Width: 113' - 0"

Depth: 91' - 0"

Foundation: Slab

Price Code: L1

1-800-850-1491 • EPLANS.COM

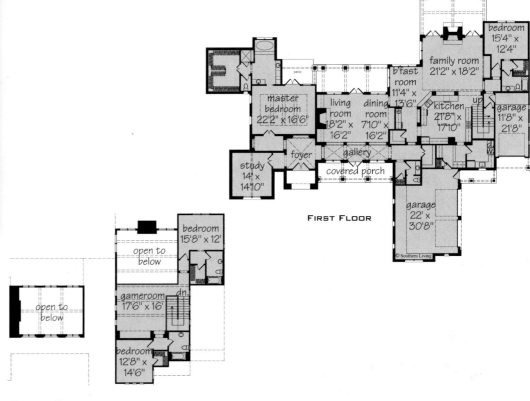

FIRST FLOOR

SECOND FLOOR

5,040 square feet

ARCHITECTURAL RENDERING: SPITZMILLER AND NORRIS, INC.

DESIGNED BY SPITZMILLER AND NORRIS, INC.

FIRST FLOOR

SECOND FLOOR

Plan# **HPK3800332**

First Floor: 2,562 sq. ft.

Second Floor: 2,478 sq. ft.

Total: 5,040 sq. ft.

Bedrooms: 4

Bathrooms: 5 ½

Width: 60' - 0"

Depth: 94' - 0"

Foundation: Unfinished Basement

Price Code: L2

1-800-850-1491 • EPLANS.COM

~CANTON CREEK~

5,128
square feet

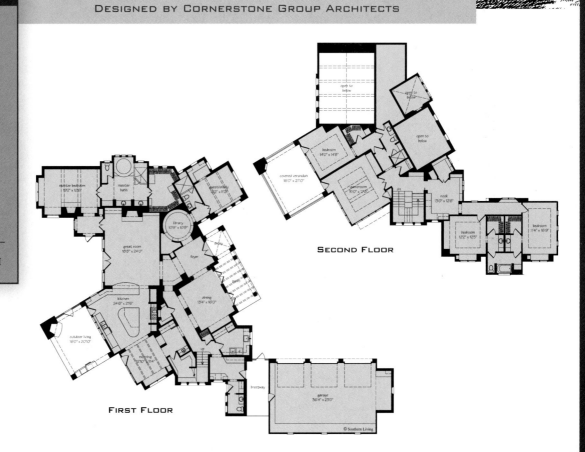

DESIGNED BY CORNERSTONE GROUP ARCHITECTS

Plan# HPK3800333

First Floor: 3,427 sq. ft.

Second Floor: 1,701 sq. ft.

Total: 5,128 sq. ft.

Bedrooms: 4 or 5

Bathrooms: 4 ½

Width: 122' - 0"

Depth: 92' - 0"

Foundation: Slab

Price Code: L2

1-800-850-1491 • EPLANS.COM

SECOND FLOOR

FIRST FLOOR

~Palmetto Court~

5,159 square feet

ARCHITECTURAL RENDERING: BRIAN BARKS

DESIGNED BY LOONEY RICKS KISS ARCHITECTS, INC.

Plan # HPK3800334

First Floor: 3,932 sq. ft.

Second Floor: 1,227 sq. ft.

Total: 5,159 sq. ft.

Bonus Space: 596 sq. ft.

Bedrooms: 5

Bathrooms: 4 ½

Width: 102' - 0"

Depth: 103' - 0"

Foundation: Slab

Price Code: L1

1-800-850-1491 • EPLANS.COM

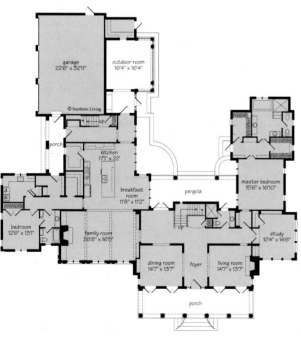

FIRST FLOOR

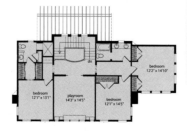

SECOND FLOOR

ARCHITECTURAL RENDERING: MILES MELTON

5,280 square feet

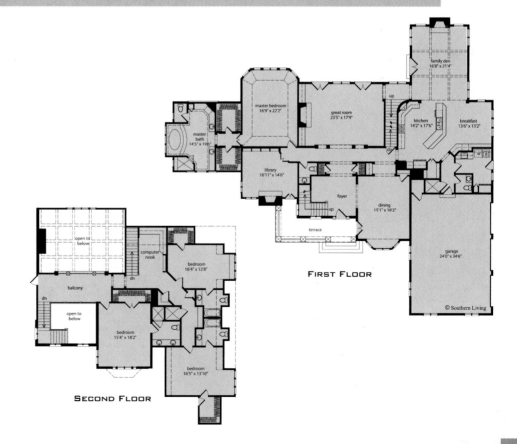

DESIGNED BY SPITZMILLER AND NORRIS, INC.

Plan# HPK3800335

First Floor: 3,608 sq. ft.

Second Floor: 1,672 sq. ft.

Total: 5,280 sq. ft.

Bedrooms: 4

Bathrooms: 4 full + 2 half

Width: 98' - 5"

Depth: 86' - 0"

Foundation: Unfinished Basement

Price Code: L2

1-800-850-1491 • EPLANS.COM

FIRST FLOOR

SECOND FLOOR

·BRITTANY·

5,203 square feet

Designed by Spitzmiller and Norris, Inc.

Plan# HPK3800336

First Floor: 3,498 sq. ft.

Second Floor: 1,705 sq. ft.

Total: 5,203 sq. ft.

Bonus Space: 460 sq. ft.

Bedrooms: 4

Bathrooms: 6 full + 2 half

Width: 88' - 0"

Depth: 92' - 0"

Foundation: Unfinished Basement

Price Code: L2

1-800-850-1491 • EPLANS.COM

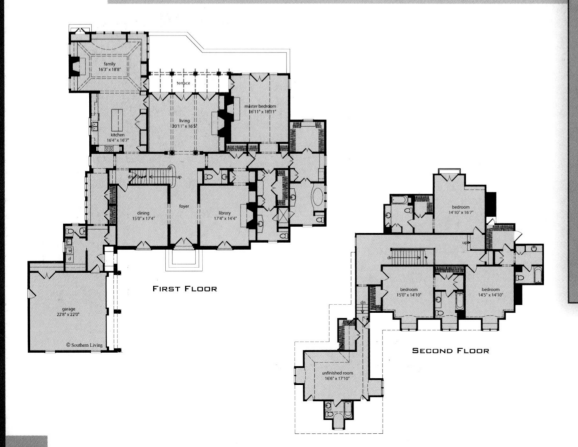

First Floor

Second Floor

5,537 square feet

ARCHITECTURAL RENDERING: GREG HAVENS

Plan# HPK3800337

First Floor: 3,150 sq. ft.

Second Floor: 2,387 sq. ft.

Total: 5,537 sq. ft.

Bedrooms: 4

Bathrooms: 3 ½

Width: 81' - 0"

Depth: 158' - 5"

Foundation: Slab

Price Code: L4

1-800-850-1491 • EPLANS.COM

DESIGNED BY BRYAN & CONTRERAS, LLC

FIRST FLOOR

SECOND FLOOR

~SUMMER LAKE~

5,378 square feet

ARCHITECTURAL RENDERING: MILES MELTON

DESIGNED BY BRYAN & CONTRERAS, LLC

FIRST FLOOR

SECOND FLOOR

Plan# HPK3800338

First Floor: 2,850 sq. ft.

Second Floor: 2,528 sq. ft.

Total: 5,378 sq. ft.

Bedrooms: 4

Bathrooms: 4 ½

Width: 101' - 2"

Depth: 62' - 10"

Foundation: Crawlspace, Slab

Price Code: L4

1-800-850-1491 • EPLANS.COM

·LAVENDALE·

5,397 square feet

DESIGNED BY GARY/RAGSDALE, INC.

Plan# HPK3800339

First Floor: 3,173 sq. ft.

Second Floor: 2,224 sq. ft.

Total: 5,397 sq. ft.

Bonus Space: 221 sq. ft.

Bedrooms: 4

Bathrooms: 3 ½

Width: 61' - 11"

Depth: 99' - 3"

Foundation: Slab

Price Code: L2

1-800-850-1491 • EPLANS.COM

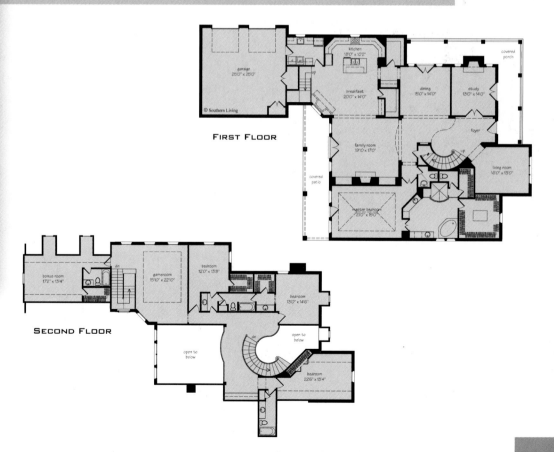

FIRST FLOOR

SECOND FLOOR

Embassy Row

5,474 square feet

DESIGNED BY SPITZMILLER AND NORRIS, INC.

Plan# HPK3800342

First Floor: 3,329 sq. ft.

Second Floor: 2,145 sq. ft.

Total: 5,474 sq. ft.

Bedrooms: 6

Bathrooms: 4 full + 2 half

Width: 100' - 0"

Depth: 62' - 0"

Foundation: Unfinished Basement

Price Code: L2

1-800-850-1491 • EPLANS.COM

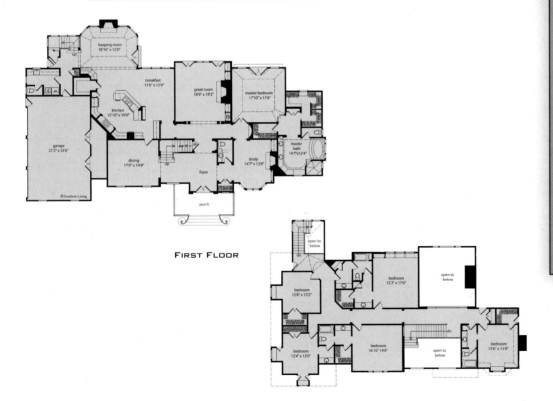

FIRST FLOOR

SECOND FLOOR

5,510 square feet

Plan # **HPK3800344**

First Floor: 3,456 sq. ft.

Second Floor: 2,054 sq. ft.

Total: 5,510 sq. ft.

Bedrooms: 5

Bathrooms: 4 ½

Width: 85' - 0"

Depth: 92' - 0"

Foundation: Unfinished Basement

Price Code: L2

1-800-850-1491 • EPLANS.COM

DESIGNED BY SPITZMILLER AND NORRIS, INC.

FIRST FLOOR

SECOND FLOOR

5,576
square feet

ARCHITECTURAL RENDERING: BRIAN BARKS

DESIGNED BY SPITZMILLER AND NORRIS, INC.

Plan# HPK3800345

First Floor: 3,875 sq. ft.

Second Floor: 1,701 sq. ft.

Total: 5,576 sq. ft.

Bonus Space: 194 sq. ft.

Bedrooms: 4 or 5

Bathrooms: 4 full + 2 half

Width: 154' - 0"

Depth: 71' - 0"

Foundation: Unfinished Basement

Price Code: L4

1-800-850-1491 • EPLANS.COM

FIRST FLOOR

SECOND FLOOR

SHELBURNE

6,290 square feet

Plan# HPK3800347

First Floor: 4,118 sq. ft.

Second Floor: 2,172 sq. ft.

Total: 6,290 sq. ft.

Bedrooms: 5

Bathrooms: 5 ½

Width: 101' - 10"

Depth: 75' - 10"

Foundation: Unfinished Basement

Price Code: L2

1-800-850-1491 • EPLANS.COM

DESIGNED BY SPITZMILLER AND NORRIS, INC.

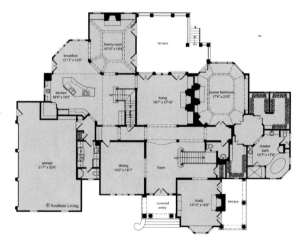

FIRST FLOOR

SECOND FLOOR

6,320 square feet

DESIGNED BY SPITZMILLER AND NORRIS, INC.

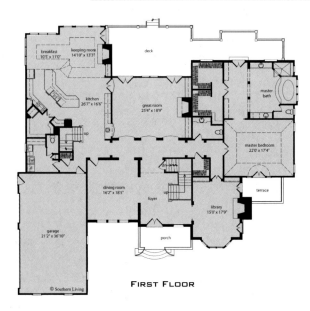

FIRST FLOOR

© Southern Living

SECOND FLOOR

Plan# HPK3800348

First Floor: 3,929 sq. ft.

Second Floor: 2,391 sq. ft.

Total: 6,320 sq. ft.

Bedrooms: 5

Bathrooms: 5 full + 2 half

Width: 88' - 9"

Depth: 82' - 3"

Foundation: Unfinished Basement

Price Code: L2

1-800-850-1491 • EPLANS.COM

DESIGNED BY SPITZMILLER AND NORRIS, INC.

Plan# HPK3800341

First Floor: 3,317 sq. ft.

Second Floor: 2,150 sq. ft.

Total: 5,467 sq. ft.

Bonus Space: 372 sq. ft.

Bedrooms: 4

Bathrooms: 4 full + 2 half

Width: 78' - 0"

Depth: 95' - 8"

Foundation: Unfinished Basement

Price Code: L4

1-800-850-1491 • EPLANS.COM

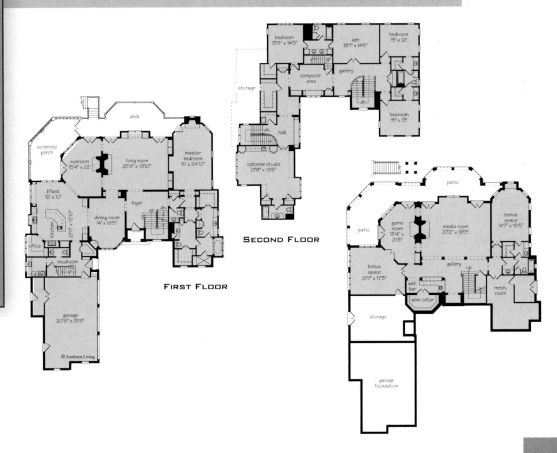

FIRST FLOOR

SECOND FLOOR

For 20 years, *Southern Living*® magazine has been collecting exclusive home plans from the South's top architects and designers. From formal and deeply elegant traditional homes, to casual and stylish vacation cottages, the *Southern Living* plan collection has been the favorite of the magazine's readers as well as other admirers of Southern architecture.

The plans gathered here represent the very best of the Southern Living portfolio. Each home finds a unique balance of historically influenced exteriors—Neoclassical, Colonial, Craftsman, European—and modern approaches to interior layout. Along with beautifully presented formal spaces, each design caters to the comfort and convenience of homeowners with the inclusion of flexible utility spaces, such as mudrooms and offices. Outdoor living areas, present as extended entertaining spaces or as private retreats, are equally important features in the *Southern Living* home.

WHAT YOU'LL GET WITH YOUR ORDER

The contents of each designer's blueprint package is unique, but all contain detailed, high-quality working drawings. You can expect to find the following standard elements in most sets of plans:

ABOUT OUR PLANS

Southern Living working drawings offer a complete conceptual design of our homes. However, our working drawings do not include fully engineered construction documents.

Square Footage Estimates

The heated square footage estimate provided on the small-scale plan does not include the garage, porches, decks, bonus spaces, storage areas, or the basement level. We recommend that your builder verify all of the plan's dimensions and square footage calculations, taking into consideration any modifications or additions.

Also keep in mind that there are several different formulas for calculating square footage, and your builder's estimate may differ slightly from ours.

Estimating Construction Costs

Accurate construction-cost estimates should be made from the working drawings. We suggest consulting with a local builder to provide an estimate of those specific costs. Sometimes your builder can give you a ballpark estimate based on the information provided in the descriptions in this magazine. However, you will need working drawings for more accuracy.

After you order the plans, you may want to get at least two separate estimates from contractors for comparison because many variables can affect cost. The contractor should provide the material quantity lists; costs may vary depending on choice of materials, availability of materials within an area, labor costs, choice of finishes, and degree of detail.

Copy Restrictions and Copyright Information

All *Southern Living* House Plans are protected under the United States Copyright Law. Blueprints may not be resold, copied, or reproduced by any means. When you purchase a blueprint from *Southern Living* House Plans, you are licensed the right to build one residence. *Southern Living* designers and architects retain all rights, title, and ownership to the original design and documents.

What's Included in a Blueprint Package

* **Foundations and floor-framing plans.** This shows the complete foundation layout, including drawings for a basement, slab, or crawlspace. Only one type is included with each plan. Support walls and all necessary dimensions are part of this sheet. Please note that there is no beam layout included with foundation plans.

* **Dimensioned floor plans.** Each floor of the house is shown in detail. The position and dimensions of floors, windows, staircases, and columns are clearly indicated.

* **Suggested electrical plans.** Included are suggestions for the placement of switches, outlets, and fixtures. Local code will dictate exact placement. This will be determined by your builder. Select plans may not include electrical plans.

* **Typical wall section.** This cross section shows a typical wall from footings to roofline.

* **Exterior elevations.** These pages provide drawings of the front, rear, left, and right sides of the house. They also suggest materials for the structure and detail work.

* **Interior elevations.** This includes detailed drawings of cabinets, fireplaces, columns, other built-in units, or suggested trim profiles. CHK Architects plans from the American Traditions Series do not include interior details.

* **Suggested exterior and interior finish schedules.**

* **Doors and window sizes.**

What's Not Included

* **Heating and plumbing plans.** These plans should be supplied by local subcontractors.

* **Material quantity lists.** Obtain these lists from the contractor you choose or from a local building materials supplier.

* **Architectural and engineering seals.** Some cities and slates require a licensed architect or engineer to review and seal, or officially approve, a blueprint prior to construction due to concerns over energy costs, safety, and other factors. Due to varying local requirements *Southern Living* House Plans is unable to offer these seals. Contact a local building official to find out if such a review is required.

Changing Your Plans

We encourage you to personalize your *Southern Living* House Plan. In an effort to make this process quicker and easier, we offer reproducible prints and electronic CAD files on selected plans. Please note that CAD and Reproducible files come with a one-time construction license and are not returnable.

Rear Elevations

If you would like to see a rear elevation, call toll-free 1–800–850–1491, or visit eplans.com. We offer a complimentary reduced sheet taken directly from our blueprints. This sheet cannot be used for construction purposes, but it will provide a detailed look at the back of the home.

Reverse Plans

Sometimes, to better site a house, it is necessary for the builder to use a reverse set of plans (often called a mirror image or flopped set). If your builder needs a reverse set, order one reverse and the rest standard sets of plans.

Building Codes

Our plans are designed to meet national building standards, but because of varying interpretations, and the fact that codes are subject to change, we cannot warrant compliance with any of the specific building codes and ordinances.

Your local builder or an engineer should review the plan you choose and ensure that it complies with all applicable building codes and subdivision restrictions. We are not responsible for any revisions or interpretations made by third parties involved in the construction of your homes.

BEFORE YOU CALL

You are making a terrific decision to use a pre-drawn house plan—it is one you can make with confidence, knowing that your blueprints are crafted by national-award-winning certified residential designers and architects, and trusted by builders.

Once you've selected the plan you want—or even if you have questions along the way—our experienced customer service representatives are available to help you navigate the home-building process. To help them provide you with even better service, please consider the following questions before you call:

■ **Have you chosen or purchased your lot?**
If so, please review the building setback requirements of your local building authority before you call. You don't need to have a lot before ordering plans, but if you own land already, please have the width and depth dimensions handy when you call.

■ **Have you chosen a builder?**
Involving your builder in the plan selection and evaluation process may be beneficial. Luckily, builders know they can have confidence with pre-drawn plans because they've been designed for livability, functionality, and typically are builder-proven at successful home sites across the country.

■ **Do you need a construction loan?**
Construction loans are unique because they involve determining the value of something that is not yet constructed. Several lenders offer convenient construction-to-permanent loans. It is important to choose a good lending partner—one who will help guide you through the application and appraisal process. Most will even help you evaluate your contractor to ensure reliability and credit worthiness.

■ **How many sets of plans do you need?**
Building a home can typically require a number of sets of blueprints—one for yourself, two or three for the builder and subcontractors, two for the local building department, and one or more for your lender. For this reason, we offer 8-set and Reproducible plan packages, but your best value is the CAD Package, which includes a copy of the digital file used to create the home design. By using CAD software, it is easy to print hard copies of blueprints. Reproducible plans are tremendously flexible in that they allow you to make up to 12 duplicates of the plan so you have enough copies of the plan for everyone involved in the financing and construction of your home.

■ **Do you have to make any changes to meet local building codes?**
While all of our plans are drawn to meet national building codes at the time they were created, many areas require that plans be stamped by a local engineer to certify that they meet local building codes. Building codes are updated frequently and can vary by state, county, city, or municipality. Contact your local building inspection department, office of planning and zoning, or department of permits to determine how your local codes will affect your construction project. The best way to assure that you can make changes to your plan, if necessary, is to purchase a Reproducible or CAD Plan Package.

■ **Has everyone—from family members to contractors—been involved in selecting the plan?**
Building a new home is an exciting process, and using pre-drawn plans is a great way to realize your dreams. Make sure that everyone involved has had an opportunity to review the plan you've selected. While Hanley Wood does have an exchange policy, it's best to be sure all parties agree on your selection before you buy.

CALL TOLL-FREE 1–800–850–1491

Source Key
HPK38

TERMS & CONDITIONS
OUR 90-DAY EXCHANGE POLICY

BUY WITH CONFIDENCE!

As the plan fulfillment partner to *Southern Living*, ePlans.com is committed to ensuring your satisfaction with your blueprint order, which is why we offer a 90-day exchange policy. With the exception of Reproducible and CAD Plan Package orders, we will exchange your entire first order for an equal or greater number of blueprints from our plan collection within 90 days of the original order. The entire content of your original order must be returned before an exchange will be processed. Please call our customer service department at 1-888-690-1116 for your return authorization number and shipping instructions. If the returned blueprints look used, redlined, or copied, we will not honor your exchange. Fees for exchanging your blueprints are as follows: 20% of the amount of the original order, plus the difference in cost if exchanging for a design in a higher price bracket or less the difference in cost if exchanging for a design in a lower price bracket. (Because they can be copied, Reproducible or CAD blueprints are not exchangeable or refundable.) Please call for current postage and handling prices. Shipping and handling charges are not refundable.

ARCHITECTURAL AND ENGINEERING SEALS

Some cities and states now require that a licensed architect or engineer review and "seal" a blueprint, or officially approve it, prior to construction. Prior to application for a building permit or the start of actual construction, we strongly advise that you consult your local building official who can tell you if such a review is required.

LOCAL BUILDING CODES AND ZONING REQUIREMENTS

Each plan was designed to meet or exceed the requirements of a nationally recognized model building code in effect at the time and place the plan was drawn. Typically plans designed after the year 2000 conform to the International Residential Building Code (IRC 2000 or 2003). The IRC is comprised of portions of the three major codes below. Plans drawn before 2000 conform to one of the three recognized building codes in effect at the time: Building Officials and Code Administrators (BOCA)

**CALL TOLL FREE
1-800-850-1491
OR VISIT
EPLANS.COM**

International, Inc.; the Southern Building Code Congress International, (SBCCI) Inc.; the International Conference of Building Officials (ICBO); or the Council of American Building Officials (CABO).

Because of the great differences in geography and climate throughout the United States and Canada, each state, county, and municipality has its own building codes, zone requirements, ordinances, and building regulations. Your plan may need to be modified to comply with local requirements. In addition, you may need to obtain permits or inspections from local governments before and in the course of construction. We authorize the use of the blueprints on the express condition that you consult a local licensed architect or engineer of your choice prior to beginning construction and strictly comply with all local building codes, zoning requirements, and other applicable laws, regulations, ordinances, and requirements. Notice: Plans for homes to be built in Nevada must be redrawn by a Nevada-registered professional. Consult your local building official for more information on this subject.

TERMS AND CONDITIONS

These designs are protected under the terms of United States Copyright Law and may not be copied or reproduced in any way, by any means, unless you have purchased a Reproducible Plan Package and signed the accompanying license to modify and copy the plan, which clearly indicates your right to modify, copy, or reproduce. We authorize the use of your chosen design as an aid in the construction of ONE (1) single- or multifamily home only. You may not use this design to build a second dwelling or multiple dwellings without purchasing another blueprint or blueprints or paying additional design fees. Multi-use fees vary by designer—please call one of our experienced sales representatives for a quote.

DISCLAIMER

The designers we work with have put substantial care and effort into the creation of their blueprints. However, because we cannot provide on-site consultation, supervision, and control over actual construction, and because of the great variance in local building requirements, building practices, and soil, seismic, weather, and other conditions, WE MAKE NO WARRANTY OF ANY KIND, EXPRESS OR IMPLIED, WITH RESPECT TO THE CONTENT OR USE OF THE BLUEPRINTS, INCLUDING BUT NOT LIMITED TO ANY WARRANTY OF MERCHANTABILITY OR OF FITNESS FOR A PARTICULAR PURPOSE. ITEMS, PRICES, TERMS, AND CONDITIONS ARE SUBJECT TO CHANGE WITHOUT NOTICE.

IMPORTANT COPYRIGHT NOTICE
From the Council of Publishing Home Designers

Blueprints for residential construction (or working drawings, as they are often called in the industry) are copyrighted intellectual property, protected under the terms of the United States Copyright Law and, therefore, cannot be copied legally for use in building. The following are some guidelines to help you get what you need to build your home, without violating copyright law:

1. HOME PLANS ARE COPYRIGHTED

Just like books, movies, and songs, home plans receive protection under the federal copyright laws. The copyright laws prevent anyone, other than the copyright owner, from reproducing, modifying, or reusing the plans or design without permission of the copyright owner.

2. DO NOT COPY DESIGNS OR FLOOR PLANS FROM ANY PUBLICATION, ELECTRONIC MEDIA, OR EXISTING HOME

It is illegal to copy, change, or redraw home designs found in a plan book, CDROM or on the Internet. The right to modify plans is one of the exclusive rights of copyright. It is also illegal to copy or redraw a constructed home that is protected by copyright, even if you have never seen the plans for the home. If you find a plan or home that you like, you must purchase a set of plans from an authorized source. The plans may not be lent, given away, or sold by the purchaser.

3. DO NOT USE PLANS TO BUILD MORE THAN ONE HOUSE

The original purchaser of house plans is typically licensed to build a single home from the plans. Building more than one home from the plans without permission is an infringement of the home designer's copyright. The purchase of a multiple-set package of plans is for the construction of a single home only. The purchase of additional sets of plans does not grant the right to construct more than one home.

4. HOUSE PLANS IN THE FORM OF BLUEPRINTS OR BLACKLINES CANNOT BE COPIED OR REPRODUCED

Plans, blueprints, or blacklines, unless they are reproducibles, cannot be copied or reproduced without prior written consent of the copyright owner. Copy shops and blueprinters are prohibited from making copies of these plans without the copyright release letter you receive with reproducible plans.

5. HOUSE PLANS IN THE FORM OF BLUEPRINTS OR BLACKLINES CANNOT BE REDRAWN

Plans cannot be modified or redrawn without first obtaining the copyright owner's permission. With your purchase of plans, you are licensed to make non-structural changes by "red-lining" the purchased plans. If you need to make structural changes or need to redraw the plans for any reason, you must purchase a reproducible set of plans (see topic 6) which includes a license to modify the plans. Blueprints do not come with a license to make structural changes or to redraw the plans. You may not reuse or sell the modified design.

6. REPRODUCIBILE HOME PLANS

Reproducible plans (for example sepias, mylars, CAD files, electronic files, and vellums) come with a license to make modifications to the plans. Once modified, the plans can be taken to a local copy shop or blueprinter to make up to 10 or 12 copies of the plans to use in the construction of a single home. Only one home can be constructed from any single purchased set of reproducible plans either in original form or as modified. The license to modify and copy must be completed and returned before the plan will be shipped.

7. MODIFIED DESIGNS CANNOT BE REUSED

Even if you are licensed to make modifications to a copyrighted design, the modified design is not free from the original designer's copyright. The sale or reuse of the modified design is prohibited. Also, be aware that any modification to plans relieves the original designer from liability for design defects and voids all warranties expressed or implied.

8. WHO IS RESPONSIBLE FOR COPYRIGHT INFRINGEMENT?

Any party who participates in a copyright violation may be responsible including the purchaser, designers, architects, engineers, drafters, homeowners, builders, contractors, sub-contractors, copy shops, blueprinters, developers, and real estate agencies. It does not matter whether or not the individual knows that a violation is being committed. Ignorance of the law is not a valid defense.

9. PLEASE RESPECT HOME DESIGN COPYRIGHTS

In the event of any suspected violation of a copyright, or if there is any uncertainty about the plans purchased, the publisher, architect, designer, or the Council of Publishing Home Designers (www.cphd.org) should be contacted before proceeding. Rewards are sometimes offered for information about home design copyright infringement.

10. PENALTIES FOR INFRINGEMENT

Penalties for violating a copyright may be severe. The responsible parties are required to pay actual damages caused by the infringement (which may be substantial), plus any profits made by the infringer commissions to include all profits from the sale of any home built from an infringing design. The copyright law also allows for the recovery of statutory damages, which may be as high as $150,000 for each infringement. Finally, the infringer may be required to pay legal fees which often exceed the damages.

PAGE	PLAN #	PLAN NAME	PRICE CODE	8-SET PACKAGE	REPRODUCIBLE PACKAGE	CAD PACKAGE
12	HPK3800001	Oak Creek	A2	$620	$765	N/A
13	HPK3800002	Beachside Bungalow	A2	$620	$765	N/A
14	HPK3800003	Hilltop	A2	$620	$765	N/A
15	HPK3800004	Crooked Creek	A2	$620	$765	N/A
16	HPK3800005	Eagle's Nest	A3	$690	$870	N/A
17	HPK3800006	Smokey Creek	A2	$620	$765	N/A
18	HPK3800007	Little Red	A3	$690	$870	N/A
19	HPK3800008	Grayson Trail	A3	$690	$870	N/A
20	HPK3800009	Mill Springs	A3	$690	$870	N/A
21	HPK3800010	Deer Run	A2	$620	$765	N/A
22	HPK3800011	The Ozarks	A3	$690	$870	N/A
23	HPK3800012	Walnut Cove	C1	$810	$1,000	N/A
24	HPK3800013	Foxglove Cottage	A3	$690	$870	N/A
25	HPK3800014	Fox River	C1	$810	$1,000	N/A
26	HPK3800015	Hunting Creek Alternate	C1	$810	$1,000	N/A
27	HPK3800016	Chestnut Lane	A3	$690	$870	N/A
28	HPK3800350	Sawgrass Cottage Alternate	C3	$910	$1,145	N/A
29	HPK3800017	Dogtrot	A3	$690	$870	N/A
30	HPK3800018	Sweet Water	A3	$690	$870	N/A
31	HPK3800019	Banning Court	C1	$810	$1,000	N/A
32	HPK3800020	Rustic Beach Cottage	C1	$810	$1,000	N/A
33	HPK3800021	Caribbean Getaway	A3	$690	$870	N/A
34	HPK3800022	Heather Place	A3	$690	$870	N/A
35	HPK3800023	River Birch	C1	$810	$1,000	N/A
36	HPK3800024	Forsythia	C1	$810	$1,000	N/A
37	HPK3800025	Gardenia	A3	$690	$870	N/A
38	HPK3800026	Hunting Creek	C1	$810	$1,000	N/A
39	HPK3800027	Ashley River Cottage	C1	$810	$1,000	N/A
40	HPK3800028	Sugarplum	A3	$690	$870	N/A
41	HPK3800029	Ellsworth Cottage	C1	$810	$1,000	N/A
42	HPK3800031	The Sage House	C3	$910	$1,145	N/A
43	HPK3800032	Redbud	A3	$690	$870	N/A
44	HPK3800033	Coosaw River Cottage	C3	$910	$1,145	N/A
45	HPK3800034	Tidewater Retreat	C3	$910	$1,145	$1,915
46	HPK3800035	Ashton	C1	$810	$1,000	N/A
47	HPK3800036	Cedarbrook	C1	$810	$1,000	N/A
48	HPK3800037	Beaufort Cottage	C1	$810	$1,000	N/A
49	HPK3800038	Sawgrass Cottage	C3	$910	$1,145	N/A
50	HPK3800039	Rosemary Cottage	C1	$810	$1,000	N/A
51	HPK3800040	Silverhill	C3	$910	$1,145	N/A
52	HPK3800041	Camellia Cottage	A3	$690	$870	N/A
53	HPK3800042	Bucksport Cottage	C1	$810	$1,000	N/A
54	HPK3800043	Wisteria	C3	$910	$1,145	N/A
55	HPK3800044	Capeside Cottage	A4	$750	$935	N/A
56	HPK3800045	Gresham Creek Cottage	A3	$690	$870	N/A
57	HPK3800046	Jasmine	C1	$810	$1,000	N/A
58	HPK3800047	Piedmont Cottage	C3	$910	$1,145	N/A
59	HPK3800048	Turtle Lake Cottage	C1	$810	$1,000	N/A
60	HPK3800049	Winonna Park	A2	$620	$765	N/A
62	HPK3800050	River Cliff Cottage	L4	$1,440	$1,850	N/A
63	HPK3800051	Windsong Cottage	A3	$690	$870	N/A
64	HPK3800052	Elizabeth's Place	C1	$810	$1,000	N/A
65	HPK3800053	Couples Cottage	C3	$910	$1,145	N/A
66	HPK3800054	Bermuda Bluff Cottage	L2	$1,195	$1,515	N/A
67	HPK3800055	River Run	A4	$750	$935	N/A
68	HPK3800056	Forestdale	C3	$910	$1,145	$1,915
69	HPK3800057	Spartina Cottage	C3	$910	$1,145	N/A
70	HPK3800058	Azalea	C1	$810	$1,000	N/A

PAGE	PLAN #	PLAN NAME	PRICE CODE	8-SET PACKAGE	REPRODUCIBLE PACKAGE	CAD PACKAGE
71	HPK3800059	Walterboro Ridge	C1	$810	$1,000	N/A
72	HPK3800060	West Bay Landing	L4	$1,440	$1,850	N/A
73	HPK3800061	Barrier Island Escape	C3	$910	$1,145	N/A
74	HPK3800062	Ogletree Lane	C1	$810	$1,000	N/A
75	HPK3800063	Glencoe Springs	C1	$810	$1,000	N/A
76	HPK3800064	Red Bay Cottage	C1	$810	$1,000	N/A
77	HPK3800065	Cotton Hill Cottage	C1	$810	$1,000	N/A
78	HPK3800066	Miss Maggie's House	C1	$810	$1,000	N/A
79	HPK3800067	Chinaberry	C1	$810	$1,000	N/A
80	HPK3800351	Chestnut Hill Alternate	L4	$1,440	$1,850	N/A
81	HPK3800068	Bayside Cottage	C1	$810	$1,000	N/A
82	HPK3800069	Williams Bluff	C1	$810	$1,000	N/A
83	HPK3800070	Lowcountry Cottage	C1	$810	$1,000	N/A
84	HPK3800071	Oakleaf	C1	$810	$1,000	N/A
85	HPK3800072	Maple Hill	C1	$810	$1,000	N/A
86	HPK3800073	Inlet Retreat	C3	$910	$1,145	N/A
87	HPK3800074	Carlisle House	C1	$810	$1,000	N/A
88	HPK3800075	Summer Cottage	C1	$810	$1,000	N/A
89	HPK3800076	Aiken Ridge	C3	$910	$1,145	N/A
92	HPK3800077	New Rustic Oaks	C3	$910	$1,145	N/A
93	HPK3800078	Bradley House	C3	$910	$1,145	N/A
94	HPK3800236	St. Helena House	C3	$910	$1,145	N/A
95	HPK3800080	Shiloh Creek	C1	$810	$1,000	N/A
96	HPK3800081	New Round Hill	C3	$910	$1,145	N/A
97	HPK3800082	Amberview Way	C1	$810	$1,000	N/A
98	HPK3800083	Angel Oak Point	C1	$810	$1,000	N/A
99	HPK3800084	Bay Harbor Cottage	C1	$810	$1,000	N/A
100	HPK3800085	River View Cottage	C3	$910	$1,145	N/A
101	HPK3800086	Richmond	L1	$1,115	$1,390	N/A
102	HPK3800087	Wildmere Cottage	C3	$910	$1,145	N/A
103	HPK3800088	Franklin House	L4	$1,440	$1,850	N/A
104	HPK3800089	Winnsboro Heights	C1	$810	$1,000	N/A
105	HPK3800090	Valensole	C3	$910	$1,145	$1,915
106	HPK3800091	Tabor Lane	A4	$750	$935	N/A
107	HPK3800092	Rambert Place	C1	$810	$1,000	N/A
108	HPK3800093	Mabry Cottage	C3	$910	$1,145	N/A
109	HPK3800094	Peachtree Cottage	C3	$910	$1,145	N/A
110	HPK3800095	Lakeside Cottage	A4	$750	$935	N/A
111	HPK3800096	Pennington Point	C3	$910	$1,145	N/A
112	HPK3800097	New Oxford	L1	$1,115	$1,390	N/A
113	HPK3800098	Montereau	L1	$1,115	$1,390	N/A
114	HPK3800099	Glen View Cottage	C1	$810	$1,000	N/A
115	HPK3800100	Beaumont	C3	$910	$1,145	N/A
116	HPK3800175	Forest Ridge	C1	$810	$1,000	N/A
117	HPK3800102	Pleasant Hill Cottage	C3	$910	$1,145	N/A
118	HPK3800103	Whitestone	C3	$910	$1,145	N/A
119	HPK3800104	Laurel Woods	C3	$910	$1,145	N/A
120	HPK3800105	Woodridge	A4	$750	$935	N/A
121	HPK3800106	Stafford Place	A4	$750	$935	N/A
122	HPK3800107	Westbury Park	C3	$910	$1,145	N/A
123	HPK3800108	Valleydale	L2	$1,195	$1,515	N/A
124	HPK3800109	Stonebridge Cottage	C3	$910	$1,145	N/A
125	HPK3800110	Our Gulf Coast Cottage	C3	$910	$1,145	N/A
126	HPK3800111	Camden Cottage	L4	$1,440	$1,850	N/A
127	HPK3800112	Asbury	C3	$910	$1,145	N/A
128	HPK3800113	Moore's Creek	C3	$910	$1,145	N/A
129	HPK3800114	Honeysuckle Hill	C3	$910	$1,145	N/A

PAGE	PLAN #	PLAN NAME	PRICE CODE	8-SET PACKAGE	REPRODUCIBLE PACKAGE	CAD PACKAGE
130	HPK3800115	Belhaven Place	C3	$910	$1,145	$1,915
131	HPK3800116	Stone Harbor	C3	$910	$1,145	N/A
132	HPK3800117	Pine Hill Cottage	C3	$910	$1,145	N/A
133	HPK3800119	Fairmont Heights	L1	$1,115	$1,390	N/A
134	HPK3800118	Sand Mountain House	L4	$1,440	$1,850	N/A
136	HPK3800120	Bluff Haven	C1	$810	$1,000	N/A
137	HPK3800354	Family Central	A4	$750	$935	N/A
138	HPK3800122	Cottage Of The Year	L4	$1,440	$1,850	N/A
139	HPK3800123	Harrison Place	C3	$910	$1,145	$1,915
140	HPK3800124	New Lynwood	C3	$910	$1,145	N/A
141	HPK3800125	Cloverdale	C1	$810	$1,000	N/A
142	HPK3800126	Poplar Creek Cottage	C3	$910	$1,145	N/A
143	HPK3800127	New Meadowlark	C3	$910	$1,145	N/A
144	HPK3800128	New Wyntuck	C1	$810	$1,000	N/A
145	HPK3800129	Mandeville Place	C3	$910	$1,145	N/A
146	HPK3800130	Spring Lake Cottage	L4	$1,440	$1,850	$3,140
147	HPK3800131	Alta Vista	L4	$1,440	$1,850	$3,140
148	HPK3800132	Overton Place	C3	$910	$1,145	$1,915
149	HPK3800133	Turnball Park	C3	$910	$1,145	N/A
150	HPK3800134	Elderberry Place	C3	$910	$1,145	N/A
151	HPK3800135	Arborview	C3	$910	$1,145	$1,915
152	HPK3800136	Grissom Trail	C1	$810	$1,000	$1,735
153	HPK3800137	Saddlebrook House	C3	$910	$1,145	N/A
154	HPK3800138	Country French Southern Charm	C3	$910	$1,145	N/A
155	HPK3800139	Whitmore	A4	$750	$935	N/A
156	HPK3800140	Bluff Towne Cottage	C3	$910	$1,145	N/A
157	HPK3800141	Bienville	L1	$1,115	$1,390	N/A
158	HPK3800142	Sea Island House	SQ5	N/A	$2,190	N/A
162	HPK3800143	Harborside Cottage	C1	$810	$1,000	N/A
163	HPK3800144	McKenzie Cottage	C1	$810	$1,000	N/A
164	HPK3800145	Woodmere Creek	C3	$910	$1,145	N/A
165	HPK3800146	Silver Springs	C3	$910	$1,145	N/A
168	HPK3800147	St. Marie	C3	$910	$1,145	$1,915
169	HPK3800148	Addison Place	C3	$910	$1,145	N/A
170	HPK3800149	New Cooper's Bluff	L1	$1,115	$1,390	N/A
171	HPK3800150	Red Springs	C3	$910	$1,145	N/A
172	HPK3800151	Stonybrook	L1	$1,115	$1,390	N/A
173	HPK3800152	Kilburne	C3	$910	$1,145	N/A
174	HPK3800153	Mayesville	C3	$910	$1,145	N/A
175	HPK3800154	New Holly Springs	L1	$1,115	$1,390	N/A
176	HPK3800155	Norfolk	L1	$1,115	$1,390	N/A
177	HPK3800156	New Shannon	C3	$910	$1,145	N/A
178	HPK3800352	Crabapple Cottage Alternate	L4	$1,440	$1,850	N/A
179	HPK3800159	Covington Cove	L1	$1,115	$1,390	N/A
180	HPK3800160	Northridge	C3	$910	$1,145	$1,915
181	HPK3800161	Iberville	L1	$1,115	$1,390	N/A
182	HPK3800162	Southberry Farm	L1	$1,115	$1,390	N/A
183	HPK3800163	Fairfield Place	C3	$910	$1,145	N/A
184	HPK3800164	Wesley	C3	$910	$1,145	N/A
185	HPK3800165	Port Gibson	C3	$910	$1,145	N/A
186	HPK3800166	Bay Point Cottage	C3	$910	$1,145	N/A
187	HPK3800167	Berrywood	C3	$910	$1,145	N/A
188	HPK3800168	Cherrybrook	C3	$910	$1,145	N/A
189	HPK3800169	River Bend Farmhouse	L4	$1,440	$1,850	$3,140
190	HPK3800170	New Brookhaven	C3	$910	$1,145	N/A
191	HPK3800171	Arden Gate	L2	$1,195	$1,515	N/A
192	HPK3800172	Allendale	L1	$1,115	$1,390	N/A

PAGE	PLAN #	PLAN NAME	PRICE CODE	8-SET PACKAGE	REPRODUCIBLE PACKAGE	CAD PACKAGE
193	HPK3800173	Lousiana Garden Cottage	C3	$910	$1,145	N/A
194	HPK3800174	Cumberland	C3	$910	$1,145	N/A
195	HPK3800177	Middleton Park	C3	$910	$1,145	N/A
196	HPK3800178	Camden Way	L1	$1,115	$1,390	N/A
197	HPK3800179	Lanier	C3	$910	$1,145	N/A
198	HPK3800180	Rosehaven	L4	$1,440	$1,850	N/A
199	HPK3800176	Bedford Cottage	L1	$1,115	$1,390	$2,500
200	HPK3800202	Poplar Grove	L4	$1,440	$1,850	N/A
204	HPK3800121	Poppy Point	C3	$910	$1,145	$1,915
205	HPK3800183	Juliette	L1	$1,115	$1,390	N/A
206	HPK3800184	Chestnut Hill	L4	$1,440	$1,850	N/A
207	HPK3800185	Barrow Lake	L1	$1,115	$1,390	N/A
208	HPK3800186	Gavinbrooke	L1	$1,115	$1,390	N/A
209	HPK3800187	Inanda House	L4	$1,440	$1,850	N/A
210	HPK3800188	Willow Bend	L1	$1,115	$1,390	N/A
211	HPK3800189	Woodlawn	C3	$910	$1,145	N/A
212	HPK3800190	Andrews	C3	$910	$1,145	N/A
213	HPK3800191	Summerfield Chase	L1	$1,115	$1,390	N/A
214	HPK3800192	Cape May	L1	$1,115	$1,390	N/A
215	HPK3800193	Clayfield Place	L1	$1,115	$1,390	N/A
216	HPK3800194	Carrington Court	L1	$1,115	$1,390	$2,500
217	HPK3800195	The Orchard House	L4	$1,440	$1,850	N/A
218	HPK3800196	Grand and Gracious	C3	$910	$1,145	N/A
219	HPK3800197	Arden	C3	$910	$1,145	N/A
220	HPK3800198	A Courtyard Home	L2	$1,195	$1,515	N/A
221	HPK3800199	Kennesaw Country House	C3	$910	$1,145	N/A
222	HPK3800200	Brookwood Cottage	L1	$1,115	$1,390	N/A
223	HPK3800201	Presque Isle	C3	$910	$1,145	N/A
224	HPK3800182	Blount Springs Retreat	L4	$1,440	$1,850	N/A
225	HPK3800203	Oldfield	C3	$910	$1,145	N/A
226	HPK3800204	Myrtle Grove	C3	$910	$1,145	N/A
227	HPK3800205	Chattahoochee Run	L1	$1,115	$1,390	N/A
228	HPK3800206	Live Oak Cottage	L4	$1,440	$1,850	N/A
229	HPK3800207	The Jefferson	C3	$910	$1,145	N/A
230	HPK3800208	River Bluff	L2	$1,195	$1,515	N/A
231	HPK3800209	2006 Cooking Light Fit House	L2	$1,195	$1,515	N/A
232	HPK3800210	Walker Ridge	C3	$910	$1,145	N/A
233	HPK3800211	Bankston	C3	$910	$1,145	$1,915
234	HPK3800212	Lamberth Way	C3	$910	$1,145	N/A
235	HPK3800213	The Shoals	C3	$910	$1,145	N/A
236	HPK3800214	Shook Hill	L1	$1,115	$1,390	N/A
237	HPK3800215	Scarborough	C3	$910	$1,145	$1,915
238	HPK3800217	Classical Retreat	L2	$1,195	$1,515	N/A
239	HPK3800291	Kensington Place	L1	$1,115	$1,390	N/A
240	HPK3800216	Howell Park	L1	$1,115	$1,390	N/A
241	HPK3800218	New Willow Grove	L1	$1,115	$1,390	N/A
242	HPK3800219	Planters Retreat	L4	$1,440	$1,850	N/A
243	HPK3800220	Crescent Hill	C3	$910	$1,145	$1,915
244	HPK3800222	Van Buren	C3	$910	$1,145	N/A
245	HPK3800223	Bellwoode	L1	$1,115	$1,390	N/A
246	HPK3800224	The Hamptons	L1	$1,115	$1,390	N/A
247	HPK3800225	Monet House	C3	$910	$1,145	N/A
248	HPK3800226	The Asheville	L1	$1,115	$1,390	N/A
249	HPK3800227	Denham Springs	L2	$1,195	$1,515	N/A
250	HPK3800228	Mulberry Alternate	L4	$1,440	$1,850	N/A
251	HPK3800229	Old Field House	L1	$1,115	$1,390	N/A
252	HPK3800230	Clenney Point	L1	$1,115	$1,390	N/A

PAGE	PLAN #	PLAN NAME	PRICE CODE	8-SET PACKAGE	REPRODUCIBLE PACKAGE	CAD PACKAGE
253	HPK3800231	Lexington	C3	$910	$1,145	$1,915
254	HPK3800232	Madison Place	L1	$1,115	$1,390	N/A
255	HPK3800233	New Haven Cottage	L1	$1,115	$1,390	N/A
256	HPK3800234	Montreat	L1	$1,115	$1,390	N/A
257	HPK3800235	Aaronwood	L1	$1,115	$1,390	N/A
258	HPK3800346	The Twin Gables	L2	$1,195	$1,515	N/A
259	HPK3800237	New London	L1	$1,115	$1,390	N/A
260	HPK3800238	Oak Hill Lane	L2	$1,195	$1,515	N/A
261	HPK3800240	Sope Creek	L1	$1,115	$1,390	N/A
262	HPK3800241	Brookfield	L4	$1,440	$1,850	$3,140
263	HPK3800242	Southridge	C3	$910	$1,145	N/A
264	HPK3800243	Vernon Hill	L4	$1,440	$1,850	N/A
265	HPK3800244	Kinsley Place	SQ3	N/A	$1,966	$3,361
266	HPK3800246	Danbury Oaks	L1	$1,115	$1,390	N/A
267	HPK3800247	Crestview Park	L1	$1,115	$1,390	N/A
270	HPK3800245	Rucker Place	L1	$1,115	$1,390	N/A
271	HPK3800275	Rockwell House	L1	$1,115	$1,390	N/A
272	HPK3800248	Newberry Park	L4	$1,440	$1,850	N/A
273	HPK3800249	Avington Place	L1	$1,115	$1,390	N/A
274	HPK3800250	Arborview Alternate	L2	$1,195	$1,515	$2,575
275	HPK3800251	Cumberland River Cottage	L4	$1,440	$1,850	N/A
276	HPK3800252	Cypress Garden	L1	$1,115	$1,390	$2,500
277	HPK3800253	Linden	L1	$1,115	$1,390	N/A
278	HPK3800254	Smythe Park House	L4	$1,440	$1,850	N/A
279	HPK3800255	Amelia Place	L4	$1,440	$1,850	N/A
280	HPK3800256	Belfield Bend	L2	$1,195	$1,515	N/A
281	HPK3800257	Chatham Hall	L2	$1,195	$1,515	N/A
282	HPK3800258	Brenthaven	L4	$1,440	$1,850	N/A
283	HPK3800259	Belvedere	L1	$1,115	$1,390	N/A
284	HPK3800260	Centennial House Alternate	L4	$1,440	$1,850	$3,466
285	HPK3800261	Ansley Park	L1	$1,115	$1,390	N/A
286	HPK3800262	Ash Lawn	L2	$1,195	$1,515	N/A
287	HPK3800263	Habersham	C3	$910	$1,145	N/A
288	HPK3800264	Swannanoa River House	L4	$1,440	$1,850	$3,140
289	HPK3800265	Weston House	L4	$1,440	$1,850	N/A
290	HPK3800266	Surrey Crest	L1	$1,115	$1,390	N/A
291	HPK3800267	Cannon Creek	C3	$910	$1,145	N/A
292	HPK3800268	Crabapple Cottage	L4	$1,440	$1,850	N/A
293	HPK3800269	Sterett Springs	L1	$1,115	$1,390	N/A
294	HPK3800270	Chickering Country House	SQ3	N/A	$2,069	N/A
295	HPK3800271	Brittingham	L1	$1,115	$1,390	N/A
296	HPK3800272	All The Comforts Of Home	L1	$1,115	$1,390	N/A
297	HPK3800273	Lakeland Hall	L1	$1,115	$1,390	N/A
298	HPK3800274	Greywell Cottage	L4	$1,440	$1,850	N/A
302	HPK3800276	Wentworth Heights	L1	$1,115	$1,390	N/A
303	HPK3800277	Braden House	L4	$1,440	$1,850	N/A
304	HPK3800278	Martha's Vineyard	L1	$1,115	$1,390	N/A
305	HPK3800279	Sagewick House	L1	$1,115	$1,390	N/A
306	HPK3800280	Claremont	L1	$1,115	$1,390	$2,500
307	HPK3800281	Abberley Lane	L4	$1,440	$1,850	N/A
308	HPK3800282	St. Anne Georgian	L1	$1,115	$1,390	N/A
309	HPK3800283	Normandy Manor	L1	$1,115	$1,390	N/A
310	HPK3800284	Whitfield II	L1	$1,115	$1,390	N/A
311	HPK3800285	Hansell Park	L1	$1,115	$1,390	N/A
312	HPK3800286	Amsterdam Avenue	L1	$1,115	$1,390	N/A
313	HPK3800287	Weatherford	L1	$1,115	$1,390	N/A
314	HPK3800288	Mulberry Park	L4	$1,440	$1,850	N/A

PAGE	PLAN #	PLAN NAME	PRICE CODE	8-SET PACKAGE	REPRODUCIBLE PACKAGE	CAD PACKAGE
315	HPK3800289	Brentwood Cottage	L1	$1,115	$1,390	N/A
316	HPK3800290	Stones River Farm	L4	$1,440	$1,850	$3,140
318	HPK3800292	Crabapple Grove	L1	$1,115	$1,390	N/A
319	HPK3800293	Avalon Alternate	L4	$1,440	$1,850	N/A
320	HPK3800294	Sabine River Cottage	L2	$1,195	$1,515	N/A
321	HPK3800295	Kennesaw Ridge	L2	$1,195	$1,515	N/A
322	HPK3800296	Brookhollow	L4	$1,440	$1,850	N/A
323	HPK3800297	Colonial Lake Cottage	L1	$1,115	$1,390	N/A
324	HPK3800298	Walker's Bluff	L4	$1,440	$1,850	$3,140
325	HPK3800299	Avery's Bluff	L1	$1,115	$1,390	N/A
326	HPK3800300	Pine Glen	L2	$1,195	$1,515	$2,575
327	HPK3800301	Sienna Park	L2	$1,195	$1,515	N/A
328	HPK3800302	Forest Glen	C4	$970	$1,225	N/A
329	HPK3800303	Montcrest	L2	$1,195	$1,515	N/A
330	HPK3800304	Luberon	L1	$1,115	$1,390	$2,500
331	HPK3800305	Travis Ridge	L4	$1,440	$1,850	N/A
332	HPK3800306	Riddley Park	L2	$1,195	$1,515	$2,575
333	HPK3800307	Garden Court	L1	$1,115	$1,390	N/A
334	HPK3800308	Carter Hall	L1	$1,115	$1,390	N/A
335	HPK3800309	Harwood Park	L1	$1,115	$1,390	N/A
336	HPK3800310	Somerset	L1	$1,115	$1,390	N/A
337	HPK3800343	Charles Towne Place	L2	$1,195	$1,515	N/A
338	HPK3800340	Bella Maison	L2	$1,195	$1,515	N/A
339	HPK3800311	Wilmington Place	L1	$1,115	$1,390	N/A
340	HPK3800312	Stanton Court	L1	$1,115	$1,390	N/A
341	HPK3800313	Cambridge	L1	$1,115	$1,390	$2,500
342	HPK3800314	Hunter's Glen	L2	$1,195	$1,515	N/A
343	HPK3800315	Ivy Manor	L2	$1,195	$1,515	N/A
344	HPK3800316	Cordova Place	L2	$1,195	$1,515	N/A
345	HPK3800317	Strathmore	L1	$1,115	$1,390	N/A
346	HPK3800318	Whitfield	L1	$1,115	$1,390	N/A
347	HPK3800319	Everett Place	L1	$1,115	$1,390	N/A
348	HPK3800320	Parkside Place	L1	$1,115	$1,390	N/A
349	HPK3800321	Beacon Hill	L2	$1,195	$1,515	N/A
350	HPK3800322	Ocean House	SQ3	N/A	$2,399	N/A
351	HPK3800323	Oak Hill Lane Alternate	L1	$1,115	$1,390	N/A
352	HPK3800324	Clayton Hall	L2	$1,195	$1,515	N/A
353	HPK3800325	Glendale	L1	$1,115	$1,390	N/A
354	HPK3800326	Harrod's Creek	L4	$1,440	$1,850	N/A
355	HPK3800327	Beecham Manor	L2	$1,195	$1,515	N/A
356	HPK3800328	Alouette	L1	$1,115	$1,390	N/A
357	HPK3800329	Hyannis Port	L2	$1,195	$1,515	N/A
358	HPK3800330	Cuscowilla	SQ3	N/A	$2,604	N/A
359	HPK3800331	Rocksprings	L1	$1,115	$1,390	N/A
360	HPK3800332	Boxwood	L2	$1,195	$1,515	N/A
361	HPK3800333	Canton Creek	L2	$1,195	$1,515	N/A
362	HPK3800334	Palmetto Court	L1	$1,115	$1,390	N/A
363	HPK3800335	Newport Valley	L2	$1,195	$1,515	N/A
364	HPK3800336	Brittany	L2	$1,195	$1,515	N/A
365	HPK3800337	Carriage Park	L4	$1,440	$1,850	N/A
366	HPK3800338	Summer Lake	L4	$1,440	$1,850	N/A
367	HPK3800339	Lavendale	L2	$1,195	$1,515	N/A
368	HPK3800342	Embassy Row	L2	$1,195	$1,515	N/A
369	HPK3800344	Fairmount Heights	L2	$1,195	$1,515	N/A
370	HPK3800345	Centennial House	L4	$1,440	$1,850	$3,140
371	HPK3800347	Shelburne	L2	$1,195	$1,515	N/A
372	HPK3800348	Argonne Manor	L2	$1,195	$1,515	N/A
373	HPK3800341	Avalon	L4	$1,440	$1,850	N/A